Creating a Profitable Catalog

Creating a Profitable Catalog

Everything You Need to Know to Create a Catalog That Sells

JACK SCHMID

Foreword by Laura Beaudry, Editorial Director, *Catalog Age*

NTC Business Books
NTC/Contemporary Publishing Group

Library of Congress Cataloging-in-Publication Data

Schmid, Jack.
    Creating a profitable catalog : everything you need to know to create a catalog
that sells / Jack Schmid.
        p.   cm.
    Includes index.
    ISBN 0-658-00064-0 (cloth)
    1. Commercial catalogs.   2. Advertising, Direct-mail.   I. Title.
HF5862.S35   2000
659.13′3—dc21
                                                99-57871
                                                  CIP

Interior design by Hespenheide Design

Published by NTC Business Books
A division of NTC/Contemporary Publishing Group, Inc.
4255 West Touhy Avenue, Lincolnwood (Chicago), Illinois 60712-1975 U.S.A.
Copyright © 2000 by NTC/Contemporary Publishing Group, Inc.
Printed in the United States of America
International Standard Book Number: 0-658-00064-0
00 01 02 03 04 05 HP 15 14 13 12 11 10 9 8 7 6 5 4 3 2 1

Contents

Credits

Interior

Exhibit 2.1: Reprinted with permission of Three Dog Bakery.

Exhibit 2.3: Reprinted with permission of Electric Outlet.

Exhibit 3.3: Used by permission of the DMA, 1999.

Exhibit 3.8: Used by permission of the DMA, 1999.

Exhibit 4.3: Reprinted with permission of Quill Corporation, Lincolnshire, IL, 1-800-789-1331; www.quillcorp.com. Reproduction prohibited.

Exhibit 5.3: Used by permission of Plow & Hearth "Products for Country Living."

Exhibit 6.2: Reprinted with permission of Electric Outlet.

Exhibit 8.6: Reprinted with permission of Belcaro Group, Inc. (Shop at Home). Reprinted with permission of Publishers Inquiry Services, Inc. (The Best Catalogs in the World).

Exhibit 8.7: Used by permission of Omaha Steaks, Inc.

Photo Insert

Page 1c. Provided courtesy of New Pig Corporation.

Page 1g. Provided courtesy of New Pig Corporation.

Page 1h. Reprinted with permission of Fingerhut Companies, Inc.

Page 2b. Courtesy of L. L. Bean, Inc.

Page 2c. Reprinted with permission of Fingerhut Companies, Inc.

Page 2d. Reprinted with permission of Cushman Fruit, Inc.

Page 2e. Reprinted with permission of Wolferman's Inc.

Page 2f. Reprinted with permission of Bath & Body Works.

Page 3a. Luminescence Catalog, your inside source for professional skincare and body care. 1-800-364-6637.

Page 3b. "Garfield Stuff"® is a registered trademark of Paws, Inc. "Garfield" and "Garfield Stuff"® Catalog: © Paws, Inc.

Page 3c. Used by permission of Cushman Fruit, Inc.

Page 3d. Courtesy of Sokkia Corporation, Overland Parks, KS.

Page 4a. Used by permission of Mammoth Sports Group.

Page 4b. Hello Direct, Telephone Productivity Tools, 1-800-444-3556 or www.hellodirect.com.

Page 4c. Used by permission of Foster & Gallagher.

Page 4d. King Schools, Inc., San Diego, CA.

Page 5a. Thanks to Annette Zientek and Robert Brost of Christine Columbus.com.

Page 5b. Reprinted with permission of Lands' End, Inc.

Page 5d. Reprinted with permission of Wolferman's Inc.

Page 6a. "Garfield Stuff"® is a registered trademark of Paws, Inc. "Garfield" and "Garfield Stuff"® Catalog: © Paws, Inc..

Page 6b. Used with permission of Drs. Foster & Smith.

Page 6c. Used by permission of Cushman Fruit, Inc.

Page 7b. Courtesy of Macomber Inc. and L. L. Bean, Inc.

Page 7c. © Sharper Image Corporation.

Page 7e. Coldwater Creek—A Northcountry catalog: www.coldwater-creek.com 1-800-262-0040

Page 8a. Used with permission of Drs. Foster & Smith.

Page 8b. Used with permission of Draper's & Damon's.

Page 8c. Used with permission of Electric Outlet, Inc.

Page 8d. Lillian Vernon Catalogs: www.lillianvernon.com

Page 8e. Gooseberry Patch®

Page 8f. Coldwater Creek—A Northcountry catalog: www.coldwater-creek.com 1-800-262-0040

Foreword

As the editorial director of *Catalog Age* magazine for the past decade, I've been lucky in that I have been able to observe the growth and evolution of the catalog industry from a broad vantage point. I have watched this business move from the kitchen-table start-up to the Internet start-up, with all the trials and growing pains that came in between. It's a complex and demanding business, and it doesn't suffer fools gladly. To succeed, you cannot just be more attractive or less expensive than the other guy. You must be superior in every way: creative, production, merchandising, marketing, operations, and customer service.

I've learned a lot in my ten-plus years. When I started with *Catalog Age* in 1989, I was a confident journalist who had no qualms about being able to edit a magazine known by many catalogers as the "bible of the catalog industry." I was such a naif! "So what if I have no previous experience writing about catalogs?" I asked myself. "I get catalogs in the mail; I shop from catalogs—what else is there to know?"

I quickly found out what else. I began hearing terms like *square-inch analysis*, *lifetime value*, and *database marketing* and became overwhelmed by the complexity of this business. I also came to realize how incredibly smart catalogers have to be in order to succeed.

I learned as much as I could as fast as I could, but I could barely keep up. In the 1980s, cataloging was growing as much as 15 to 20 percent annually, far outpacing the revenue growth of the retail sector. New techniques in database marketing, production, operations, and service were reshaping the catalog landscape.

In the early 1990s, I watched cataloging suffer through an economic recession, a series of painful postal and parcel delivery rate increases, paper price volatility, and a fickle customer base. I was a wide-eyed witness as the business changed from an industry dominated by large, general-merchandise mass mailers to one defined by niche or specialty catalog brands focused on unique product segments and database-driven marketing techniques.

Over time, I also watched the culture of the business change, as well as its image. People who were once ashamed to say they shopped by catalog—fearing that the catalog connotation would bring to mind only the low-end mailers that had once defined the industry—now began to proudly announce their dependency on mail-order catalogs. The busier and more time-restrained Americans became, the more catalogs became a mainstream shopping option. At the same time, the more that people needed fast and easy shopping, the better catalogers' services became. The toll-free phone line for ordering and customer service, as well as the express delivery option, became mainstays of the business, all in response to escalating customer-service demands.

Today, U.S. cataloging has grown to a more than $100 billion business. Nearly 60 percent of all adult Americans have purchased something from a mail-order catalog, and more than 40 percent of catalogers are conducting some sort of international catalog activity. But the growth and evolution of cataloging doesn't stop there.

Always savvy to evolving customer needs, some visionary catalogers became Internet commerce pioneers in the mid-1990s. While many other types of retailers remained skeptical about the future of Web-based selling, a number of catalogers recognized that future buyers would want options for how they interacted with sellers, and that one of those options would be the Internet. They were right. As we enter the 2000s, we are in the midst of an Internet-commerce feeding frenzy, with catalogers in the center of the fray.

Yet despite this current emphasis on the electronic frontier, I see no end to the printed catalog. Nor do I see a lack of brave souls looking to create the next "great catalog idea." In *Catalog Age* magazine, we write about scores of new catalog ideas every year, and I continue to be amazed at the variety of ingenious marketing concepts that no one ever thought of before!

But succeeding in cataloging continues to become increasingly difficult. That's where catalog consultant Jack Schmid and this book come in.

I met Jack in the early 1990s. As I recall, I introduced myself after hearing him speak at our annual catalog conference. I felt compelled to wait in line with dozens of other admirers so that I could compliment him on the content of his highly instructive session—as well as ask him to write for *Catalog Age* magazine.

We have been working together—either in the pages of the magazine, during *Catalog Age*'s Annual Catalog Awards judging process, or at The Annual Catalog Conference—ever since. Jack's in-depth knowledge of the catalog market and his exceptional talent for articulating a precise set of how-tos for seemingly every aspect of this complex business are unrivaled. In this outstanding new book, *Creating a Profitable Catalog*, he takes the reader through the basics and beyond in critical areas of cataloging including concept development, creative, design and production, merchandising, circulation planning, database marketing, operations, and financial management. All of these topics are analyzed in intricate and careful detail as Jack vigilantly guides the reader through every step of building a catalog business. Each chapter provides useful graphics and examples, as well as worksheets to help the aspiring cataloger plot his or her future. As an appendix, Jack also includes a detailed new catalog start-up feasibility study with three hypothetical models: a conservative scenario; a most likely scenario; and an optimistic scenario.

In short, this book details everything you ever wanted to know about starting and running a successful catalog operation. I think it is a masterful how-to volume on a highly complex and challenging topic, written by one of the best catalog consultants around. I know my copy of *Creating a Profitable Catalog* will always be kept in a handy spot for any time I am stumped on a question about cataloging.

Read, learn, and prosper!

LAURA M. BEAUDRY
Editorial Director,
Catalog Age

Catalog Age, an Intertec/Primedia publication, is published thirteen times annually. Introduced in 1983, *Catalog Age* is today considered "the bible of the catalog industry." The magazine, which is the premier source of primary research on the catalog business, sponsors the prestigious Annual Catalog Awards, publishes the *Catalog Age* 100 listing of the nation's top catalog companies, and cosponsors the largest catalog industry conference and exhibition, The Annual Catalog Conference.

Acknowledgments

I dedicate this book to the people who have helped make it possible.

To Anne Basye, the developmental editor who organized and made sense of the manuscript. What a quick study!

To Lois Boyle, my colleague and friend, who was of infinite help on the creative chapters.

To Alan Weber, former coworker and also coauthor of *Desktop Database Marketing*, for his contribution on database marketing.

To Errett Schmid, my wife and personal editor, for her constant support and encouragement.

To the staff at J. Schmid & Assoc. Inc. for their help and input.

And finally, I dedicate this book to our catalog clients and former clients who have helped me as much as I hope we have helped them over the years.

Introduction
The Current Catalog Environment:
Issues, Trends, Risks, and Opportunities

In his book, *Successful Direct Marketing Methods*, Bob Stone called catalogs "America's long-standing love affair." How true his statement is! In the past few decades, cataloging has grown from its modest, almost frail beginning to an industry that employs thousands, has revenues in the billions, and encompasses everything from retailing to direct-consumer, business-to-business, and selling on the Internet.

Cataloging in the United States can be traced to the late 1660s when William Lucas, an English gardener, mailed his first seed and nursery catalogs to the American colonies. George Washington and Thomas Jefferson were among the mail-order customers of a fruit tree catalog published by William Prince of Flushing, New York in the 1770s. At the same time, Benjamin Franklin's publishing firm produced a catalog of six hundred books and periodicals. In the 1830s, the Orvis company of Vermont began selling sporting and fishing gear by mail throughout New England.

Modern cataloging got its start in 1860, when a traveling salesman named Aaron Montgomery Ward published an eight-page listing of 163 items for direct sale to midwestern farm families. Rapid success made the catalog grow, and by 1884 the catalog had 240 pages and listed over 10,000 items. Sears, Roebuck and Company followed Montgomery Ward into cataloging in 1893, and both became standards by which future catalogers would measure themselves. Some historians call Montgomery Ward and Sears catalogs "encyclopedias of American history." They carried every imaginable item that might be needed by families in remote areas, as the following letter from a farm woman in Minnesota attests

> *Do you still sell embalming fluid? I saw it in your old catalog, but not in your new one. If you do, send me enough for my husband who is five feet eleven and weighs 160 pounds when in good health. Henry has been laying around the house looking mighty peaked lately and I expect him to*

kick off any time now. He'd like to have gone last night. When you send the stuff, please send instructions with it. And please rush.

The Spiegel catalog came along in 1905. Neiman Marcus launched a mail-order operation five months after opening its Dallas store in the early 1900s, and L. L. Bean started publishing its catalogs in 1912. Northwest fruit growers Harry and David, nearly ruined by the depression, turned in the 1930s to selling baskets of fruit to business executives by mail. The 1950s and early 1960s saw the debut of specialty mail-order catalogs such as the Kenton Collection (to become Horchow), Williams-Sonoma, Tiffany, and Talbot's.

Cataloging exploded in the 1970s and 1980s, fueled by a number of social and economic factors. The growing number of working women and two-income families discovered they had more disposable dollars but less time to shop. Shopping in retail stores became more grueling as parking, crowds, and indifferent salespeople created hassles. For time and convenience, these families began shopping by mail and phone. Credit cards, suddenly available to all, eliminated the necessity of house credit and COD deliveries and made purchasing easier than ever. In fact, without credit cards, cataloging as we know it would not exist.

The computer also drove catalog growth. Before computers, companies stored their customers' names and addresses on 3 × 5 cards or in manual logs—a task that became impossible when thousands of names were involved. Computers helped catalogers easily store and retrieve data on merchandise and inventory, purchase transactions, and credit card authorization.

Computers also enabled companies to offer specialized products to carefully selected target audiences. Rather than trying to be everything to everybody, catalogers began to identify and focus on small, profitable niches. Gradually, consumers came to prefer highly specialized catalogs, and the general, big books like Sears or Montgomery Ward began to fade.

Beginning in the 1970s, merchandise quality and creative product presentation also improved, as upscale companies like Williams-Sonoma helped the catalog industry shed its downscale or "schlocky" image. Creative presentations, photography, color separations, paper, and printing all increased the medium's credibility.

Improved fulfillment and customer service also spurred consumer confidence and industry growth. The four-to-six-week wait for a catalog item was shaved to two to four weeks, and today most successful catalogs turn around orders in twenty-four hours and guarantee delivery in three to four days. Business catalogers emphasize overnight delivery and some even offer "same-day delivery." How times have changed.

Business-to-business catalogs increased in number and profitability as the cost of making a sales call soared. Business-to-business sellers looking to sell directly and eliminate costly on-the-road expenses, found that a combination of a catalog and inbound and outbound telephone sales could sufficiently replace a salesperson. As companies of all kinds began to demand measurable, accountable advertising and marketing, catalogs became an attractive alternative to general advertising. By measuring revenue per catalog mailed, companies could determine the profitability of each catalog or campaign.

As a result of these trends, increasing numbers of nontypical marketers have joined the traditional consumer and business catalogers such as Fingerhut, Lillian Vernon, Quill, and Reliable. Today, retailers such as Radio Shack, Hallmark Cards, and Bath and Body Works use catalogs to entice direct orders or to build store traffic. Banks use catalogs to introduce new customers to their full range of financial products and services, allowing customers to apply by telephone or in person. Not-for-profit organizations use catalogs to sell products that complement their mission. I've helped develop catalogs for speakers' bureaus, seminar companies, religious publishers, wholesalers, and a whole array of clients I never would have anticipated twenty years ago.

These nontraditional companies do share some characteristics. All of them sell multiple products or services and use catalogs as part of their selling mix instead of as their only selling channel. But no matter what kind of product or service they sell, catalogers must combine the same elements in order to succeed: the right merchandise, the right audience, the right creative approach, and top-quality fulfillment.

Cataloging in the New Century

The phenomenal acceptance and growth of the Internet as a complementary channel of marketing for cataloging has opened major new vistas for traditional paper catalogs and retailing. The Internet is rejuvenating a catalog industry that many felt suffered from serious "glut." New, nontraditional mail-order buyers are shopping on the Web and in many cases have been driven to the Internet with a printed catalog. One cannot talk about cataloging today without mentioning and considering the Internet. The two media are becoming interconnected. The new century will be a most exciting and challenging time for business, consumer, and retail catalogers who attempt to understand and embrace the Internet. Almost every aspect of cataloging is being impacted by the Internet as we move to what many describe as a "marketing revolution." Fortunately, the Internet is a direct marketing medium and those mailers who understand and use proven direct response techniques will be the ones who win.

New catalogers can expect to face a number of new issues as the market continues to mature.

Look for Fewer Start-Ups and More Consolidation

More competition for the same customers in a mature industry means it will be increasingly difficult to launch a new catalog that can quickly generate a profit. Unless a company is prepared to regard a new start-up as a longer-range investment (and has the capital to support it), many catalogs will die in planning. Those that survive will face increased competition from Hanover, Federated, CML Group, Spiegel, Arizona Mail Order, Williams-Sonoma, Sara Lee, Campbell Soup, and other companies that have acquired existing catalogs or started new ones to complement their product offerings, secure the seasonal market, ensure financial stability, protect against recessions, or leverage their warehousing and fulfillment operations and customer database.

The ongoing acquisition and consolidation of catalog companies does have a plus side: it will be easier to find a buyer when a company decides to recoup its investment in a new catalog venture.

Expect to Spend More on Postage and Shipping

Printing and paper are no longer a cataloger's highest expenditure. Today, it's postage and shipping charges, which are expected to increase as the United States Postal Service and alternative delivery services such as United Parcel Service continue to raise their prices.

Respond to Customer Concerns About Privacy and the Environment

The sophisticated list and database marketing systems that drive the catalog industry also lead to concerns about consumer privacy. Catalogers simply must participate in industry initiatives that ensure customers are able to avoid unwanted mailings or telephone calls and that protect information about consumers. The cost of not participating may be legislation that hampers future marketing efforts and growth.

In the environmental arena, catalogers have been criticized for mailing millions of catalogs on difficult-to-recycle, coated paper and using packing materials such as styrofoam peanuts. Smart catalogers will respond to these and other environmental concerns by switching to recycled and recyclable paper and packing materials, and offering mail preference service to those who don't want to receive unsolicited catalogs.

Expect Changes in Sales and Use Taxes

Deciding who must collect sales tax and when, will only become a more heated discussion as states seek new sources of revenue and retailers complain about direct marketers being exempt from sales tax regulations. The growth of sales on the Internet will also drive the question, which has been tossed from the Supreme Court to Congress and back again as the government seeks to determine whether "nexus" or physical presence in a state is the criterion for determining whether a company is required to collect and remit sales taxes to a state.

Take Advantage of New Technology

Some positive news is that catalogers are reducing costs through new approaches to design, separate color, print, and mail catalogs. Desktop publishing is now commonplace in page production, but digital photography and direct-to-plate color separations and printing will drive future technology change. Selective binding, personalized laser-printed messages, and improved papers and printing are a few of the additional changes that will reduce creative and prepress costs and will ultimately decrease the cost of mailing catalogs to customers. Internet-based catalogs are allowing catalogers to create them faster and more cheaply and may eventually be a reliable and very inexpensive alternative to multiple annual catalog mailings.

Look for Growth from the Internet

The paper catalog is unlikely to be replaced by electronic commerce in the next decade because the two selling channels—catalog and Internet—are quite complementary. The Internet is passive; catalogs are intrusive. Together they will promote growth in direct selling while enhancing the credibility and authority of each marketing channel to turn them into international marketing phenomenons.

Enter the Global Village

Cataloging is no longer just an American phenomenon. Many American mailers are mailing to Japan, the United Kingdom, and Europe. Canadian markets are being tested by scores of U.S. catalogers, and Canadian catalogers are eyeing American markets. Ownership of catalogs is becoming more international. Expect significant growth in the international arena, especially Canada, Central and South America, eastern and western Europe, and the Pacific Rim. With less competition, the growth of direct selling and cataloging outside the U.S. will probably outpace the domestic business by 40 to 60 percent in the next decade.

Catalogs that do enter these markets would be well advised to pay close attention to production issues. In many emerging overseas markets such as the United Kingdom or Argentina, the image and quality problems that plagued U.S. catalogers in the '60s still exist. Catalogs that offer high-quality merchandise and high-class creativity will make an impact.

Domestic business-to-business and retail cataloging will also remain on a strong growth curve for the future.

Who Will Succeed?

Which catalogers will succeed in the coming decades?

- Catalogers that provide the greatest customer focus. Time and convenience are *still* the most important drivers of mail-order sales, which is why the competitive edge goes to catalogers who let customers buy when and where they wish to buy, as well as how they care to buy—via phone, fax, store visit, or Internet.
- Catalogers that meet or exceed the operational standards set by such benchmark organizations as Lands' End and Reliable. Their superb telephone operations,

on-line customer databases and inventory information, and twenty-four-hour turnaround in shipping set the standard that customers expect. If you don't meet the standard, you may be out of business.

- Catalogers that clearly differentiate themselves, their products, and their positioning from the others. Highly targeted, specialized catalogs are not just a specter of the future . . . they are realities today. New catalogers will find ample opportunity if they can identify a unique niche. "Me too" catalogs will not be so fortunate.

Above all, success will go to catalogers that master the process of creating and producing a catalog. After three decades in cataloging, I believe that creating and producing a catalog is a process, supported by subprocesses, which can be mastered and refined. When a catalog company can competently handle every step of this process with its own staff or a competent outsourcing partner, it will greatly enhance its chances for success.

Creating a Profitable Catalog outlines the catalog process one step at a time, so you can implement it correctly from the outset and avoid the pitfalls that trap many new catalogers. It also introduces state-of-the-art catalog techniques that permit you to move very quickly up the experience and sophistication ladder. When you can do things faster, better, and smarter, you increase the chances that your catalog will be profitable and mature five years hence.

Whether a catalog is intended for a business or consumer market, certain ingredients are essential to success: the right merchandise, the right audience, creative, sharp prospecting and customer circulation strategies, and high-quality fulfillment. *Creating a Profitable Catalog* will set you on the road to success in these areas, so your catalog will live long and prosper.

Creating a Profitable Catalog

CHAPTER 1

Planning and Staffing the Start-Up Catalog

When Columbus left Spain, he didn't know where he was going. When he got there, he didn't know where he was. When he got back, he didn't know where he had been. But he got there and back four times in ten years without getting lost.

Although the Christopher Columbus School of Management worked in the fifteenth century, it won't work for catalogers today. Every catalog venture benefits from a strategic business plan. Whether you are launching a new catalog, repositioning an existing catalog, or spinning off a catalog from an existing venture, it makes sense to define the conditions, strategies, and tactics you need to employ to build a successful and profitable business.

Why Planning Matters

There are plenty of good reasons to invest time in strategic planning before launching a new catalog. First, planning lets you determine how much capital is needed for the new venture, and helps you secure financing. Working with companies seeking internal financing for a catalog, I've heard plenty of CFOs say, "There is as much money as you need, but not one dime until you present the business plan." Venture capitalists and other investors feel the same way. The funds *are* there. But only a business plan will persuade someone to lend them to you.

Even more important, your chances of success go up dramatically with a plan. Without one, they diminish. The statistics aren't good. Only about three out of ten U.S. catalogs that start this year will still be in business three years from now. The outlook is somewhat rosier for business-to-business catalogers, for whom direct selling is often a new selling channel rather than a totally new business, and for companies launching catalogs in the United Kingdom, South America, or Canada.

Why is the success ratio for domestic consumer catalogs so low? Here's my list of the top ten reasons why catalogs fail:

10. The company lacks a sound inventory management plan.
9. Fulfillment and customer service are not equal to the competition.
8. The company lacks the financial and analytical skills needed to effectively manage the catalog.
7. The company underestimates the time it takes to build critical mass in a buyer file.
6. The acquisition of new customers is haphazard at best.
5. The company doesn't understand the creative subtleties of cataloging.
4. The company does not know its target audience(s) or how to reach that target.
3. The catalog fails to establish a clear identity or niche for its merchandise or company.
2. The company has difficulty obtaining financing or is undercapitalized.
1. The company fails to have a plan.

I've seen venture after venture falter due to lack of planning—especially those led by entrepreneurs. Big companies practice planning because they understand the process and know how important it is. But planning is often new to entrepreneurs, and some unwisely choose to wing it. If you're an entrepreneur, don't be tempted to skip this essential stage. Acquaint yourself with the basics of planning, and formulate a plan before you attempt to execute your idea.

Planning Defined

Planning a new catalog is like starting a trip, and the strategic plan is the road map that helps tell you where to go and how to get there. Although the map doesn't spell out every detail, it gives the planners a solid direction . . . and when no direction is clear, success is seldom achieved.

Planning also provides an orderly, informed, proactive response to changing conditions. It is orderly and organized because it is a logical, step-by-step process. It is informed because planners gather all relevant information and are totally knowledgeable about facts, issues, and conditions of the project. And it is proactive because instead of merely guessing at or responding to conditions, planning seeks to use that information to make decisions.

Planning is also a communication process. Constructing a business plan for the launch of a new catalog lets you communicate upward to superiors and others to whom you report. It lets you communicate sideways to your peers and third-party vendors who are asked to support the catalog effort. And it facilitates communication downward to subordinates who are responsible for the daily catalog execution.

Altogether, planning is a process, a systematic way of approaching problem solving. As the *Harvard Business Journal* noted several years ago, "the process is more important than the product." In other words, while strategies, financials, and other end products of planning are important, the process of constructing the plan and communicating it within your organization is more important.

Two Levels of Catalog Planning

Two levels of strategic plans are outlined in the following pages: a feasibility study and a full-blown strategic business plan.

The catalog feasibility study outlined in Exhibit 1.1 on page 4 addresses six critical areas. It defines the purpose and objectives of the catalog, closely analyzes the market, summarizes the business concept, sets forth financial objectives, details the problems and risks of entering the business, and establishes a timetable. A feasibility study should be your first step in planning. As its title suggests, it enables you to decide whether your catalog venture can get off the ground.

If a feasibility study gives your project a green light, it's time to develop a full-length catalog strategic business plan like the one in Exhibit 1.2 on page 5. A new cataloger meeting a private investor, a venture capitalist, or even a bank must be prepared to answer questions about the five areas of planning and strategy that comprise the five sections of the plan: merchandise plan and strategies, marketing plan and strategies, fulfillment plan and strategies, financial plan, and people plan. The financial section is typically extensive and includes three different financial scenarios: conservative, most likely, and optimistic. A model financial plan is presented in the Appendix.

SOURCES OF FUNDS

- Friends, family, and relatives
- Banks and other financial institutions
- Small Business Administration
- Venture capital firms
- Private placement
- Public offering
- Partnering with a merchandising company, a printer, a fulfillment company, or another vendor
- Overseas investors

These two types of plans are partners. The feasibility plan lets you determine whether a catalog venture can make money, and the business plan serves as your implementation

Specialists in Direct Marketing

Strategic, Creative,
Analytical & Database
Services for:
- Catalogs–
  Consumer & Business
- Direct Marketers
- Retailers
- New Start-ups

4550 West 90th Street
Shawnee Mission KS
66207-2307
Ph: 913-385-0220
Fax: 913-385-0221

FEASIBILITY STUDY

I. Statement of Purpose and Objectives

II. Market Analysis
1. Market Segmentation (size, growth rates, trends, etc.)
2. Competitive Analysis
3. Target Consumer Definition (primary and secondary)
4. Consumer Needs
5. Problems of Entering the Market
6. Prior Direct Marketing Experience

III. Business Concept Description
1. The Product
2. Promotion, Advertising, and Creative Execution
3. Fulfillment
4. Staffing
5. Relationship to the Base Business

IV. Financial Objectives
1. Sales
2. Earnings
3. Budgeting
4. Funding Requirements
5. Payout/Payback
6. Return on Investment
7. Breakeven Analysis

V. Problems/Risks of Entering the Business
1. Effect on the Base Business
2. Inventory Risk

VI. Timetable

©J.Schmid & Assoc. Inc.

EXHIBIT 1.1

Specialists in Direct Marketing

Strategic, Creative,
Analytical & Database
Services for:

- Catalogs—
  Consumer & Business
- Direct Marketers
- Retailers
- New Start-ups

4550 West 90th Street
Shawnee Mission KS
66207-2307
Ph: 913-385-0220
Fax: 913-385-0221

STRATEGIC BUSINESS PLAN

I. Merchandising Plan
1. Product Selection (the method)
2. Inventory Control (turns, buying, rebuying, projecting)
3. Product Analysis
4. Excessive Inventory Disposal

II. Marketing Plan
1. Customer List Development (name acquisition)
2. The Creative Image (niche)
3. Creative Execution (inside or outside)
4. Test Plan and Method of Evaluation
5. Annual Mailing Schedule

III. Fulfillment Plan
1. Order Processing
2. Data Processing
3. Warehousing, Picking, Packing, and Shipping
4. Customer Service
5. Credit and Controls

IV. Financial Plan
1. Breakeven Analysis
2. Annual Financial Plan
3. Name Flow
4. Order Flow
5. Five-Year Financial Plan
6. Cash Flow
7. Return on Sales
8. Return on Investment

V. People Plan

©J.Schmid & Assoc. Inc.

EXHIBIT 1.2

plan by outlining how you will make your idea reality. Together, they provide a "reality check" for your venture and answer the following five essential questions:

1. Does the catalog business make sense for your company? Does it complement the business you are presently in?
2. What do the numbers say? Can you be successful in this channel of marketing?
3. How much capital do you need to launch this business, and how much will be needed during the first three-year period or until the business breaks even?
4. Do you have any core competencies in place, or can you easily acquire them?
5. What are the sources of funding?

Exhibit 1.3 identifies five more questions that must be answered during the planning process. The most important question appears in the middle of the diagram: What is the catalog's competitive difference?

I cannot overstress the importance of differentiating your catalog from others in the market. Any new catalog must differentiate itself from its competition through its merchandise, creative presentation, and mailing strategy. Operational aspects are less important differentiating points; they should be as similar as possible to the operations of the industry's best catalogs and should meet or exceed industry standards.

The answers to these five questions will drive your catalog's creative differentiation. When you know your target customers and their needs, you can more easily find ways to meet them using your company's strategic skills and core competencies in a manner that

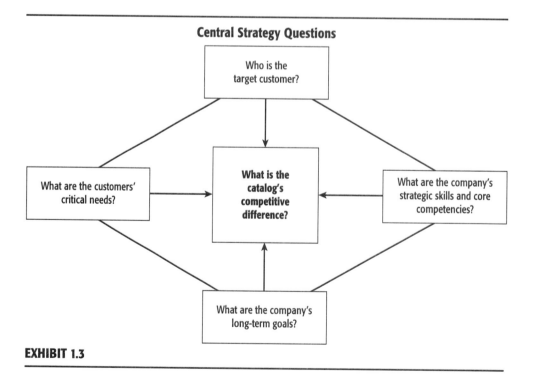

EXHIBIT 1.3

also meets your company's long-term goals. When the planning team can answer these questions, they will have succeeded in the planning process.

If your company is developing feasibility studies for a number of new ventures, Exhibit 1.4, the new venture rating chart, might be useful in prioritizing or comparing a new catalog with other business options. It lets you quickly compare a number of opportunities using five criteria.

				New Venture Evaluation		Rate each from 1 to 10
New Venture	**Capital**	**Time**	**Expertise**	**Success Potential**	**Hassle Factor**	**Total**
	Initial $ needed to be profitable. (Consider facility, people, equipment, and promotional costs.)	Initial time needed to be profitable. (Consider research and preparatory time as well as rollout interval.)	Is this something the company knows about, and is it closely related to what it is currently doing?	How large and/or profitable can this venture become? (Consider competition, market size, and niche.)	How easy or difficult is this business to run? (Consider vendor reliability, customer credit, lifetime value.)	
	1 = much capital 10 = little capital	1 = much time 10 = little time	1 = know little about 10 = know lot about	1 = little potential 10 = great potential	1 = lots of problems 10 = few problems	

EXHIBIT 1.4

Beware the Pitfalls of Strategic Planning

The planning process is full of problems. They vary with the size of the company, the nature of management's involvement in planning, and the company's attitude toward the need to plan. Here is a quick, ten-point checklist of some of the problems that typically plague planning in a corporate context:

1. Top management not being involved in any way in the planning process—assumes function can be delegated to others.
2. Management saying, "We've been successful without planning; why do it?"
3. Ignoring the fact that planning is a learning process.
4. Assuming that planning is easy and won't take much effort.
5. Forgetting (especially in larger companies) that planning is as much a political as a rational process.
6. Assuming that comprehensive planning is something apart from the entire management process.
7. Seeking precise numbers throughout the planning process.
8. Assuming that equal weight can be given to all elements of planning.
9. Failing to identify the fundamental differences that distinguish your catalog's products and services from the competition.
10. Assuming that plans, once made, are cast in stone or are like blueprints for construction of a building that must be rigorously followed.

You can probably name another dozen pitfalls that might impact your company. The secret is to be aware of them and avoid them in your planning.

Planning Is the Beginning of the Catalog Process

Sound catalog planning draws investors when it identifies a merchandise concept that is strongly differentiated from the competition. But companies and individuals also invest in people—people who know what cataloging is all about.

Producing a catalog is a process. Once defined and refined, a process can be used over and over again. To start and grow a profitable catalog, your company needs to understand the catalog process inside and out.

Exhibit 1.5 outlines the overall process of creating a catalog. It looks simple, until you realize that within each of these areas lies a subsystem of functions, most of which take place simultaneously. Hundreds of decisions and activities go into selecting and purchasing merchandise, for example. Merchandising, like each of the other stages of the process, is a *core competency*—a skill that your company or an outsourced partner must have or master in order to succeed. A cataloger cannot be good at merchandising and creative, for example, and horrible at fulfillment. All core competencies need to be developed and managed for success.

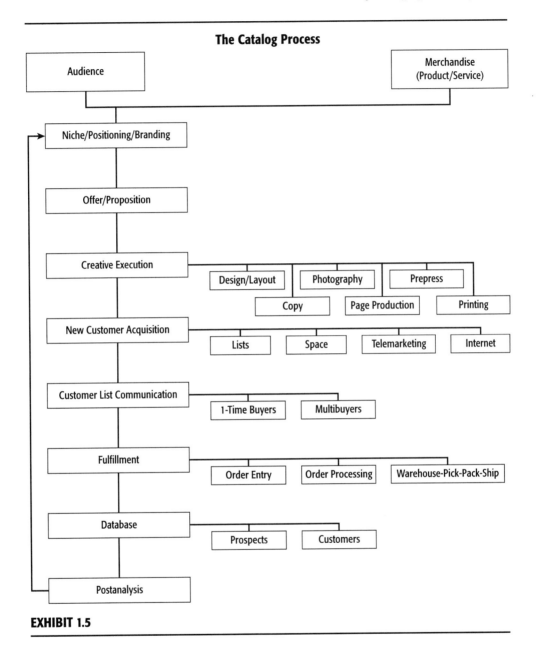

EXHIBIT 1.5

In a successful catalog, every core competency is a well-honed subsystem or sub-process, and each one operates in a tightly interconnected way. One subprocess supports and feeds information to another. For example, in the course of a year, a cataloger might run five or six promotion campaigns, some at the same time. All subsystems of the catalog work together to run the campaigns: merchandising, inventory, creative marketing, database fulfillment, and analysis.

The catalog process begins when a catalog is launched and never ends unless the catalog calls it quits. In the months or years between those two events, the process is circular: some function is always under way. Because it is circular, smart catalogers have the opportunity to fine-tune the process each time a catalog is produced. Doing so will make the process smoother and the catalog more profitable.

Let's take a brief look at each of the functions or competencies.

Core Competency #1: Merchandising

Like the foundation of a building, the product is the starting point—the structure without which no catalog can exist. Fundamental to the success of the business, merchandising is the number one core competency. Necessary skills that will be described in more detail in Chapters 2 and 3 include:

- Understanding the target audience(s) to whom the catalog is being positioned
- Preparing a competitive analysis of product with respect to pricing, product categories, and positioning
- Developing a product pool
- Negotiating terms and conditions for purchase and rebuying of product
- Postanalyzing product by item, price point, category, and page
- Establishing inventory procedures and practices to manage the product supply

Core Competency #2: Niche, Positioning, and Branding

Be they retail, consumer, or business-to-business, winning catalogs have one thing in common: a well-defined, well-executed *persona* that clearly differentiates them from their competition. This is sometimes called the "voice of the catalog" and is reflected in the design, photography, and copy style that is used.

Ten years ago, few catalogers discussed branding. While niche and positioning were important, they left branding to packaged goods companies like Procter & Gamble. Today and in the future, catalogers work to build strong brands by staking out clear niches and making sure that all merchandising, creative, and marketing decisions support that brand. A strong brand creates brand loyalty, as Chapter 4 will explain. Customers who are loyal to a brand will spend more time with the catalog and make more purchases.

Core Competency #3: The Offer or Proposition

The **proposition** is what you are willing to give to your customers in return for their business. Examining the competition and understanding the target audience and the niche and brand of the catalog help catalogers determine which offers will best motivate customers or prospects to action. Offers need to be tested and retested to ensure that they are paying for themselves. Every offer must be examined in light of whether it enhances the brand. Different types of offers are presented in Chapter 4.

Core Competency #4: Creative Execution: Design, Photography, and Copy

Once the niche and brand have been determined and the offer or proposition decided, it's time to develop the creative execution—a winning combination of design, photography, and copy. The process takes about 120 days and includes the following subtasks, all discussed in Chapters 5 and 6:

- Defining format, specifications, and number of pages
- Building a detailed production schedule
- Paginating the catalog
- Developing concepts for the cover and pages
- Laying out the pages and order form
- Photography and copywriting
- Computer page production

Core Competency #5: Color Separations, Printing, Binding, Addressing, and Mailing

Printing and mailing the catalog is the final step of the creative process. Most catalogers work with outside vendors for prepress, printing, and mailing. Increasingly, all three of these tasks are offered by a single printer who can be relied on to effectively execute this final creative phase. The tasks involved in the last thirty days of the creative schedule, covered in Chapter 7, include:

- Selecting a color separator, a printer/mailer, and an order-form printer on the basis of bids and capabilities
- Reviewing color-separation scatters or scans to ensure that they are true to color
- Adjusting color
- Attending press approvals to ensure quality of printing
- Coordinating the mailing plan with the printer/mailer
- Monitoring binding and mail drop against the schedule

Core Competency #6: New Customer Acquisition

Building the customer list is critical to a cataloger's success. Prospecting efforts are expensive but necessary, because this is where growth comes from. Historically, catalog and direct marketing firms have relied heavily on mail-order rental names to build their customer lists. Instead of generating new buyers, they trade lists with and rent lists from other companies. Chapter 8 presents a new paradigm in customer acquisition: thinking more broadly and using public relations, customer referrals, space advertising, and alternative media such as the Internet to supplement the name-gathering process.

Circulation is the term for the mail-planning strategy process covered in Chapter 8, which includes:

- Planning the overall prospect mailing strategy for the year
- Preparing a detailed mailing plan complete with source codes, quantities mailed, and forecasting response from each list segment
- Calculating the breakeven for outside names
- Researching possible lists to test
- Developing alternative-media tests
- Coordinating merge-purge of outside names and house names for each mailing
- Postanalyzing lists to determine cost per name by source, lists that are exceeding breakeven, and other variables

Core Competency #7: Customer List Communication

The customer list is where profit comes from. Not only are customer names already paid for, but also customer lists will respond to an offer two, four, or even ten times more than a prospect list—generating the profits the company needs to expand.

Proper database and circulation management skills are essential for long-term profitability of the business. Too many catalogers undermail or undercommunicate with their customers, or treat customers as identical, instead of segmenting lists and mailing the best customers more often and poor customers less often, as well as reactivating old segments. Chapters 9 and 10 discuss the following tasks involved in managing the contact strategy with customers:

- Planning the overall customer mailing strategy for the year, including number of drops, remailings, and catalog variations
- Developing a list history and strategy with the database provider
- Preparing a detailed mailing plan for each segment of each mail drop, complete with source codes, quantities mailed, and forecasting response for each list segment
- Calculating the breakeven for the customer names
- Postanalyzing all customer list segments to determine profitability by source and lists that are exceeding breakeven
- As the list grows and ages, developing an RFMP (recency, frequency, monetary, and product category) segmentation scheme to obtain better results from each mail effort

Core Competency #8: Database

With a good database, a company can track prospect and customer mailings, gather purchase history, and develop more profitable mailing strategies. The tasks and process of database marketing as discussed in Chapter 9 include:

- Defining the prospect and customer file layout
- Ensuring that the specifications built into the fulfillment system will support all aspects of the database
- Building a customer list segmentation and strategy designed around RFMP (recency, frequency, monetary, and product category)
- Modeling buyer names for clues on how to emulate the catalog's top buyers in prospecting efforts
- Warehousing data

Core Competency #9: Fulfillment

Once considered a "nice-to-have" skill, today catalog fulfillment is a primary core competency that supports the niche and brand and can differentiate one catalog from another. Just think of Lands' End, L. L. Bean, and England's Marks & Spencer—all catalogs known for their outstanding fulfillment and customer service. These companies work hard to make sure that every time a customer makes an inquiry or places an order, they respond promptly, courteously, and efficiently. Chapter 11 defines and charts the fulfillment process and its six subfunctions:

- Receiving orders or requests from customers and order entry
- Filling the order, including warehousing; pick, pack, and shipping; and handling returns
- Inventory management systems
- Database management systems
- Accounting and credit card authorization
- Management information reporting

Core Competency #10: Testing, Measurement, and Analysis

Cataloging is a numbers business. Profitable catalogers understand and excel at testing, measuring, and analyzing results to make each new promotional campaign better than the last. By examining the quantitative details of every aspect of the catalog, it's possible to improve the effectiveness of each subsequent mailing or communication. As Exhibit 1.5 (see p. 9), again, makes clear, the postanalysis stage is ultimately connected back to the start of the flowchart. Testing, measurement, and analysis are discussed in several chapters; Chapter 12 covers the following analyses:

- Determining what merchandise is selling by looking at each item, price point, product category, and placement in the catalog
- Examining each outside list, space ad, or other medium used to acquire new customers
- Examining each house name by list segment
- Determining which offer, timing, or other test is producing the best results
- Ascertaining whether each creative aspect of the catalog is working to achieve maximum results
- Tracking all parts of fulfillment (fill rate, back orders, returns, cancellations, call center functions, etc.)
- Establishing catalog response cycles (by week) to better track performance during the life of the catalog
- Preparing a detailed post mailing profit and loss statement (P&L)and comparing it with the campaign plan

Note: The P&L may or may not show mark downs or liquidations mentioned on p. 52.

Staffing the Competencies

Profitable catalogers practice these core competencies in the everyday management of their business. Starting or growing catalogers need to build their skill levels in each of these ten areas. Exhibit 1.6 identifies seven areas of people expertise that catalogs must have in the first five years. Not all seven need to be on staff; for new catalogers, it is often less expensive to turn to strong outside partners to supply some of these skills. After five years, when a new venture has matured and is presumably making a profit, the catalog can consider bringing more of the competencies in-house.

Merchandising skill needs to be on staff as soon as possible. Although it is possible to hire top-notch merchandise consultants to assist in product sourcing, positioning the book, and building a merchandise vendor database, inside skills are important. Try to build from within from day one.

Circulation—deciding when, how often, and to whom to mail—is a skill that is often outsourced for the initial two or three years.

Most new catalogers opt to buy *creative skills* outside rather than building an internal team. Once the company is mailing six or more times a year, it may pay to have design and creative skills inside.

Analytical skills are often combined with circulation in small companies and together comprise the marketing function. These skills are closely related to the financial ones that are so important to the start-up process.

Unless a start-up cataloger is a business-to-business company or retailer with an existing warehouse and shipping operation, the *fulfillment* function should probably be farmed

Required Expertise–First Five Years

Merchandising
>	Product sourcing and selection
>	Inventory forecast and management
>	Merchandise database and postanalysis

Circulation
>	Building the customer list
>	Customer mailings
>	Promotion planning
>	Testing

Creative
>	Catalog execution
>	Design, copy, photography
>	Color separation and print buying
>	Mailing

Analytical
>	Breakevens
>	Buying/rebuying, inventory management
>	Campaign postanalysis

Fulfillment
>	Call center
>	Order processing
>	Data processing
>	Warehousing, pick-pack-ship, returns handling
>	Credit

Financial
>	Budgeting
>	Cash flow
>	Financing-investment
>	ROI

Database
>	Customer and prospect list maintenance
>	Merge-purge and list preparation for mailing
>	List segmentation and modeling

EXHIBIT 1.6

out. At least a half dozen full-line catalog fulfillment vendors have complete catalog operating systems and can handle call center and warehousing/pick-pack functions.

Financial acumen is a crucial area for new catalogs. No outside investor will be interested in a company that lacks this skill. Knowing what it takes to build a profitable catalog and how to get there is important.

Database management, which drives marketing and circulation, can be outsourced through the fulfillment company and its operating system, or via a data warehousing firm. As the fulfillment function is brought on staff, so should the database function be.

If you decide to search for companies, consultants, or potential employees to provide any core competency, screen them carefully. Ask whether they have worked on catalogs before. Look at samples, and contact references. Find out what the candidates know about your particular marketplace or product category. If you're developing a fashion catalog, you want a circulation person who understands the fashion business; if you're planning to sell ostrich and other exotic meats, you need somebody who knows the mail-order food segment.

The Role of the Catalog Consultant

The catalog consultant can be a cost-effective source of expertise for start-up catalogers that can't afford a full staff. Consultants can assist with the entire process of planning, developing, and launching a catalog, or just lend a hand with a specific project or stage, such as design, new customer acquisition, or testing and analysis. A catalog with in-house merchandising and marketing staff might turn to a consultant to design, photograph, and write copy for the catalog. When it's time to bring creative skills in-house, the consultant can help train the new hires.

Generally speaking, consultants are strong either in creative or in the "numbers" areas of analytical/financial/circulation, merchandising, and fulfillment—but seldom both. On the numbers side, the consultant can determine whether a new venture is feasible and how great the investment, cash flow, and return on investment (ROI) it will require. For an existing catalog, a consultant can audit operations to find ways to increase the bottom line, suggest improvements to processes and systems, and evaluate potential employees and train new ones.

Because very few consultants offer expertise in all areas, it may be necessary to hire more than one consultant, or to select a consultant with partners in several areas. Ask consultants about their strengths when you interview them. Like good doctors, they should be candid about areas in which they have less expertise.

❖ KEY POINTS

- Strategic planning will help determine whether a new venture is financially feasible, pinpoint how much capital will be required, and make it easier to secure funding.
- Careful strategic planning will also help identify the critical differences that distinguish a catalog's products and services from the competition.
- For the planning process to succeed, top management must be involved.
- A catalog must have access to all ten core competencies—either on staff or through a consultant—in order to increase its chances of success. Examine your resources carefully to find where your competencies need to be improved and where they can be outsourced.
- Perhaps an understanding of, and a facility in using, the Internet should be added as another core competency for profitable catalogers. The rapid acceptance of the Internet has already changed the marketing and merchandising landscape for catalogers.

PART 1

Merchandising

In a sense, a catalog is a "store without walls." Instead of a storefront and windows, a catalog has covers. Instead of a floor plan and departments, a catalog is organized by pages, spreads, and product categories. Where a store has a checkout counter, a catalog has an order form, telephone and fax numbers, and a website. And instead of people to sell the products, a catalog has copy.

Like stores, a catalog can be product driven or market driven. A product-driven catalog might be a business book produced by a lighting manufacturer, or a safety catalog produced by a safety product distributor. This type of company already produces a line of products and needs to ascertain who its buyers are. A retail example of a product-driven store is a plumbing supply outlet that needs to create a pool of plumber and contractor customers.

Most gift and apparel catalogs are market or audience focused. The Horchow Collection, Gump's, Coldwater Creek, and similar catalogs identify a target audience and develop or produce products that are right for them. These catalogs are similar to retail department stores that seek to entice a large customer base with a variety of unique products.

Whichever the focus—product or market—the two functions ultimately need to come together. A successful catalog is the blend of reaching the right audience with the right product or service.

Food-by-mail catalogs such as Wolferman's English Muffins, Honey Baked Ham, and Cushman Fruit Company are excellent examples of specialty-food catalogs that mail to both businesses and consumers during the holidays and year-round.

The success of a catalog's brand has everything to do with its merchandising "panache." In the next two chapters, you'll find out how to pinpoint the right audience, develop or source the right merchandise, and manage inventory profitably.

CHAPTER 2

Merchandising: Building Successful Products

Merchandising is the first and foremost core competency for any cataloger.

It's as important as the foundation of a house. Unless the foundation is solid, all aspects of the building and its construction may be in jeopardy. Without a solid product concept, a catalog's short- and long-term viability is questionable. If the merchandising idea is a fad without long-term customer interest, the catalog's future is probably limited. Survival will also be doubtful if the product concept is not unique.

In today's competitive catalog industry, new catalogs that succeed are highly niche driven. They find a narrow merchandise niche and drive it deep. A good example is a catalog from Three Dog Bakery (Exhibit 2.1). This young company combined its baking skills with its knowledge of the anthropomorphic relationship that many dog owners have with their pets. It doesn't try to be a full-line pet catalog, but concentrates instead on building retail stores and a supporting catalog—two separate selling channels—to grow the business. Talk about a narrow niche. But it works!

At one time, my company regularly received calls from prospective clients who hadn't a clue about their product and hoped we could help them "discover" the right one for their catalog. Fortunately, few new ventures today choose this long and expensive path to success. Most companies considering catalogs have a strong interest, skill level, and knowledge in a particular product or service. In short, they have a merchandise idea and are seeking an audience.

Fingerhut is a great example of a company that used a strong merchandise idea to find a market. In the 1940s, Manny Fingerhut and his brother were installing seat covers in cars when they decided to sell covers instead. A mail-order circular to Minnesota car owners generated so many sales that they branched out to other states. During the war, people purchased new seat covers because war production made new cars hard to come by. In the prosperous postwar years, however, purchasers of seat covers tended to be people who couldn't afford a new car. Thus, the focus on seat covers created a largely downscale base of customers who needed the house credit that eventually became Fingerhut's

EXHIBIT 2.1
Three Dog Bakery

unique selling proposition. Although Fingerhut added other merchandise, seat covers were still bringing in $10 million a year when I joined the company in the 1970s.

After fifty years of selling to their audience, Fingerhut's merchandise buyers know exactly how to match products and market. But they haven't stopped trying to learn more about their customers. A standout catalog continually seeks to gather more information about its market so that its merchandise buyers (the people responsible for sourcing, screening, and selecting products *for* the catalog, as opposed to the customers who purchase products *from* the catalog) can search for and select the right products. Whether your catalog is in its first year or its twentieth, you need to constantly ask, "Who is my target audience?"

Finding a Target Audience

There are three kinds of target markets or audiences:

1. A primary target audience that can be defined as the ideal customers
2. A secondary target audience of people who might be interested in the product but are judged to be not quite as good as the primary group
3. A tertiary target audience of people whose interest in the product is less pronounced than those in the primary or secondary groups

While a new cataloger with a proven product already selling in other channels *may* be able to identify its primary, secondary, and tertiary audience right off the bat, most new catalogers have to experiment first. Before it mailed its first catalog, a gymnastics apparel catalog believed that its primary target audience would be gymnastic clubs that purchase team uniforms, its secondary audience would be parents of gymnasts who belong to gymnastic clubs, and its tertiary audience would comprise the owners of gymnastic facilities who often stock apparel and staple gymnastic workout gear. Actual sales countered the catalog's expectations: parents were number one in sales, gymnastic facilities were second, and gymnastic clubs were third. In response, the catalog kept its product mix but reconfigured its mailing strategy to better concentrate on parents.

Finding and focusing on your best customers is a long-term process, not a one-shot project. A company with a customer list can start by profiling and segmenting current customers or sending out a research questionnaire to gather more demographic and psychographic information. A start-up catalog must begin with hypothetical primary, secondary, and tertiary customers and refine its definition as purchases are made.

As a catalog discovers who buys as well as what products and categories are being purchased, it can apply that knowledge to each subsequent mailing. Every mailing can make a company smarter, if new information is analyzed and applied to future decisions in a timely manner. As it moves up the experience curve, it will make better decisions about products and categories, price points and offers, lists, and mailing strategy. Every successful company—even Fingerhut—is continually fine-tuning its customer knowledge and assessing customer merchandise needs.

Wanted: Mail-Order Buyers

Not everyone in your target audience will want to purchase by mail. Exhibit 2.2, based on research that differentiated between people who make frequent mail-order purchases and those who do not, describes differences that all consumer catalog publishers should understand.

As the chart shows, frequent mail-order buyers find catalog shopping convenient, time-saving, and easy. They have confidence in mail-order shopping, and they expect to find unique, new items and good values. They trust catalog companies with strong brand

The Psychology of Catalog Buyers

Frequent Buyers	Infrequent Buyers
Convenience	
Quick and easy way to shop Comfortable alternative to retail A way to avoid crowds	Hassles in dealing with post office Waiting for an order Returning merchandise
Merchandise	
Unusual merchandise New products and styles Found merchandise that fits	Cannot see or feel merchandise Hard to judge quality Problems with fit, color, etc.
Customer's Outlook	
Confident In control Excitement, anticipation Dream fulfillment	Skeptical Afraid of losing control Fear of "rip offs"
Value	
Lower prices on special promos No driving to store Can comparison shop with other catalogs	Can shop around at retail More sales at retail Can control bills
Brand	

Experience in dealing with direct-
  mail companies selling uncommon
  brand names
Trust direct-mail companies
	Lack of experience in buying
	  unknown brands
	Uncertain about the reputation
	  of direct-mail companies

Need	
Can wait for products Order well in advance of special need	Want immediate gratification at time of purchase Waiting time is frustrating

EXHIBIT 2.2

recognition and are willing to wait for products. Infrequent mail-order buyers, on the other hand, are "touch-and-feel" people who love to shop retail but are negative about shopping by mail. They want the immediate satisfaction of trying on a product and taking it with them, and so they are skeptical and afraid of being "ripped off" by mail-order operators.

Don't waste time and energy trying to turn infrequent mail-order buyers into your customers. Focus on people who love to buy by mail. Chapter 8 introduces strategies to segment and select known mail-order customers from rental lists in order to build your house list of proven buyers.

Finding Information About Your Customers

"Know your customer" is the number one rule of merchandising. It is impossible to search for and select the right product unless the merchandise buyer thoroughly understands the target audience to whom the catalog sells.

Companies rely on three methods to find out about their customers and their needs: market research, customer dialogue, and customer advisory boards.

Conduct Market Research

Conduct some type of research on your customer list at least every eighteen to twenty-four months, and if possible, more often. It doesn't matter whether you use telephone interviews, a mail survey, focus groups, or even an in-the-box customer survey like the one in Exhibit 2.3. What's important is to do it and keep doing it on a regular basis. Position every survey to gather both specific and demographic information.

Very new catalogs can call customers to find out what they thought of the catalog and ask more detailed questions about who they are and why they purchased. Find out what other kinds of products they would like to be offered, and how they felt about product quality. Important information can also be gained by calling customers who have returned product. If most products have a return rate of 5 percent but one or two are being returned in larger quantities, call and find out the problem. When products go wrong, merchandisers need to know why.

Initiate a Dialogue with Customers When Taking Phone Orders

Because customer service staff and order specialists talk to customers and prospects every day, they often know more about customers than anyone else in the organization. Some catalog companies ask every management team member to spend one hour a month taking orders or fielding customer service calls as a way to stay in touch with customers and pass along important information to merchandisers. Other companies pose one research question monthly at the end of the ordering process. One month, they may ask about

Electric Outlet New Customer Survey

1. Please check the statement that best describes how you feel about catalog/direct-mail shopping.
   - ☐ I prefer to do my shopping through catalogs.
   - ☐ I prefer to shop at local stores but occasionally purchase from catalogs.
   - ☐ I am just as likely to shop at local stores as I am to order from a catalog.

2. How many items did you order from this catalog?
   - ☐ 1   ☐ 2   ☐ 3   ☐ 4   ☐ 5 or more

3. Did you have any problems on this order with: (check all that apply)
   - ☐ Out-of-stock merchandise
   - ☐ Back-ordered merchandise
   - ☐ Wrong item shipped
   - ☐ Other (please specify) _____

4. If you experienced any problems with your order, did you contact Customer Service at Electric Outlet?
   - ☐ Yes   ☐ No

5. If you contacted Customer Service, please tell us whether you agree or disagree with the following statements:

	Strongly Agree	Agree	Disagree	Strongly Disagree	Don't Know
Person was courteous.	☐	☐	☐	☐	☐
Person was knowledgeable.	☐	☐	☐	☐	☐
It was easy to contact Customer Service.	☐	☐	☐	☐	☐
The problem was handled to my satisfaction.	☐	☐	☐	☐	☐

6. Were the items you ordered:
   - ☐ For your own use
   - ☐ Gift(s)
   - ☐ Some items were for me; others were gift(s)

7. Compared to other direct-mail catalogs from which you have ordered, how would you rate the catalog, products, and services of Electric Outlet (EO)?

	EO Is Better	EO Is About the Same	EO Is Not as Good	Don't Know
Length of time it took to receive the order	☐	☐	☐	☐
Variety of merchandise	☐	☐	☐	☐
Products are unique and cannot easily be found in other places	☐	☐	☐	☐
Depth of products offered	☐	☐	☐	☐
Value of the merchandise for the price	☐	☐	☐	☐
Quality of the merchandise	☐	☐	☐	☐
Price	☐	☐	☐	☐
Clear and accurate product descriptions	☐	☐	☐	☐
Overall appeal of catalog	☐	☐	☐	☐
Ease of placing an order	☐	☐	☐	☐
Shipping and handling charges	☐	☐	☐	☐

8. Please check any catalogs from purchases in the past year.
   - ☐ Alsto's
   - ☐ Bloomingdale's
   - ☐ Hammacher Schlemmer
   - ☐ Charles Keath, Ltd.
   - ☐ Spiegel
   - ☐ Exposures
   - ☐ Norm Thompson
   - ☐ Self Care
   - ☐ Lifestyle Fascination
   - ☐ L.L. Bean
   - ☐ Brookstone
   - ☐ Frontgate
   - ☐ Lands' End
   - ☐ Tiffany & Co
   - ☐ Crate & Barrel
   - ☐ Solutions
   - ☐ Smith & Hawken
   - ☐ Williams-Sonoma
   - ☐ Neiman Marcus
   - ☐ Signals
   - ☐ The Sharper Image
   - ☐ Herrington
   - ☐ Talbots
   - ☐ Victoria's Secret
   - ☐ Preferred Living
   - ☐ Fingerhut

   Others (please specify) _____

9. Did you place this order from Electric Outlet by:
   - ☐ Telephone
   - ☐ Mail (skip to question 11)
   - ☐ Fax (skip to question 11)
   - ☐ Internet (skip to question 11)

10. If you placed your order by telephone, how would you rate the way your order was handled?

	Strongly Agree	Slightly Agree	Slightly Disagree	Strongly Disagree
Person was very courteous.	☐	☐	☐	☐
Person was able to answer all questions to my satisfaction.	☐	☐	☐	☐
I felt confident that my telephone order was handled properly.	☐	☐	☐	☐

11. Based on your ordering experience, how likely would you be to order again from Electric Outlet? (check one answer)
    - ☐ Definitely will order
    - ☐ Probably will order
    - ☐ May or may not order
    - ☐ Probably will not order
    - ☐ Definitely will not order

12. Are you: ☐ Male   ☐ Female

13. Are you:
    - ☐ 24 years or younger
    - ☐ 25 to 34
    - ☐ 35 to 44
    - ☐ 45 to 54
    - ☐ 55 to 64
    - ☐ 65 or older

14. Are you:
    - ☐ Single   ☐ Married   ☐ Separated/Divorced   ☐ Widowed

15. Last level of education you personally completed: (check one)
    - ☐ High school graduate
    - ☐ Some college
    - ☐ College graduate
    - ☐ Post-graduate work or degree

16. Children under 18 living at home: ☐ Yes   ☐ No

17. Total yearly income before taxes of your household:
    - ☐ Under $20,000
    - ☐ $20,000 to $39,999
    - ☐ $40,000 to $59,999
    - ☐ $60,000 to $79,999
    - ☐ $80,000 to $99,999
    - ☐ Over $100,000

EXHIBIT 2.3

Dear Electric Outlet Customer,

Thank you for your order! We hope you enjoy the "electric wonders" we've delivered to your door. We're interested in your opinion of the catalog and want to learn more about your needs so that we can serve you even better.

Please take a few moments to complete the survey on the reverse side of this sheet. Your response is anonymous and completely confidential. To mail the survey back, just fold it along the dotted lines and seal it with tape. No postage is necessary.

Thank you!

Fold Here

Thank You
For Sharing Your
Opinions With Us!

Fold Here

NO POSTAGE
NECESSARY
IF MAILED
IN THE
UNITED STATES

BUSINESS REPLY MAIL
FIRST CLASS   Permit No. 74   Duluth, MN
POSTAGE WILL BE PAID BY ADDRESSEE

Electric Outlet, Inc.
30 W. Superior St.
Duluth, Minnesota 55802-9986

EXHIBIT 2.3 (continued)

children at home; the next, about magazines or business periodicals that customers read. Tabulate responses to each question, and before long, you have a much better idea of who your customers are.

What You Need to Know About Your Customers

Merchandise buyers are hungry for information about who customers are, how they feel about catalog purchasing, and why they react the way they do. Answers to the "why" question are the hardest to gather and understand. Following are lists of the basic information that merchandise buyers must have in order to find products that complement their customers' needs.

Consumer Catalogs

- Name and address
- Phone, fax, and E-mail numbers
- Age
- Marital status
- Presence of children in the home, by age and perhaps gender
- Household income level
- Occupational information on members of household
- Type of dwelling
- Avocations/interests
- Mail-order or Internet buying history
- Primary method of buying (phone, fax, mail, on-line)

Business-to-Business Catalogs

- Name and address of company
- Who in the company makes buying decisions
- Who influences buying decisions
- Who places the orders
- Key contact(s)
- Phone, fax, and E-mail numbers of key contact(s)
- Size of the company (in sales or employees)
- Type of business, by SIC (standard industrial classification) code
- Number of locations or branches
- Is this a headquarters or branch
- Central or decentralized buying
- Mail-order or Internet buying history
- Method of buying (purchase order, phone, fax, mail, on-line)

Create an Advisory Board

Some companies select and employ an advisory board of actual customers to provide feedback on new product ideas, creative presentations, and merchandise ideas. For example, a sounding board can uncover regional preferences that, if they had gone undetected, could lead to product mistakes in food and gardening products, two areas in which regional differences matter a great deal. They may also advise catalogs on product quality concerns, pricing/value issues, and appropriateness of product offerings. Managing and compensating the advisory board panel is not difficult, and the feedback is valuable to product development. Advisory boards may grow in importance as more catalogs move into the international arena.

Selecting Successful Catalog Products

Use the following nine characteristics of successful mail-order products as a starting point or benchmark for selecting new items.

1. **Not readily available at retail.** If a product is a commodity available at every corner grocery or drugstore or at Kmart or Wal-Mart, it is unlikely to sell in a catalog. The more unusual a product, the better its chance for success.

2. **Easily shipped with little risk or damage.** Look for items that are sturdy, are simple to pack, and don't weigh a ton. When I was managing the Halls catalog, an upscale gift catalog, for Hallmark, the merchandise buyer showed us three magnificent glass candleholders that were two, three, and four feet high. They were exceptionally striking. We elected to put them in the holiday catalog, and sales were excellent. The only problem was that the product had about a 90 percent breakage rate in shipment because they were so fragile. Great item but bad for mail order.

3. **Visual, easily understood through photography or illustration.** Remember, a catalog is a "store without walls." There are no salespeople, and the photography or illustrations will be all that customers see. If they cannot understand what a product is or how it works, there is a limited chance of selling it. This point is discussed further in Chapter 6.

4. **Items, items, items—not lines of product.** Retail stores deal with product "lines," while catalog merchandisers concentrate on items. In catalogs, single items sell better than groups or lines of product. Most catalog photos and copy blocks focus on a single item, although it may come in several colors and sizes.

5. **Available in simple sizing with limited choices.** In mail order, too many choices tend to reduce response. Sears Roebuck's catalog product positioning was brilliant. It offered and built a business around three versions of an item:

good, better, and best. Another reason to offer men's shirts in only small, medium, large, and extra large rather than exact neck and sleeve size is that every version requires a separate SKU, or stock keeping unit. It's easier to manage four SKUs than thirty!

6. **Perceived value.** Consumer and business buyers perceive that buying directly from a catalog will keep prices lower. While eliminating the middleman leads to lower costs and increased value, this concept is not universally true. It is in every catalog's best interest to push the value perception, regardless of whether the entity is a discounter or the most upscale in positioning.

7. **Exclusive in color, size, features, or number of pieces.** In the competitive catalog world, offering some type of exclusivity—in configuration, size, pattern, or product bundle—will help eliminate retail comparison shopping. Copperbottom Revere Ware pots and pans, available in nearly every hardware and kitchenware store in the country, might not seem like an exclusive product. But Fingerhut sells Revere Ware in a set that features three pots and pans not available in any retail store— an "exclusive" bundled set that appeals to buyers.

8. **Broad appeal on a national level.** Here is another difference between retailers and catalogers. Many retailers concentrate on products for a small, often tight geographic market. Catalogers think nationally or even globally. Unless your catalog is mailing in a tight geographic area, the broader an item's appeal, the stronger the response will be.

9. **Margin.** Cataloging is a margin-driven business. Pick up an extra point of margin, and it will drop directly through to the bottom line. Lose a point, and your profits will shrink accordingly. Retailers typically work on what is called a *keystone margin*, or a 50 percent cost of goods. A store buys a product for $5.00 and sells it for $10.00. Traditional catalog giants such as Lillian Vernon, Fingerhut, and others that import products from overseas strive for a two-thirds, or 67 percent, margin—or a 33 percent cost of goods. The leverage of proper margins is discussed in the testing, measurement, and analysis chapters at the end of the book.

Other Customer Perceptions That Affect Merchandising

Three other customer perceptions about catalog merchandise also influence the merchandising effort. The first of these is ***perceived availability***. In a store, a prospective buyer can see how many units of a certain item are in stock. But to a catalog buyer, a catalog appears to be loaded with goods, whether it's three days or six months after the catalog is received. Perceived availability creates natural problems with inventory management. People hang on to catalogs . . . and orders are often received months and even years after mail date. Adding an expiration date or a "prices guaranteed until . . ." message to the covers or order form will help.

The second customer assumption, ***perceived authority and credibility*** favors new and start-up catalogs. To customers, a beautiful new catalog has as much credibility as a long-established one. And compared with retail trade, the cost of producing the first catalog is much less than opening a store; the catalog can create a virtual plush corporate office while operating out of a basement or an industrial park, outsourcing fulfillment, and using vendors to drop-ship product while maintaining only a minimal stock of goods.

The final perception is one of ***satisfaction***—a major differentiator between catalogs and retail stores. An important tenet of direct marketing is the "guarantee of satisfaction." Every catalog needs to bang this point home regularly in its pages, on the order form, in the opening spread, and even on the back cover. Very few retailers mention these words, even though shop owners will usually exchange or take back a product from a dissatisfied customer.

Building on Your Product Winners Through Effective Analysis

Merchandising has a strong emotional, gut feel, and intuitive side as well as a serious left-brain, or quantitative, side. Many items are selected for inclusion because the merchandise buyer instinctively knows that a product is "right." But in every catalog, some products, some price points, and some product categories do better than others. When it comes to reviewing product performance, instinct must give way to analysis. Analyzing how customers respond to the merchandise in each catalog can help merchandise buyers eliminate the losers and give customers more of what they are willing to purchase.

The following three analytical tools can help you "build on your winners" by refining your ability to select products that appeal to your target audience.

Marked-Up Catalog

Start the merchandise analysis process by physically marking up a catalog to show unit sales for each item. Write sales figures next to items directly on the page or a self-adhesive note. Summarize the pages and spread in the same manner. Exhibit 2.4 provides an example to follow.

Reviewing a marked-up book will make winners and losers apparent. You'll discover how various product categories performed, which position on the pages or spreads consistently produced winners, how different sections of the catalog performed, and how design and photo treatment—model versus no model, photo versus illustration, and so forth—affected response. The marked-up book also gives the merchant and the creative team a quick, visual way to assess:

- The relative importance and strength of "hot spots" versus all other catalog pages

- Sales per item and the relative strength of an item compared with the others on that spread
- Sales per page or per spread against a predetermined sales goal per page

Mark up every catalog, study it carefully, and apply the lessons you take away to future catalogs.

EXHIBIT 2.4
Space Store Catalog Example of a Marked-Up Catalog

Square-Inch Analysis

The second analytical technique, the "squinch" or square-inch analysis report, looks at every product's performance against other products and the amount of space used for each item on the page. This fairly simple spreadsheet analysis is sometimes a by-product of the catalog's operating system. Exhibit 2.5 illustrates how to organize this spreadsheet by sorting

EXHIBIT 2.4 (continued)
Space Store Catalog   Example of a Marked-Up Catalog

Merchandise Square-Inch Analysis (Analysis Shown by Page)

Advertising Cost: $11,169

Item No.	Description	Cost	Retail	Cost of Goods—%	Actual Units Sold	Sales	Cost of Goods—$	Gross Margin	Space Allocation	Space Cost—%	Space Cost—$	Contribution to OH & Profit
Page 1												
MLQKA1	Recipe box	$9.00	$18.00	50.0%	15	$270.00	$135.00	$135.00	5.0%	1.30%	$145.05	($10.05)
MLQKA2	Coupon keeper	$4.50	$9.00	50.0%	24	$216.00	$108.00	$108.00	5.0%	1.30%	$145.05	($37.05)
MLQKA3	Recipe binder	$12.50	$25.00	50.0%	25	$625.00	$312.50	$312.50	5.0%	1.30%	$145.05	$167.45
MLQKA4	Organizer	$8.00	$16.00	50.0%	12	$192.00	$96.00	$96.00	5.0%	1.30%	$145.05	($49.05)
MLQKA5	Extra recipe cards—set of 50	$1.75	$3.50	50.0%	62	$217.00	$108.50	$108.50	5.0%	1.30%	$145.05	($36.55)
MLQKA6	Extra binder pages—set of 75	$2.50	$5.00	50.0%	14	$70.00	$35.00	$35.00	5.0%	1.30%	$145.05	($110.05)
SAGS	Plaque	$13.00	$26.00	50.0%	34	$884.00	$442.00	$442.00	10.0%	2.60%	$290.10	$151.90
GMR	Rug	$6.25	$12.50	50.0%	91	$1,137.50	$568.75	$568.75	15.0%	3.90%	$435.16	$133.59
BDPH2	Pot holder	$1.50	$3.00	50.0%	114	$342.00	$171.00	$171.00	10.0%	2.60%	$290.10	($119.10)
BDOM2	Oven mitt	$2.05	$6.00	34.2%	82	$492.00	$168.10	$323.90	10.0%	2.60%	$290.10	$33.80
BDTP2	Tea towel	$2.00	$6.00	33.5%	145	$870.00	$290.00	$580.00	10.0%	2.60%	$290.10	$289.90
	Page Summary				618	$5,315.50	$2,434.85	$2,880.65	85.0%	22.08%	$2,465.88	$414.77
Page 2												
TEGH1	Tumbler A, large	$3.50	$7.00	50.0%	108	$756.00	$378.00	$378.00	5.0%	1.30%	$145.05	$232.95
TEGH2	Tumbler A, small	$3.50	$7.00	50.0%	45	$315.00	$157.50	$157.50	5.0%	1.30%	$145.05	$12.45
TEGB1	Tumbler B, large	$3.50	$7.00	50.0%	67	$469.00	$234.50	$234.50	5.0%	1.30%	$145.05	$89.45
TEGB2	Tumbler B, small	$3.50	$7.00	50.0%	35	$245.00	$122.50	$122.50	5.0%	1.30%	$145.05	($22.55)
LTB1	Birdhouse A	$30.00	$60.00	50.0%	8	$480.00	$240.00	$240.00	8.0%	2.08%	$232.08	$7.92
LTB2	Birdhouse B	$30.00	$60.00	50.0%	10	$600.00	$300.00	$300.00	8.0%	2.08%	$232.08	$67.92
LTB3	Rose	$30.00	$60.00	50.0%	4	$240.00	$120.00	$120.00	8.0%	2.08%	$232.08	($112.08)
TEBUT	Butler's tray	$20.00	$48.00	41.7%	18	$864.00	$360.00	$504.00	13.0%	3.38%	$377.14	$126.86
TEC & D	Chip and dip tray	$16.00	$32.00	50.0%	17	$544.00	$272.00	$272.00	10.0%	2.60%	$290.10	($18.10)
TEPI	Pitcher	$18.00	$36.00	50.0%	9	$324.00	$162.00	$162.00	7.0%	1.82%	$203.07	($41.07)
SAGP	Plant plaque	$25.00	$50.00	50.0%	20	$1,000.00	$500.00	$500.00	16.0%	4.16%	$464.17	$35.83
AMOC	Outdoor companion	$12.48	$24.95	50.0%	24	$598.80	$299.52	$299.28	10.0%	2.60%	$290.10	$9.18
	Page Summary				365	$6,435.80	$3,146.02	$3,289.78	100.0%	25.97%	$2,901.04	$388.74
Page 3												
GASUMP	Half-gallon pitcher	$22.22	$36.00	61.7%	48	$1,728.00	$1,066.56	$661.44	9.0%	2.34%	$261.09	$400.35
GASUMR	Platter, 15"	$25.56	$56.00	45.6%	23	$1,288.00	$587.88	$700.12	9.0%	2.34%	$261.09	$439.03
GASUMM	Big fruit bowl	$16.67	$38.00	43.9%	57	$2,166.00	$950.19	$1,215.81	9.0%	2.34%	$261.09	$954.72
STP	Plaque	$14.00	$35.00	40.0%	11	$385.00	$154.00	$231.00	10.0%	2.60%	$290.10	($59.10)
STS	Planter A	$10.00	$29.00	34.5%	64	$1,856.00	$640.00	$1,216.00	13.0%	3.38%	$377.14	$838.86
STP1	Planter B	$22.00	$49.00	44.9%	31	$1,519.00	$682.00	$837.00	13.0%	3.38%	$377.14	$459.86
STP2	Planter C	$18.00	$49.00	36.7%	14	$686.00	$252.00	$434.00	13.0%	3.38%	$377.14	$56.86
CAWC1	Wind chime A	$11.50	$23.00	50.0%	18	$414.00	$207.00	$207.00	8.0%	2.08%	$232.08	($25.08)
CAWC2	Wind chime B	$11.50	$23.00	50.0%	16	$368.00	$184.00	$184.00	8.0%	2.08%	$232.08	($48.08)
CAWC3	Wind chime C	$11.50	$23.00	50.0%	20	$460.00	$230.00	$230.00	8.0%	2.08%	$232.08	($2.08)
	Page Summary				302	$10,870.00	$4,953.63	$5,915.37	100.0%	25.97%	$2,901.04	$3,015.33
Page 4												
BDBT	Beach towel	$8.75	$17.50	50.0%	59	$1,032.50	$516.25	$516.25	20.0%	5.19%	$580.21	($63.96)
PET	Tote bag	$6.90	$15.00	46.0%	40	$600.00	$276.00	$324.00	8.0%	2.08%	$232.08	$91.92
SVSS1	T-shirt A	$7.00	$14.00	50.0%	318	$4,452.00	$2,226.00	$2,226.00	13.0%	3.38%	$377.14	$1,848.86
SVSS2	T-shirt B	$7.00	$14.00	50.0%	46	$644.00	$322.00	$322.00	13.0%	3.38%	$377.14	($55.14)
PUD2	Doll	$32.00	$64.00	50.0%	45	$2,880.00	$1,440.00	$1,440.00	15.0%	3.90%	$435.16	$1,004.84
ANSS2	Stamp book	$12.50	$25.00	50.0%	135	$3,375.00	$1,687.50	$1,687.50	15.0%	3.90%	$435.16	$1,252.34
AMCB	To Do Book	$4.48	$8.95	50.1%	242	$2,165.90	$1,084.16	$1,081.74	16.0%	4.16%	$464.17	$617.57
	Page Summary				885	$15,149.40	$7,551.91	$7,597.49	100.0%	25.97%	$2,901.04	$4,696.45
GRAND TOTAL					2170	$37,770.70	$18,086.41	$19,684.29	385.0%	100.00%	$11,169.00	$8,515.29

EXHIBIT 2.5

products by page. It shows, for each item, the cost, actual selling (or retail) price, units sold, sales, cost of goods, gross margin, cost of the space, and, in the far right column, the product's contribution to fulfillment, overhead, and profit.

Don't worry about measuring space for each item down to the tenth of a millimeter. Rather, allocate space on the basis of one-quarter of a page or one-eighth of a page, and so on. Nonselling space such as the president's letter, testimonials, and editorial sidebars need to be allocated as well so that all space in the catalog is accounted for. Nonselling space is important in a catalog, but it must be paid for by all the products.

This initial spreadsheet can be sorted several ways to help merchants determine the relative strength of different subgroups. Exhibit 2.6 shows products sorted and ranked by contribution, with the largest contributors listed first. The report can be sorted as well by units sold, sales per item, product category, or price point ($0 to $10, $10.01 to $20, $20.01 to $30, etc.). It can also compare the performance of new items against repeat items to ascertain when to "rest" a product before repeating it or when to reduce its space.

Ultimately you will have a solid analytical comparison of each item based on the amount of space it occupies in the catalog. Understanding the profit contribution of each item can help the merchandising and creative staff determine where and how to adjust future product offerings, allocate space, and paginate catalogs. Merchandisers likewise can use its conclusions to increase or decrease space allocated to a product, or drop the item altogether. There is no emotional evaluation here. It is all hard facts—what has sold, how much it cost, and how much space on the page it took to sell it.

Merchandise Category and Price Point Grid

The final analytical planning tool used by merchandisers is the merchandise category and price point grid. Exhibit 2.7 (see p. 35), an example from a gift cataloger, summarizes the products by two key variables—product category (the left vertical column) and price point (the top row).

This analysis indicates whether there are "holes" in the product mix in either product category or price point. It also can be used to estimate a catalog's average order value. If the average price of a product in your catalog is $25 and you anticipate receiving two line items per order, your average order value, or AOV, will be $50.

This is a most useful tool for planning and reviewing a new catalog's product mix and can also help analyze competitive catalogs to determine their product and price coverage. Discovering the products and prices that competitors are emphasizing can help make your launch more successful.

Merchandise Square-Inch Analysis (Analysis Ranked by Profit Contribution)

Advertising Cost: $11,169

Item No.	Description	Cost	Retail	Cost of Goods—%	Actual Units Sold	Sales	Cost of Goods—$	Gross Margin	Space Allocation	Space Cost—%	Space Cost—$	Contribution to OH & Profit
SVS1	T-shirt A	$7.00	$14.00	50.0%	318	$4,452.00	$2,226.00	$2,226.00	13.0%	3.38%	$377.14	$1,848.86
ANSS2	Stamp book	$12.50	$25.00	50.0%	135	$3,375.00	$1,687.50	$1,687.50	15.0%	3.90%	$435.16	$1,252.34
PUD2	Doll	$32.00	$64.00	50.0%	45	$2,880.00	$1,440.00	$1,440.00	15.0%	3.90%	$435.16	$1,004.84
GASUMM	Big fruit bowl	$16.67	$38.00	43.9%	57	$2,166.00	$950.19	$1,215.81	9.0%	2.34%	$261.09	$954.72
STS	Planter A	$10.00	$29.00	34.5%	64	$1,856.00	$640.00	$1,216.00	13.0%	3.38%	$377.14	$838.86
AMCB	To Do book	$4.48	$8.95	50.1%	242	$2,165.00	$1,084.16	$1,081.74	16.0%	4.16%	$464.17	$617.57
STP1	Planter B	$22.00	$49.00	44.9%	31	$1,519.00	$682.00	$837.00	13.0%	3.38%	$377.14	$459.86
GASUMR	Platter, 15"	$25.56	$56.00	45.6%	23	$1,288.00	$587.88	$700.12	9.0%	2.34%	$261.09	$439.03
GASUMP	Half-gallon pitcher	$22.22	$36.00	61.7%	48	$1,728.00	$1,066.56	$661.44	9.0%	2.34%	$261.09	$400.35
BDTP2	Tea towel	$2.00	$6.00	33.3%	145	$870.00	$290.00	$580.00	10.0%	2.60%	$290.10	$289.90
TEGH1	Tumbler A, large	$3.50	$7.00	50.0%	108	$756.00	$378.00	$378.00	5.0%	1.30%	$145.05	$232.95
MLQKA3	Recipe binder	$12.50	$25.00	50.0%	25	$625.00	$312.50	$312.50	5.0%	1.30%	$145.05	$167.45
SAGS	Plaque	$13.00	$26.00	50.0%	34	$884.00	$442.00	$442.00	10.0%	2.60%	$290.10	$151.90
GMR	Rug	$6.25	$12.50	50.0%	91	$1,137.50	$568.75	$568.75	15.0%	3.90%	$435.16	$133.59
TEBUT	Butler's tray	$20.00	$48.00	41.7%	18	$864.00	$360.00	$504.00	13.0%	3.38%	$377.14	$126.86
PET	Tote bag	$6.90	$15.00	46.0%	40	$600.00	$276.00	$324.00	8.0%	2.08%	$232.08	$91.92
TEGB1	Tumbler B, large	$3.50	$7.00	50.0%	67	$469.00	$234.50	$234.50	5.0%	1.30%	$145.05	$89.45
LTB2	Birdhouse B	$30.00	$60.00	50.0%	10	$600.00	$300.00	$300.00	8.0%	2.08%	$232.08	$67.92
STP2	Planter C	$18.00	$49.00	36.7%	14	$686.00	$252.00	$434.00	13.0%	3.38%	$377.14	$56.86
SAGP	Plant plaque	$25.00	$50.00	50.0%	20	$1,000.00	$500.00	$500.00	16.0%	4.16%	$464.17	$35.83
BDOM2	Oven mitt	$2.05	$6.00	34.2%	82	$492.00	$168.10	$323.90	10.0%	2.60%	$290.10	$33.80
TEGH2	Tumbler A, small	$3.50	$7.00	50.0%	45	$315.00	$157.50	$157.50	5.0%	1.30%	$145.05	$12.45
AMOC	Outdoor companion	$12.48	$24.95	50.0%	24	$598.80	$299.52	$299.28	10.0%	2.60%	$290.10	$9.18
LTB1	Birdhouse A	$30.00	$60.00	50.0%	8	$480.00	$240.00	$240.00	8.0%	2.08%	$232.08	$7.92
CAWC3	Wind chime C	$11.50	$23.00	50.0%	20	$460.00	$230.00	$230.00	8.0%	2.08%	$232.08	($2.08)
MLQKA1	Recipe box	$9.00	$18.00	50.0%	15	$270.00	$135.00	$135.00	5.0%	1.30%	$145.05	($10.05)
TEC & D	Chip and dip tray	$16.00	$32.00	50.0%	17	$544.00	$272.00	$272.00	10.0%	2.60%	$290.10	($18.10)
TEGB2	Tumbler B, small	$3.50	$7.00	50.0%	35	$245.00	$122.50	$122.50	5.0%	1.30%	$145.05	($22.55)
CAWC1	Wind chime A	$11.50	$23.00	50.0%	18	$414.00	$207.00	$207.00	8.0%	2.08%	$232.08	($25.08)
MLQKA5	Extra recipe cards—set of 50	$1.75	$3.50	50.0%	62	$217.00	$108.50	$108.50	5.0%	1.30%	$145.05	($36.55)
MLQKA2	Coupon keeper	$4.50	$9.00	50.0%	24	$216.00	$108.00	$108.00	5.0%	1.30%	$145.05	($37.05)
TEPI	Pitcher	$18.00	$36.00	50.0%	9	$324.00	$162.00	$162.00	7.0%	1.82%	$203.07	($41.07)
CAWC2	Wind chime B	$11.50	$23.00	50.0%	16	$368.00	$184.00	$184.00	8.0%	2.08%	$232.08	($48.08)
MLQKA4	Organizer	$8.00	$16.00	50.0%	12	$192.00	$96.00	$96.00	5.0%	1.30%	$145.05	($49.05)
SVSS2	T-shirt B	$7.00	$14.00	50.0%	46	$644.00	$322.00	$322.00	13.0%	3.38%	$377.14	($55.14)
STP	Plaque	$14.00	$35.00	40.0%	11	$385.00	$154.00	$231.00	10.0%	2.60%	$290.10	($59.10)
BDBT	Beach Towel	$8.75	$17.50	50.0%	59	$1,032.50	$516.25	$516.25	20.0%	5.19%	$580.21	($63.96)
MLQKA6	Extra binder pages—set of 75	$2.50	$5.00	50.0%	14	$70.00	$35.00	$35.00	5.0%	1.30%	$145.05	($110.05)
LTB3	Rose	$30.00	$60.00	50.0%	4	$240.00	$120.00	$120.00	8.0%	2.08%	$232.08	($112.08)
BDPH2	Pot holder	$1.50	$3.00	50.0%	114	$342.00	$171.00	$171.00	10.0%	2.60%	$290.10	($119.10)

EXHIBIT 2.6

Merchandise Category and Price Point Grid

Category	$0–25	$26–50	$51–75	$76–100	$101–125	$126–150	$151–200	$201–250	$251–300	$300+	Total	%
Decor	1	1		2							4	1.5%
Entertainment	8	4	2	5		5		1		4	29	11.0%
Home Comfort	5	4	2	2		1		1			15	5.7%
Home Protection							1		1	1	3	1.2%
Household	13	15	5	2		1	3			1	40	15.2%
Kitchen Products	3	2	2	2							9	3.4%
Lighting	36	19	6	3		1	1				66	25.1%
Massage				2			3				5	1.9%
Medical	2	2		2							6	2.3%
Phone		3	2	3	1		3				12	4.6%
Recreation	3	4		3						5	15	5.7%
Satellite Packages	12	2									14	5.3%
Tools	6	8	1	2			1				18	6.8%
Miscellaneous	12	6	4	2		1	2				27	10.3%
Total	101	70	24	30	1	9	14	2	1	11	263	
Percent	38.4%	26.6%	9.1%	11.4%	0.4%	3.4%	5.3%	0.8%	0.4%	4.2%		100.0%

EXHIBIT 2.7

❖ KEY POINTS

- Define your target audience(s), and build your product line with them in mind. Remember that target audiences may shift or need to be reprioritized.
- Review and understand the research that differentiates between "frequent catalog buyers" and "infrequent catalog buyers."
- Learn and understand as much as you can about who your customers are and why they are buying your products. Consider regular contact with your customers through surveys, phone contact, and other types of research.
- Examine the characteristics of a successful mail-order product when selecting items and categories of product.
- Use all available postanalysis tools to better understand what your customers are buying. Build on and apply that knowledge in expanding (or contracting) your product line.

CHAPTER 3

Sourcing New Products and Managing Inventory

Woody Hayes, the outstanding Ohio State football coach noted for his commitment to the "running game," expressed deep concern about passing the football. Three things can happen when a team throws the forward pass, he said, and two of them are bad. The pass can be caught, usually for a gain in yardage, but it can also be dropped or intercepted. That's why during Woody's era, Ohio State stuck to running the football.

Inventory management is like the forward pass. If a catalog forecasts to sell 1,000 pieces of an item, three things can occur, and two of them can be trouble. Positive things happen if the catalog actually sells 1,000 of the item—but problems develop if it receives orders for 4,000 or 250. Skillful buying, rebuying, and managing inventory can solve these problems; poor inventory management will only aggravate them.

Selecting new products for a catalog is an emotion-driven process, and many merchandisers let their "gut" instincts guide them. Back in the 1970s, a gift and apparel catalog called Kaleidoscope was a model of successful catalog merchandising. The owners displayed uncanny taste and acumen in selecting and displaying unique products. The catalog's creative presentation enhanced the wonderful products, and the printing was a step above other mailings of the time. Customers flocked to this new catalog for unique and special items. But in spite of its great products and stunning creative, Kaleidoscope fell victim to poor inventory management and fulfillment practices.

Instinct and emotion need to be laid aside when it's time to forecast, order, and reorder products. Inventory management is a quantitative process—a core competency that is a key to catalog profitability in every industry. Apparel catalogs can expect high returns and cancellations—up to 25 percent or 30 percent of sales—and typically have very few items repeated from season to season. Business catalogs, conversely, often have a high number of repeated items from catalog to catalog, with only 20 percent to 25 percent new products. No matter what the industry, inventory is a major asset that needs careful attention and management. This chapter examines the merchandise buying process diagrammed in Exhibit 3.1 and shows how to carefully manage the product development, buying, and rebuying cycle.

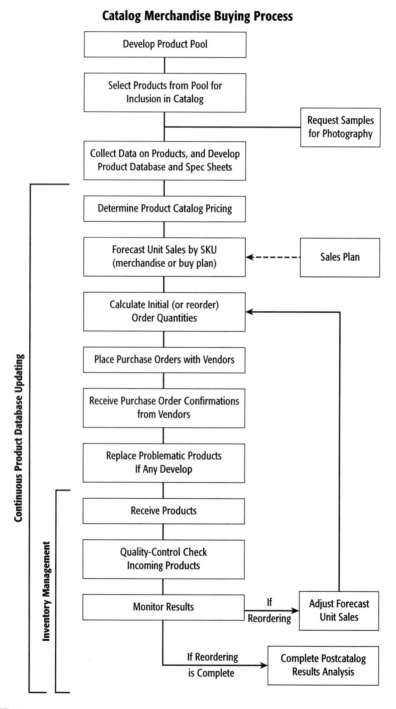

Catalog Merchandise Buying Process

EXHIBIT 3.1

Sourcing and Selecting Product

The merchandiser's first job is to develop and source great product. New product development is a highly proactive process that requires tenacious observation and tracking of the competition, active attendance at relevant trade shows, aggressive vendor pursuit, talking with and soliciting ideas from customers, staff brainstorming, and being open and responsive to new ideas. Good product buyers are like blotters in absorbing and seeking new concepts and items.

Most companies look to the product sources shown in Exhibits 3.2 and 3.3, the results of surveys conducted by the Direct Marketing Association and W. A. Dean & Associates. While few companies actually take the time to manufacture their own products, many do work with importers and foreign manufacturers to reproduce a concept less expensively. A direct-import version of a popular product can improve catalog margins tremendously, but it is fraught with inventory risk. The longer manufacturing and shipping schedule means you may need to forecast and place orders for two catalog seasons rather than one. If the product is a winner, reordering merchandise may be difficult or impossible; if it bombs, you will be stuck with unreturnable merchandise. Quality control is also a challenge for some imported products.

A product buyer needs to find many more products than will ultimately be used in the catalog. For a forty-eight-page book with 4 to 5 items per page, approximately 190 to 240 items will be selected. To narrow the final product selection to this number, at least

---

Source of New Product Ideas

This year respondents reversed a trend we had been observing in past surveys. In the past, we have observed a trend toward internal product development and away from such insular sources as buying trips, vendor presentations, and trade shows. This year, for both consumer and hybrid, trade shows were the second most important source of ideas. Similarly, vendor presentations in the office, which slid to third overall, remain a very strong source of ideas.

	All Respondents	Consumer	Hybrid	B-to-B
Internal Product Development	27%	27%	30%	26%
Trade Shows	18%	21%	15%	12%
Vendor Presentations in Office	13%	12%	14%	19%
Competitors	9%	7%	7%	14%
Your Customers	9%	5%	14%	17%
Domestic Buying Trips	8%	10%	3%	3%
Overseas Buying Trips	5%	8%	0%	1%
Trade Journals	5%	4%	10%	5%
Other	4%	4%	4%	4%
Consumer Media	2%	3%	4%	1%

Source: W. A. Dean & Associates, The Annual Catalog Survey, 1997 Results.

EXHIBIT 3.2

Top Five Sources of Merchandise

Catalogers were asked to rate nine sources of merchandise using a five-point scale, where 5 represents a very important merchandise source and 1 represents a very poor one. The percentages below represent those ranked in the top 2, in terms of importance.

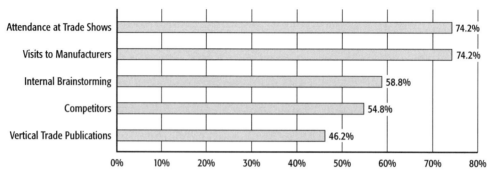

Source: *Catalog Age*, Merchandising Benchmark Report, 1997

EXHIBIT 3.3

300 to 350 items will be needed to form the merchandise pool. A number of backup products should be selected and kept in the wings, because some of the desired items will not be available during the catalog production process.

Finding 300 unique items is a formidable task, and some seasons it's harder than others. Sometimes there is simply a dearth of good products available, even from your best sources; other seasons, there is a plethora of great merchandise. Sourcing is also time consuming. A manufacturer or retailer with an established product line may be able to source additional products in less than 60 days; a cataloger starting from scratch should allow between 90 and 180 days for the process.

Developing Product Specification Sheets and a Merchandise Database

Once items have been selected, data on each product need to be collected on a specification sheet that is included in the product folder. (See examples in Exhibits 3.4 and 3.5.) A product folder contains everything pertinent to the product: vendor tear sheets and information, terms, product photographs, samples, and so forth. Ultimately, the folder is handed over to the creative team, where it becomes the copywriter's source for sell copy as well as size, color, price, and other details included in the copy block. The designer will also review the information to place products in the page layouts. Vendors are the best source for the information gathered in the file and the specification sheet. Be sure to ask vendors about each product's benefits as well as its features.

The Catalog Company Product Specification Sheet   Date _____

Manufacturer

Company Name _____

Address _____

City/State/Zip _____

Contact Person _____

Phone No. (   ) _____ Toll-Free No. (   ) _____ Fax (   ) _____ E-mail _____

Terms

Payment Terms _____ Discounts _____ Advertising Allowance _____

Minimum Order $ _____ Minimum Reorder $ _____ Other _____

Return Policy _____

Packaging & Shipping

Shipping & Requirements/Carrier _____

F.O.B. Point _____ Freight Allowance _____

Product Information (Please complete for each product requested)

Product _____ Description _____ Yes ___ No ___

Mfg. Stock. No. _____ Style/Design No. _____ Spanish Instructions Available? _____ Yes ___ No ___

Size(s) _____ Weight _____ Color(s) _____

Cost _____ Suggested Retail _____ Country of Origin _____

Availability

Date Available _____ Guaranteed Availability Until _____ Lead Time _____

Is the product individually boxed? _____ Yes ___ No ___ Can box be reshipped? _____ Yes ___ No ___

Case Pack _____ Case Lots Purchase Required _____ Direct Import Available? ___ Yes ___ No ___

Copy Information _____

Special Features: Warranty, specifications, approvals. Benefits, unique uses, limitations, etc. (Attach descriptive material.) _____

_____

Is product currently offered by direct mail or catalog in the U.S.? Yes ___ (List catalogs and attach tear sheets.) No ___

Catalogs/Media _____

Return to The Catalog Company c/o

EXHIBIT 3.4

Catalog Specifications

Catalog No. _____
Promotional Period _____ thru _____
Date Form Sent _____

The item noted below is being considered for our Mail Order Catalog. Please fill out form as completely as possible and return it to us within 7 days. Inclusion of your item in this catalog cannot be considered without your signed specification sheet.

Vendor:

Item: _____

_____

Phone #:

Cost and Discount Information	Suggested Retail _____ Unit Cost (before discounts and allowances) _____ Catalog/Advertising Allowance _____ % Net Cost _____ Quantity Discount _____ % What Quantity _____ Freight Allowance _____ Mail Order Exclusive _____ Payment Terms _____ F.O.B. Point _____ Have you dealt with a mail-order catalog in the past? _____ Is this item being considered by any other catalogs? _____ To help defray costs of photographing your product, a deduction of $50 will be taken off the initial invoice. _____
Product Description	Imported or Domestic? (circle one) Country of Origin _____ Dimensions of single piece _____ Weight of single piece _____ Made of what materials _____ Colors or variations available _____ Do you carry product liability insurance? _____ Do you have plans to discontinue this item? _____ If so, when? _____
Shipping Information	Master Pack _____ Minimum Order _____ Individually boxed? _____ Is box reshippable? _____ Is reshipper available? _____ Any extra cost _____ Normal on-hand supply? _____ Do you cancel back orders? _____ Lead time needed on reorders _____ At season's end, it may be necessary for us to order less than master pack. _____ Is drop-shipping available? _____ Give details regarding cost, turnaround time, etc. _____
Copy Tips	Examples: history, name of artist, unique uses, U.L. approved, dishwasher or microwave oven safe, handmade, warranty. Include catalog sheets or descriptive material. Any specifications of limitations _____
Catalog Company	May safely include this item in the catalog. It is understood that the commitment made above with the terms and conditions on the back of this form constitute an agreement for the catalog promotion period listed. _____ Vendor Authorized Signature

Please indicate address to which orders are to be sent if not the same as above: _____

A sample of your item has already been obtained through _____

Please sign and return all three copies. When we have made our final selections, we will send you a confirming copy, to be followed by a purchase order.

EXHIBIT 3.5

The information in the product folder and specification sheet also needs to be entered in a simple, off-line merchandising database. A product and vendor database makes it easier to gather, say, all the products from one vendor in order to negotiate the entire purchase, or to see quickly how many products are in a certain category or at a certain price point. An organized database also makes it easier to track open purchase orders and to transmit payment information to the accounting department. The merchandise database chart in Exhibit 3.6 shows the broad role of the database for each product.

The database should track every product or item in the catalog in the following ways:

- **By item description and specification.** Provide a physical description, including sizes and colors, along with selling price, cost, lead times for ordering, and minimum order quantities for every SKU (stock keeping unit).
- **By vendor.** Enter information about the company, its key contacts, and how to reach them by phone, fax, and E-mail. Additional vendor information typically includes payment and credit terms, minimum order quantity and reorder quantity, warehouse location, return policy, drop-shipping capability, freight allowance, and advertising allowance.
- **By category.** Every SKU is part of a larger product category or grouping such as those shown in the exhibit.
- **By purchase order.** For every SKU, create a record of purchase activity that includes the date, purchase order number, quantity ordered, cost of that particular purchase order, and shipping cost.

Information about customer purchases, returns, and cancellations—all important to the merchandising inventory process—is maintained in the customer database but should be relayed to the merchandising team. Returned products or product orders canceled due to back orders may indicate problems with vendors or quality control that merchandising staff needs to address as quickly as possible.

Creating the Product Forecast and Buy Plan

Once the marketing group estimates how many catalogs will be printed and mailed (see circulation planning in Chapters 8 & 9), the inventory management team can create a ***buy plan*** that forecasts to the best of their ability how many of each item are planned to be sold in the catalog. A sample is shown in Exhibit 3.7. Pricing is usually finalized at this time so that margin or cost of goods can be determined and checked against the catalog's financial benchmarks or model.

A product buy plan is typically organized by catalog page number and identifies each item or SKU and the following information:

- Item name
- Item number

Merchandise Database

Product			
Vendor	**Purchase Order**	**Product Specifications**	**Category**
Contact 1	Date	Model No.	Apparel
Address 1	P. O. No.	Description	Collectibles
Address 2	Ship-To Address	Size	Automotive
City	SKU	Color	Books
State	Quantity ordered	MSRP	Electronics
Zip	Base Cost	Minimum Order	Food
Contact 2	Total Cost	Quantity/Case	Housewares
Phone 1	FOB	Product Dimension	Jewelry
Phone 2		Product Weight	Novelty
Fax 1		Lead Time	Stationery
Fax 2		Advertising Allowance	Misc.

EXHIBIT 3.6

- Description
- Cost
- Retail or catalog selling price
- Cost of goods, shown as a percentage (cost of the product divided by selling price; for a $12.00 item that will be sold for $24.95, the cost of goods is $12.00 ÷ $24.95, or 48.1%)
- Quantity carried over from a previous catalog
- Forecast total for the catalog's life
- Initial order quantity
- Backup or "hold for confirmation" quantity

Product Buy Plan

Marketing Forecast

Mail	1,250,000
Response	2.49%
Order Unit Resp.	3.99
Orders	31,105
Units/Order (1.6)	49,768

Average Order	$59
Cancels	1%
Returns	2%

Item Summary

Item	Cost	Retail	On Order	Hold for Conf.	Forecast	Repeat Carryover	On-Order Cost	Forecast Cost	On-Order Retail	Forecast Retail
1	$48	$145	300	300	600		$14,400	$28,800	$145,000	$87,000
2	$48	$105	300	300	500		$14,400	$24,000	$31,500	$52,500
3	$38	$85	250	150	400		$9,500	$15,200	$21,250	$34,000
4	$32	$70	125	75	150		$4,000	$5,800	$8,750	$10,500
5	$99	$200	100	75	125		$9,900	$12,375	$20,000	$25,000
6	$59	$140	300	175	450		$17,700	$26,550	$42,000	$63,000
7	$66	$146	150	100	200		$9,900	$13,200	$21,900	$29,200
8	$68	$150	150	100	200		$10,200	$13,600	$22,500	$30,000
9	$79	$175	150	75	190		$11,850	$15,010	$26,250	$33,250
10	$18	$40	250	250	500		$4,500	$9,000	$10,000	$20,000
11	$70	$160	140	80	160		$9,800	$11,200	$22,400	$25,600
12	$47	$105	300	200	500		$14,100	$23,500	$31,500	$52,500
13	$21	$45	100	75	200	54	$3,126	$4,200	$6,930	$9,000
14	$30	$65	250	100	300		$6,000	$9,000	$13,000	$19,500
15	$19	$45	250	150	400		$475	$76,000	$11,250	$18,000
16	$35	$80	200	200	300		$7,000	$10,500	$16,000	$24,000
17	$16	$35	200	200	275		$3,200	$4,400	$7,000	$9,625
18	$16	$35	200	200	275		$3,200	$4,400	$7,000	$9,625
19	$14	$30	400	275	500		$5,600	$7,000	$12,000	$15,000
20	$63	$135	100	60	120		$6,250	$75,000	$13,500	$16,200
Total		$2,226,019	31,231 (items)		48,574 (items)		$643,592		$1,532,051	

Category Summary

	Cost	Retail	On Order	Forecast	On-Order Cost	On-Order Retail	Net COG	Average Cost	Average Retail
A	$473,760	$1,095,110	11,319	15,440	$363,650	$866,430	43.3%	$30.68	$70.92
B	$117,587	$267,139	3,666	6,027	$64,493	$146,599	44.1%	$19.51	$44.32
C	$197,382	$470,995	6,377	10,967	$115,068	$277,376	42.0%	$17.99	$42.94
D	$111,641	$268,225	6,919	10,395	$76,335	$184,877	41.6%	$10.73	$25.80
E	$51,638	$124,550	2,950	5,745	$24,046	$56,769	41.5%	$8.99	$21.97
Total	$952,008	$2,226,019	31,231 (items)	48,574 (items)	$643,592	$1,532,051	42.8%	$17.58	$41.13

EXHIBIT 3.7

This information can then be projected into financial numbers as shown on the right-hand side of the buy plan. Also, products are summarized into their respective categories at the bottom of the chart. This chart becomes a working tool for buyers in preparation for placing purchase orders.

How does a buyer know how many to forecast? This is where merchandise selling history, knowledge of vendors, and good common quantitative sense come in. Typically, a forecaster looks at the selling history of an item or similar items in a product category. Sales of products with a similar price point are another clue. The forecaster also asks other questions about the product, such as:

- How much space is being devoted to the product?
- What is its position on the page and in the catalog—is it in a "hot spot" in the book?
- How have comparable items sold before? Many catalogs keep statistics on units sold per 1,000 catalogs mailed.
- Is this a "high-impulse" item?
- Is the product seasonal—for example, heavy sweaters and coats in an early-fall catalog?

For a first catalog or an item with no relevant history, the forecaster relies on knowledge of the vendor, including the required lead time, shipping time, and vendor reliability.

The buy plan is not created in a vacuum. It must be coordinated with the sales or marketing plan. Note that at the top of the buy plan in the exhibit is a marketing forecast for a particular catalog mailing campaign. In this case, the plan is to mail 1,250,000 catalogs, have an order response rate of 2.49 percent, and receive 31,105 orders with an average of 1.6 line items per order, or 49,768 total unit or item orders. Unit response (units sold divided by total pieces mailed) is expected to be 3.99 percent; average order value (AOV) is expected to be $59; and 1 percent cancellations and 2 percent returns are anticipated.

Ultimately, the buy plan and the marketing plan need to be in sync. If marketing is expecting to sell almost 50,000 units, but product development forecasts and buys merchandise based on 75,000 units, substantial goods will remain at the end of the catalog's life cycle. A different problem will develop if the buy plan is based on selling 25,000 units. In small companies, where the same person may be developing the marketing plan and the buy plan, this problem is less likely. In any event, the coordination of the two plans is fundamental to good inventory management.

Forecasting new catalogs and new items in a catalog is always tricky. After a year of research, Fingerhut Corporation found that the level of variance from forecast on new catalog items with little or no sales history was astounding: plus or minus 400 percent. In other words, if an item was expected to sell 100 pieces, actual demand ranged between 400 pieces on the top side and 25 pieces on the bottom side. Fortunately, forecasting gets easier as time passes and a catalog and product categories amass a track record. By maintaining a sales history for all products in your catalog, you can increase the accuracy of your forecast.

Reviewing the Buy Plan After Seeing Layouts

Smart merchants give the buy plan a final review after seeing the creative layouts of the catalog, preferably with copy and photography in place. During the creative kickoff meeting, discussed in Chapter 5, the product development team briefs the creative team about the selling points of each product. Once layouts are created, the product development team should review them to make sure that it is positioned, described, and illustrated correctly, and to see how it is presented. Because a great photograph or a full-page presentation will always influence sales, the buy plan may need final "tweaking" before purchase orders are issued to make sure larger orders are placed for products given an unexpectedly generous presentation.

Placing Purchase Orders

Once products have been selected, vendors investigated, and the catalog's forecast and buy plan developed, it's time to place purchase orders. Written purchase orders should be placed in sufficient time that product will arrive at your warehouse two to three weeks before mail date. This gives the warehouse staff time to receive, inspect, perform quality checks, apply bar codes or item numbers, and place the goods in stock.

Advertising and freight allowances should be negotiated before purchase orders are placed. Determine exact pricing and payment schedules for goods, and make certain who is paying shipping and how goods are being shipped. Shipping or freight to the catalog's warehouse is a part of cost of goods and is often underestimated or not considered at all. This is a significant cost and must not be missed in budgeting, costing, and profitability analysis.

Purchase orders should be in writing. Faxed purchase orders should be confirmed by mail. Ask the vendor for confirmation of the purchase order and a specific delivery schedule.

In an ideal world, a catalog expects the vendor to back up initial orders with one or more secondary orders called "hold-for-confirmation" orders. Let's say you expect to sell 600 units of an item. The initial order is for 300 pieces, and you ask the vendor to hold an additional 300 units (at the vendor's expense and ownership) for a later time-dated second or third order. (In a holiday catalog, for example, you want those initial 300 pieces of the item in the warehouse two weeks before your September 1 mailing.) A second, hold-for-confirmation order is dated October 1 for 150 units, and another hold-for-confirmation order for 150 units is dated November 1. In the real world, every vendor backup must be planned and negotiated before purchase orders are placed. Not all vendors will be cooperative.

Drop-shipping from vendor to customer may be an option for higher-ticket items or items that are more cumbersome to ship. However, drop-shipping must be controlled and monitored to ensure timely delivery and good customer service.

INVESTIGATING VENDORS AND DEVELOPING RAPPORT

All potential merchandise vendors need to be carefully investigated to make sure they can deliver on their promises. Use these questions as a guide:

- Is the vendor financially sound?
- Does it manufacture the products or purchase them from others?
- Are the products imported or domestically sourced?
- Has the vendor worked with catalogs and mail-order companies before? Can it provide references from those companies?
- Does the vendor understand mail-order margins and requirements?
- What type of exclusivity can your catalog receive on the product(s) you have selected?
- What level of backup is the vendor willing to provide?
- Does the vendor understand that catalogs place orders for only 30 percent to 50 percent of their total forecast and expect the vendor to reserve merchandise on a "hold-for-confirmation–time-dated orders" basis?
- What is the lead time for placing reorders?
- Does the vendor accept returns? Is there a stocking fee for returned goods?
- How does the vendor handle smaller orders, typical of smaller, new catalogs?
- How does the vendor handle large orders?
- How well does the vendor know mail-order packaging requirements?
- Does the vendor have an advertising allowance or freight allowance policy? If so, what is it? If not, will this supplier give you better pricing?
- What happens if a large cataloger like Spiegel, Lands' End, Viking, or Quill wants the same item?
- Is the vendor still able to make money, even though you have negotiated the "last cent" out of his or her cost?
- What background information can the vendor provide on the relative sales history of items under consideration?
- Who will be the vendor's specific contact with your catalog?

Developing new vendors is like performing due diligence in a public offering or company purchase. The better the rapport and the more information the product buyer has on each vendor, the better the chance of working successfully in the longer term. Understand that most vendors are not good at keeping information confidential about products sold. If your catalog has a winner, they want to place it in other catalogs. They know exactly how many units your catalog has sold and are eager to "tell the world" of your success.

It is important to maintain regular communication with vendors once purchase orders have been placed. Don't place orders and forget them. Copies of purchase orders must be given to the warehouse or receiving so that they can monitor deliveries, and to accounting so that they can control payment to vendors and monitor open orders.

Receipt of Product and Quality Control

Quality control is everyone's responsibility. It starts with the merchandise or product buyer, who must be certain that products selected meet the quality standards of the catalog's image and brand. Next, the warehouse checks products against purchase order specifications to confirm that the right item and quantity were shipped to the facility, that nothing has been damaged in transit, and that product quality meets expectations. If quality questions arise, warehouse staff should notify the product buyer immediately. Warehouse pickers and packers make a final quality check before packing an item for shipment to the customer. Marketing also plays a role in developing a customer follow-up survey to ascertain consumer reactions to product value and quality. Exhibit 3.8 describes how different types of catalogers check quality of merchandise.

Rebuying

Once the catalog is mailed, rebuying, or control buying, takes place. In most catalogs, control buying is the job of an analytical group that monitors daily and weekly orders and tracks

Merchandise Quality Checking

The first function of operations is to ensure that merchandise not only matches what is shown in the catalog, but also that it meets company quality standards. About half of all respondents inspected their merchandise in every shipment.

By Business Type	All Respondents	Consumer	Hybrid	B-to-B
Initial Shipments Only	13%	11%	8%	19%
All Shipments	49%	54%	33%	43%
At the Manufacturer	10%	9%	0%	19%
Statistical Sample	16%	21%	8%	5%
No Quality Check	13%	5%	50%	14%
By Business Size	**<$5MM**	**<5–20MM**	**$20–50MM**	**>$50MM**
Initial Shipments Only	100%	13%	8%	16%
All Shipments	45%	57%	38%	47%
At the Manufacturer	0%	13%	8%	11%
Statistical Sample	15%	9%	31%	16%
No Quality Check	30%	9%	15%	11%

Source: DMA Sourcebook

EXHIBIT 3.8

the top sellers against the forecast. Item product forecasts are revised, and the product is repurchased throughout the cycle of a catalog's life span. In a mature catalog, one with more than $15 million in sales, sales begin to be monitored two to three days after the first customer order, and rebuying follows in the first and second weeks.

Three types of product situations will quickly become apparent during the control buying phase.

- Products that are on-forecast—expected to generate as many customer orders as the buy plan originally forecast—cause no problems; a second or third shipment order can be placed with the vendor in week three or four.
- "Highfliers," products that are ahead of forecast, need immediate attention as soon as the overresponse can be quantified. Alerting the vendor of the overpull is a first step. Activating reorders or hold-for-confirmation orders is a second step. The important thing is to act quickly so as to minimize back orders. A cataloger cannot manage inventory from a back-order report. It will have missed the trigger date to get product moving from the vendor.
- Products that are underpulling are yet another problem. As soon as under-forecast response can be quantitatively confirmed, rebuyers have to cancel hold-for-confirmation orders and start planning how to dispose of excess product.

Most catalog operating systems have some inventory-forecasting subsystems and reports that can help the rebuyer project response based on one to two weeks' results. Exhibit 3.9 shows a catalog forecasting report, which is tied into a stock status report and a historical weekly response curve. Marrying the three reports gives the rebuyer a quantitative tool to project total sales of any item in the catalog.

Part of most catalog operating systems, the catalog forecasting report estimates future demand for each item based on sales to date. Sorted by item number, color, size, and description of the item, it shows how many units are "on order" but not yet in the warehouse, how many products are on hold because of a quality problem ("qlty hold"), how many returns have been made during this catalog season, and how many products are on hand in the warehouse ready for shipment. It also indicates how many items have been sent to customers, shown accumulated for the campaign ("accum issued"), how many items are on back order awaiting receipt of a vendor shipment, and the size of the hold-for-confirmation order ("HFC").

The most important columns are the last five. These show the computer's estimate of total units to be sold of an item based on where the catalog is in the selling cycle and customer demand thus far. For example, if an item has sold 100 units through week 4 and the catalog's historical response curve indicates that response is 40 percent complete, the computer will estimate final sales at 250 units (100 ÷ 40% = 250). Since some product categories sell faster than others, the range of percents gives the rebuyer an at-a-glance choice of calculations, based on category behavior. For example, in a gift and apparel catalog, hard goods sell more slowly than apparel. A control buyer can refer to the respective percentages to estimate different subcategories in a catalog.

DM050 — **Catalog Forecasting**

Item #	On Order	Qlty Hold	Accum Return	On Hand	Accum Issued	Total B/Os	Hold for Confirmation (HFC)	86%	89%	95%	99%	99%
6606	11				8	14		25	24	23	22	22
6606	14				12	10		25	24	23	22	22
6606	7		1		24	10		39	38	35	34	34
6606	2				20	8		32	31	29	28	28
6606	6		1		16	2		20	20	18	18	18
6606	5		1		11	4		17	16	15	15	15
6607	24		2	3	291	4		343	331	310	297	297
6608	750		37	1,971		437		2,800	2,705	2,534	2,432	2,432
6612				18	2			2	2	2	2	2
6613			4	57	32			37	35	33	32	32
6613			7	80	31			36	34	32	31	31
6613				43	17			19	19	17	17	17
6614			1	1,678	227			263	255	238	229	229
6615			1	17	4			4	4	4	4	4
6616			1	7	36			41	40	37	36	36
6617			3	13		1		16	15	14	14	14
6617			5	25				29	28	26	25	25
6617			9	9	27			31	30	28	27	27
6617			8	7	37			43	41	38	37	37
6617			7	47		8		63	61	57	55	55

EXHIBIT 3.9

The catalog forecasting report is used in conjunction with ***response curve by week.*** Successful catalogers understand and can accurately track seasonality (response by month) and response by week within a catalog's selling season. Exhibit 3.10 depicts the typical catalog response curve reported in the 1998 DMA *Statistical Fact Book*; Exhibit 3.11 is a more detailed comparison of five catalogs showing orders by week. Curves vary by season—a spring catalog response curve might be drastically different from fall or holiday—and from company to company. Your response curve will depend on a number of variables:

- Whether you are a business, consumer, hybrid (selling to both business and consumer), or retail catalog
- How many times a year you mail—for example, twelve times, versus four times, versus one time
- Type of offers used to induce early ordering
- Type of product

A new catalog will have to build its first response curve with industry averages like the one shown in Exhibit 3.10, but as orders come in, it can calculate a custom weekly

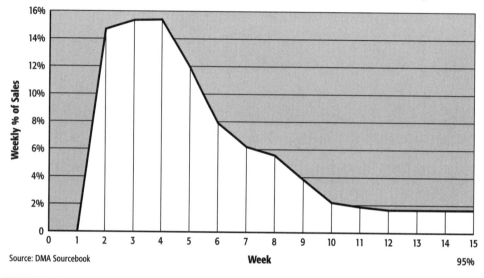

Typical Catalog Response Curve

Developing response curves, which indicate the percent of sales for each week of the catalog response period, can be an effective way to gauge how much inventory is required for any given product. Often, the first week's response can give a reliable indication of final sales, especially for hot-selling items that will need to be reordered immediately.

Source: DMA Sourcebook

EXHIBIT 3.10

response curve and enter this information into the computer for use with inventory forecasting. What rebuyers are looking for in the curve is the "doubling point," the place when 50 percent of the orders are in. From that point, it is possible to project with a fair degree of accuracy how many items will be needed to complete the selling season. The more accurate the response curve is within a season, the greater the chance of improving your merchandise turnover each year and eliminating needless excess product at the end of a catalog selling season.

Control buying is vital for most catalogs. The more volatile the product line and the longer the vendor lead time in replenishing orders, the more important this function is.

Disposing of Excess Inventory

The final phase in inventory management is disposing of overstocks. The sooner overstocks can be identified, the sooner they can be liquidated. Catalogs use dozens of ways to liquidate excess product, as Exhibits 3.12 and 3.13 show. During a catalog's campaign season, telemarketing up-selling and an in-the-box shipment package insert sale are the most effective.

Example of an Actual Catalog Order Response

Week	Spring Year 1	Spring Year 2	Fall Year 1	Fall Year 2	Fall Year 3	
1	2.7	7.1	1.2	1.7	2.8	
2	18.1	20.9	10.7	10.6	10.2	
3	18.1	14.1	15.8	15.3	18.5	Look for
4	12.2	8.4	10.8	13.0	12.8	"doubling
5	6.4	7.0	7.6	9.0	10.7	point" =
6	9.1	9.5	5.9	6.5	9.5	50% of
7	8.3	7.4	7.0	6.6	7.1	orders in
8	5.3	6.6	7.1	6.4	6.0	
9	3.8	4.3	4.8	5.8	4.1	
10	3.2	2.9	4.3	5.2	3.5	
11	2.7	2.5	3.4	3.7	3.1	
12	2.1	2.6	2.6	3.2	2.4	
13	1.9	2.0	2.4	2.7	1.9	
14	1.4	1.3	1.7	1.0	1.4	
15	1.4	1.3	2.2	2.1	1.6	
16	1.0	1.1	1.6	1.8	1.8	
17	1.0	1.0	1.6	1.5	1.2	
18	0.1	1.5	1.4	0.8		
19	0.6	1.4	1.4	0.5		
20			1.4			
21			1.4			
22			1.0			
23			1.3			
24			0.8			
25			0.4			
Total	100	100	100	100	100	

EXHIBIT 3.11
Response Curve by Week

New catalogers must remember that inventory that must be liquidated or marked down is an addition to the cost of goods. With adequate vendor backup (and the ability to return excess product) and good day-to-day rebuying, catalogers should be able to minimize significant excesses. It is unlikely that new catalogs can operate without any overstocks. If a catalog can recapture the cost of goods through timely liquidation and smart special sales, extra charges to the cost-of-goods part of the P&L can be minimized (see note on p. 14).

Final Merchandise Postanalysis

When customer order activity has run its course, the analytical staff summarizes the product demand and response curve for that campaign and reports on returns, cancellations,

Devices Catalogers Use to Reduce Inventory

Catalogers use a wide variety of options to reduce inventory, the top three being order-taker up-sell, package inserts, and sales catalogs.

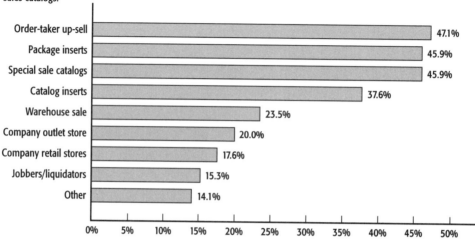

Source: *Catalog Age,* Operations Benchmark Report

EXHIBIT 3.12

How Catalogers Liquidate Returns

More than one-third of catalogers restock returned merchandise, but more than one-quarter indicate that they destroy it.

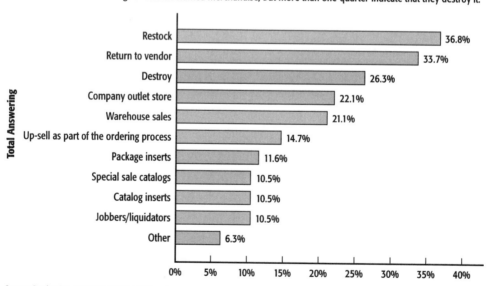

Source: *Catalog Age,* Operations Benchmark Report

EXHIBIT 3.13

and excess inventory. Disposition of excess goods is planned by the merchandise buyer, rebuyer, and marketing staff. The cycle is now complete, and planning starts afresh for the next catalog campaign.

❖ KEY POINTS

- Inventory management is a quantitative process that every cataloger must master in order to achieve and maintain profitability.
- Use **product specification sheets** and a **merchandise database** to collect and track essential product and vendor information for use throughout the catalog development and creative process.
- A product **buy plan** that captures the forecast and initial purchases for a catalog promotion must be tied into the sales and marketing plan for accurate inventory management.
- Make vendors solid partners by investigating them carefully before placing orders and then establishing a good working relationship.
- By using the **catalog forecasting report** and **response curve by week**, forecasting will become easier, rebuying will be more accurate, and you will have less excess inventory to dispose of at the end of the promotion.

PART 2

The Creative Concept

Is your catalog a Wal-Mart or a Tiffany?

A clear understanding of the catalog's identity—its unique positioning, niche, and brand—is the starting point of the creative process. Once everyone in the company agrees on who the catalog is and what it stands for, the art director can begin to create a presentation that conveys its identity. A clear identity establishes the parameters for everything from products and pricing strategy to typography, photography, and color.

The following chapters discuss the process of creating a catalog and trace every step from identifying a niche and building a brand to developing a creative concept and bringing it to life through design and production.

CHAPTER 4

Establishing Your Niche, Positioning, and Branding

No catalog company knows more about niche and branding than L. L. Bean. At a recent conference, I heard Bean's merchandising vice president describe how its merchandising team looked at every product in terms of "Beanness" and ranked each one on the following scale:

Brand Enhancing	Brand Neutral	Brand Negative
5 ———————	2.5 ———————	0

For example, measuring slow-selling rustic furniture and flannel bedding against this scale revealed that the products were at best brand neutral and many were negative to the brand. They were quickly dropped.

L. L. Bean knows the importance of its brand and ensures that every product in its catalog reinforces and enhances its brand image and identity. Every cataloger should do likewise.

Why Niche, Positioning, and Branding Are Important

The 40/40/20 rule is a direct marketing concept that reflects the importance of niche, positioning, and branding. As the chart in Exhibit 4.1 shows, three sectors contribute to the success or failure of a mailing program. Forty percent of success or failure is attributable to niche, positioning, brand, and offer; another 40 percent depends on reaching the right audience; and the remaining 20 percent depends on the elements that go into the creative execution: format, paper, design, copy, photography, use of color, and quality of printing.

Some veteran catalogers consider niche, positioning, and branding to be the most important factor in the long-term success of a catalog. A clear niche, position, and brand image correlate with strong sales. An inconsistent presentation and brand image raises doubts in the minds of consumers, which leads to lowered response rates and lower average order values.

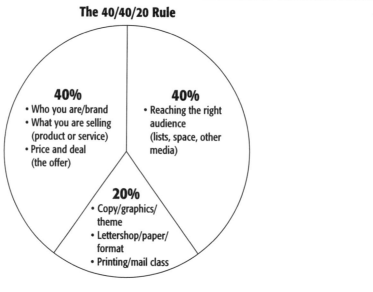

The 40/40/20 Rule

40%
- Who you are/brand
- What you are selling (product or service)
- Price and deal (the offer)

40%
- Reaching the right audience (lists, space, other media)

20%
- Copy/graphics/theme
- Lettershop/paper/format
- Printing/mail class

EXHIBIT 4.1
The Success (or Failure) of Any Catalog Program

Branding is the outcome of the entire process of identifying who you are and how you want customers to relate to and think about your catalog and its products.

Questions to Answer Before You Start the Creative Execution

Before you begin sketching cover and page concepts, photographing products, or writing copy for a new catalog, it's important to take the time to answer six basic questions. Even if you think you already know the answers, discipline yourself to consider each one with a fresh and open mind.

These questions should also be answered whenever a catalog is repositioned. When a catalog's performance begins to slip, sales diminish, and things just seem to be going awry, chances are good you've forgotten the answers to these basic questions. Answer them all over again, and use them to keep your niche and position firmly in mind.

Question 1: Who are you?

This is really two questions: What are you selling, and who is the company behind the catalog? Defining the products or services to be sold is relatively easy for prospective catalogers; defining the company is harder.

It isn't just the customer who needs to know who you are. Everyone in your company needs to agree on the company's identity. In my seminars, I often ask people to liken their company to a car. One president in attendance described his company as a Mercedes. Unfortunately, the staff present at the seminar called it a Ford Escort. Such conflicting perceptions no doubt made themselves felt in the company's catalog. A business must agree on who it is and what it stands for before merchandisers can buy product and designers can translate that identity into an appearance.

Companies more than ten years old—including experienced retailers venturing into the catalog arena, as well as manufacturers changing their marketing channel strategy to sell directly to end users—already have an identity and a positioning, although these may not have been formally articulated. A start-up catalog will need to use two documents to help answer the "Who are you?" question: a brand identity statement and a mission statement.

A ***brand identity statement*** succinctly explains who a company is to its customers. In a sense, it is a look at the external identity of the company. The following example from the Halls catalog helped define who and what the catalog was all about, and explained the relationship between the catalog and Hallmark Cards, the parent company.

> *I am the Halls Catalog. I am feminine and assertive. I'll never tell my age, but you'd guess me to be 25 to 39 (heavens, never 40!) years old. I'm contemporary, yet down to earth. I love beautiful, even clever, things around me. Often, I'm quite expensive, but well worth it because my goal in life is to be the single source of only the most special items demanded by those with impeccable taste. Sometimes I'm eccentric, often I'm practical—but always I plan on being the spectacular leader of all my compatriots. I exist because my parents, Hallmark Cards, and Halls retail stores mated with the express intent of creating a superior individual. And, in that tradition, each Halls Catalog will be better than the last.*

When that statement was first written, it was regarded as a great starting place in defining the catalog. Retrospect reveals some serious flaws in the statement, namely that it doesn't differentiate the Halls catalog from any other upscale women's gift catalog. Black out several key words, and this statement could apply to almost any catalog such as Gump's, Horchow, or Neiman Marcus.

> *I am the ~~Halls~~ Catalog. I am feminine and assertive. I'll never tell my age, but you'd guess me to be 25 to 39 (heavens, never 40!) years old. I'm contemporary, yet down to earth. I love beautiful, even clever, things around me. Often, I'm quite expensive, but well worth it because my goal in life is to be the single source of only the most special items demanded by those with impeccable taste. Sometimes I'm eccentric, often I'm practical—but always I plan on being the spectacular leader of all my compatriots.*

> *I exist because my parents, ~~Hallmark Cards~~, and ~~Halls~~ retail stores mated with the express intent of creating a superior individual. And, in that tradition, each ~~Halls~~ Catalog will be better than the last.*

A catalog must be clearly differentiated from its competition. If it can't be differentiated in the brand identity statement, no amount of differentiation in pricing, offers, layout, photography, or appearance will help. Before you venture further, make sure your brand identity statement clearly sets the catalog apart from all others.

Where a brand identity statement focuses on a catalog's external appearance, a ***mission statement*** explains its internal purpose for being. A mission statement defines the tenets or principles upon which the catalog is built. Lands' End's mission statement, Exhibit 4.2, often excerpted in its catalog and advertising during the early '90s, is an excellent expression of what the company is and how it intends to manage its catalog business. The state-

---

Lands' End Direct Merchants Principles of Doing Business

Principle 1: We do everything we can to make our products better. We improve material, and add back features and construction details that others have taken out over the years. We never reduce the quality of a product to make it cheaper.

Principle 2: We price our products fairly and honestly. We do not, have not, and will not participate in the common retailing practice of inflating markups to set up a phony "sale."

Principle 3: We accept any return for any reason, at any time. Our products are guaranteed. No fine print. No arguments. We mean exactly what we say: GUARANTEED. PERIOD.

Principle 4: We ship faster than anyone we know of. We ship items in stock the day after we receive the order. At the height of the last Christmas season the longest time an order was in the house was 36 hours, excepting monograms which took another 12 hours.

Principle 5: We believe that what is best for our customer is best for all of us. Everyone here understands that concept. Our sales and service people are trained to know our products, and to be friendly and helpful. They are urged to take all the time necessary to take care of you. We even pay for your call, for whatever reason you call.

Principle 6: We are able to sell at lower prices because we have eliminated middlemen; because we don't buy branded merchandise with high protected markups; and because we have placed our contracts with manufacturers who have proved that they are cost conscious and efficient.

Principle 7: We are able to sell at lower prices because we operate efficiently. Our people are hard working, intelligent and share in the success of the company.

Principle 8: We are able to sell at lower prices because we support no fancy emporiums with their high overhead. Our main location is in the middle of a 40-acre cornfield in rural Wisconsin. We still operate our first location in Chicago's Near North tannery district.

EXHIBIT 4.2

---

ment addresses almost all the salient aspects of a catalog business, including products, pricing, returns, shipping time, and customer service. A second example of a mission statement is the Quill Customer Bill of Rights in Exhibit 4.3 on pages 64–65. Quill has been including this statement in its annual catalogs for many years, often near the order form, in order to convey its commitment to customers.

Involve everyone in your company in drafting your brand identity and mission statements. The better you can define your company, the stronger your ultimate creative effort can be.

Question 2: What is your niche, and how do you get one and keep it?

The terms *niche* and *positioning* are often used interchangeably. Often defined as "unique positioning" or "unique identity," a niche is a special place in the market where there is a void that is not met or filled by the competition.

It's easy to list catalogs that occupy a specialized, unique place in the market. Current, Inc., for example, is uniquely positioned as an inexpensive source of social expressions or greeting cards by mail. While greeting cards, wrapping paper, and holiday gift items are available in many retail stores, Current sets itself apart through a pricing structure that saves customers money, yet increases the value of an average order. To set itself apart from other office supply catalogs, the Reliable Home Office catalog sells furniture and supplies to the "SOHO," or small office/home office, market. Hello Direct differentiates itself by selling telephonic products and accessories to consumers.

Some catalogs set themselves apart with specialized offers or pricing, while others use design elements or the product line. The more you can differentiate your merchandise from others, the better. Design, copy, and photo consistency is another hallmark of a catalog with a strong niche.

Every new cataloging venture needs to target a niche. Establishing that niche is a gradual process of finding products that meet the needs of target customers, offering suitable pricing, and creating a catalog whose "look" supports the niche. Even fulfillment and customer service are agents in this process. Every new issue of a catalog can strengthen or weaken a niche. Make sure you have a solid grasp of your niche before your first catalog leaves the drawing board.

Question 3: What is your brand?

For many years, catalogers focused on niche and positioning and left brand development to companies like Procter & Gamble. Today, brand development is a high priority for successful catalogers, who are paying more attention to developing and enhancing a distinct brand name and to cultivating brand loyalty and brand equity.

A *brand name* is the name given a product or service, such as Kleenex or Kodak. A brand name is often trademarked to protect its exclusive use. *Brand loyalty* is customer allegiance to a specific product. Brand-loyal customers will purchase their preferred brand over

EXHIBIT 4.3
Quill Brand Customer's Bill of Rights

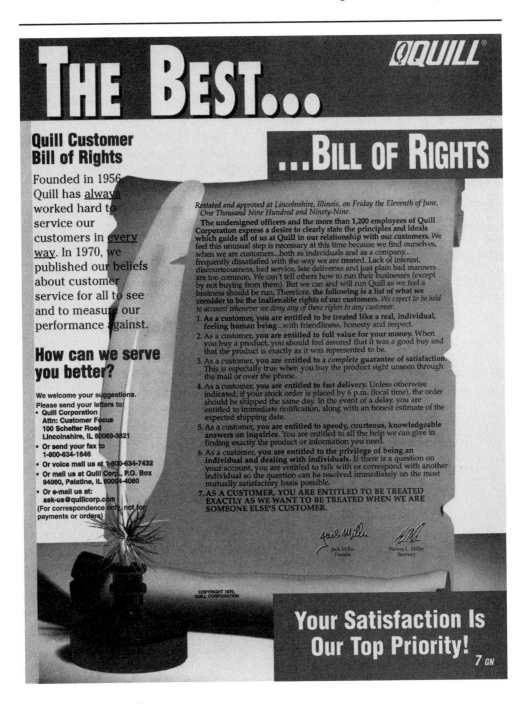

EXHIBIT 4.3 (continued)
Quill Brand Customer's Bill of Rights

generic or lesser-known brands even if the price is a bit higher. ***Brand preference*** is a worldwide phenomenon that works for catalogs, too. As an example, high acceptance of the Eddie Bauer brand has made its clothing catalog very successful in Germany and England.

When a brand has a strong name and loyal followers, it builds worth, or ***brand equity***, and achieves "top-of-mind" name recognition. Some catalogs have already earned this distinction in their respective categories. In outdoor gear and clothes, we think of L. L. Bean. In women's fashions, we think of Bloomingdale's. In chocolate products, Hershey Foods; in ham and smoked meats, Honey Baked Ham; in high-end gardening, White Flower Farm; in computers and the Internet, Dell; and in office supplies, Quill.

A brand's strength rests on a tripod of three factors, as Exhibit 4.4 shows: outstanding creative execution, superior merchandising, and quality fulfillment and customer service. Each of these core competencies has a direct impact on how a cataloger identifies, builds, and enhances its brand. Apply the L. L. Bean test to each of the three competencies to find out how well each supports your brand:

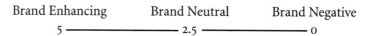

Where does the format, paper quality, printing, and overall creative execution of your catalog fall on this scale? Is your merchandise brand enhancing, brand neutral, or brand negative? What about your fulfillment and customer service? If each of these three core skill areas is not on the positive side of the ledger, you may not only fail to build brand equity but also jeopardize the long-term financial viability of your catalog.

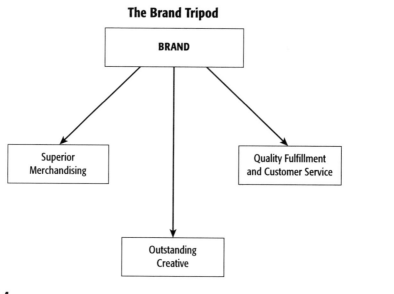

EXHIBIT 4.4

Question 4: Who is your competition, what is its niche, and how strong is its brand?

Knowing the competition inside and out will help you refine your niche and position. Track every aspect of your prime competitors' business, including:

- Best products
- Repeated products
- How they liquidate products
- Frequency of mailing
- Differences in customer contact strategy based on RFM (recency, frequency, monetary)
- Customer service and return policies
- Shipping prices and options
- Customer loyalty programs

Examine competitive mailings, and order from your competition. Get on their customer lists and track the information for the eight areas just cited. Return product, and give the companies customer service problems to solve so you can understand every aspect of how competitors think and what drives their business. By listing your prime competitors' strengths and weaknesses, it is possible to develop programs that "go for the jugular" in exploiting their shortcomings.

Question 5: How can you differentiate your catalog and its products from the competition?

When you know the competition like the back of your hand, you can more easily find ways to set yourself apart with a USP, or unique selling proposition. A catalog can differentiate itself with specialized merchandise, unique offers and pricing strategies, striking format and design elements such as layout, use of color, copy, typography, photography, and so on.

Marks & Spencer, the famous British retailer, devised a second definition for USP when it launched its catalog program: USP^2—or USP "squared." Successful product sales have two sides: the ***unique selling proposition*** and the ***unique service proposition***. To support the marvelous Marks & Spencer brand, the catalog needed a superior customer service proposition that would differentiate its efforts from other retailers and mail-order companies. It succeeded!

Question 6: Who is your target customer?

Customers are the acid test. For new catalogers in a crowded field, the ultimate challenge is finding a niche and developing the brand with customers in mind. Keep your primary, secondary, and tertiary target customers in mental view as you select products, create spreads, or plan fulfillment. Successful copywriters often address copy to a specific but imaginary customer. You can use the same technique at every step in the planning process.

Earning Customer Loyalty

Recent research by the Direct Marketing Association identified reasons why customers choose one company, supplier, or store over another. The answers are highly applicable to catalogs, especially new catalog ventures trying to build business. Buyers choose your catalog over the competition because:

- Your catalog makes them feel good when they buy.
- Your catalog has an atmosphere that they like.
- Your catalog makes them comfortable.
- Your catalog consistently gives good value for the money.
- Your catalog recognizes them by name.
- Your catalog always has a good merchandise selection.
- Your catalog always has new products.
- Your catalog makes customers feel appreciated.
- Your catalog says thank you for their business.
- Your catalog has the best customer service—anywhere.
- Your catalog makes ordering easy with every option—phone, fax, mail, and the Internet.

Take a moment to analyze why you keep returning to certain retailers or service providers. Why do you patronize your bank? Why do you shop at a certain supermarket? The answers vary dramatically from person to person. Convenience and proximity to home or work rate very high when it comes to choosing banks, gasoline stations, and grocery stores. Cleanliness, familiarity with store layout, and quality of meat and produce are exceptionally important in selecting grocery stores. Can you imagine the confusion that would ensue if the grocery store manager rearranged the store every other week? The criteria for selecting a computer company, an insurance provider, or a travel agency include experience, knowledge, and skill level. For apparel, customers typically want to shop at boutiques known for their savvy about today's fashion trends.

New catalogers and those in their formative years must work hard to build loyal customers who return to purchase again and again. Brand loyalty and top-of-mind recognition are built one order at a time. Treating every transaction as though it were the first one will help get customers back and build recognition. Satisfied customers tell others.

Every order properly completed helps lead to the next order. Conversely, every order in which there is a problem can "disconnect" a customer for a season or even forever. Pay attention to the qualities that keep customers returning. In the end, getting customers to come back is a matter of observing the golden rule: treat them as you would like to be treated!

The Offer or Proposition

The *offer* is an integral part of a catalog's niche and position. When you think of Publishers Clearing House, you think sweepstakes. When you think of Fingerhut, you think house credit and free gifts. Both of these companies have built their brand around their offer—the proposition they make to prospective customers. An offer is what a company is willing to give to customers in return for their response. Offers vary in dozens of ways; the one you choose must be in keeping with your niche, positioning, and brand.

Offers can do more than just increase response rates or improve average order values. You can design offers to trigger orders earlier in the response cycle, motivate inactive buyers and prospects to become active, convert prospects to buyers, and persuade first-time buyers to make a second purchase. Some offers can encourage low-average-order buyers to buy at a higher level on the next purchase, encourage Internet orders, or build retail store traffic.

The offer is a near-forgotten part of the creative effort, but one that is important to discuss during the creative planning of a campaign. Here are some examples of offers used by successful catalogs:

- **Special pricing.** Every item in the Current, Inc., catalog has three prices; which one the customer gets depends on the quantity ordered.
- **Volume-related pricing.** Buy one item for $100, buy two to five and pay $90, buy more than ten and pay $80, and so on; a strategy used by most business catalogs.
- **Discounts.** To support its position as a discounter, Damark runs the suggested list price next to its price, and offers special club pricing structures. At the other end of the economic spectrum, Smithsonian underscores the benefits of membership by offering discounts to members.
- **Payment terms.** Fingerhut, the Sprint catalog, and others offer deferred payment options such as six months to pay, or no payments till June 1.
- **Internal credit.** House credit is the backbone of the Fingerhut catalog, which lets customers spread payments over several months and often shows the price of an item per month. Spiegel offers its own credit card.
- **Free trial offer or send no money now.** New Pig Corporation, an industrial cleaning supplier, tells customers that if they are not happy with any product, it will cancel the invoice.
- **Guarantee.** L. L. Bean, Lands' End, and Reliable all offer money-back guarantees. L. L. Bean and Lands' End will accept product returns at any time if for any reason a customer is not totally satisfied.
- **Sweepstakes and contests.** Fingerhut and U.S. Sales regularly use sweepstakes to improve response rate.
- **Gifts and premiums with purchase.** Gifts are standard with the Fingerhut offer.
- **Deadlines and time limitation.** Many catalogs offer hurry-up orders and early-bird premiums, such as "order by March 15 and receive. . . ."
- **Clubs and continuities.** Harry and David has eight different "Fruit of the Month" clubs with four-month, six-month, or twelve-month plans.
- **Free shipping, or savings on shipping and handling.** To entice new customers and reactivate old ones, Cushman Fruit Company and others offer free shipping on orders over $70, and 50 percent off shipping for a $50 order.

- **Loyalty programs.** Sears Club members earn perks for paying with the Sears credit card; the $49.95 membership in Damark's frequent-buyer program entitles members to special benefits.
- **Offers that encourage Internet shopping.** Tweeds offers a $5 bonus gift for a minimum order placed on the Internet; Sharper Image takes $2 off any product purchased on-line.
- **Offers that drive store traffic.** Bath & Body Works binds in special coupons redeemable in its retail stores.

The list goes on. Offers can be as innovative as catalogs want them to be and can afford!

(See pp. 1 & 2 of the four-color insert for visual examples of offers.)

Ingredients of a Successful Offer

Use this five-point list to create offers that pull orders.

1. **The offer must pay for itself.** If you give a discount or a premium with every order, the offer must give you sufficient gain. In other words, if you are offering a gift worth $5, you need to generate a sufficient increase in response and average order value to cover the added cost. Offer costs can be easily calculated in a breakeven to know exactly what percentage of gain is needed (you'll find more on this in Chapter 13). You may need a 15 percent increase in sales per catalog to pay for an offer. You need to know the exact "gain needed" and measure and track results, or you could be throwing away money.
2. **Offers must be correctly tested.** Never assume that an offer is a winner. Test every offer against a control group that does not receive the same offer. For accurate results, mail the offer to identical selections of the same list at exactly the same time. Mail to a large enough quantity of people for the test to be statistically significant. Chapter 12 offers a more detailed discussion of catalog testing. To keep costs down, run the test on the front panel of the order form, on a plus-cover or wrap, or on an extra four-page cover. Special bind-in cards or dot whacks affixed to the front of the catalog also let you test inexpensively and make the offer prominent.
3. **Tracking results is crucial.** If an offer test is properly constructed, tracking and measurement are quite simple. Each test and control must be given unique source codes that are then recorded. A test is wasted if orders can't be tracked; the higher the percentage of untracked orders, the less accurate the test. Are you willing to risk being 50 percent wrong? You do so if half the orders have no source code! Looking at response rate, average order value (AOV), and sales per catalog on coded orders will allow you to compare the tests.

4. **Offers must be in keeping with the catalog's brand and niche.** Are discounts or sweepstakes right for every catalog? Hardly! Offers for upscale gift catalogs are quite different from offers for downscale gift books. Business catalogs and retail store catalogs have different objectives and therefore quite different offers. Every aspect of how products are priced and how offers are used to motivate different buyer or prospect segments must be in sync with who you are and what your catalog stands for. Discuss offers with the creative team early in the catalog's creative development stage. If a new catalog has done its positioning homework and developed a mission statement, offer development is easier.

5. **The offer must get noticed.** An offer is useless if customers don't "get it." Don't tuck messages into the gutter on the opening spread (pages 2–3) or bury them on a flap of the order form! Explain or mention offers on the front and back covers. Reiterate them on the opening spread, and play them up on the order form, especially in the ordering section. If you want an offer to motivate customers to action, make it prominent.

❖ KEY POINTS

- To establish your creative concept, you need to know your company's identity, niche, and brand, your competition's niche and brand, and your target audience.
- Differentiating your company and its products as strongly as possible from all the competition will enhance your creative concept and make designing the catalog much easier.
- Use offers to increase response rates, improve average order values, trigger orders earlier in the response cycle, reactivate dormant buyers, and convert prospects to buyers. Make sure your offer reinforces your niche, brand, and position.

CHAPTER 5

Developing the Creative Concept

Putting a catalog together can be an overwhelming task for the first-timer. Without a system, even the seasoned cataloger can waste much time and money before producing a reasonable end product. Following the four-part catalog creative process shown in Exhibit 5.1 will keep the project on track.

Phase One is devoted to developing the conceptual "blueprint" that the other phases will execute. The creative concept is pinned down in a creative kickoff meeting in which catalog staff and outside consultants gather together to brainstorm the catalog's "look" for the designer to capture in sketches and layouts. In Phase Two, the creative concept is executed as pages are laid out, copy is written, and products are photographed. In Phase Three, page production, pages are developed and composed using computer software. Color separations, film, and printing take place in the fourth and final phase.

This chapter examines the first phase, developing a creative concept.

Creating the Catalog Concept

It takes only one person to come up with a great new catalog idea, but it takes a talented group to translate that idea into a creative platform and execution. Set aside one or two days for a free-form, idea-generating concept or identity meeting, preferably in a quiet spot away from telephones and other day-to-day business interruptions.

Draw up an agenda (see Exhibit 5.2), and appoint a meeting facilitator—perhaps the catalog owner or an outside consultant who understands catalog creative. The facilitator should strive to create an attitude of openness in which brainstorming rules apply. A number of people should participate in this first phase in the creative process:

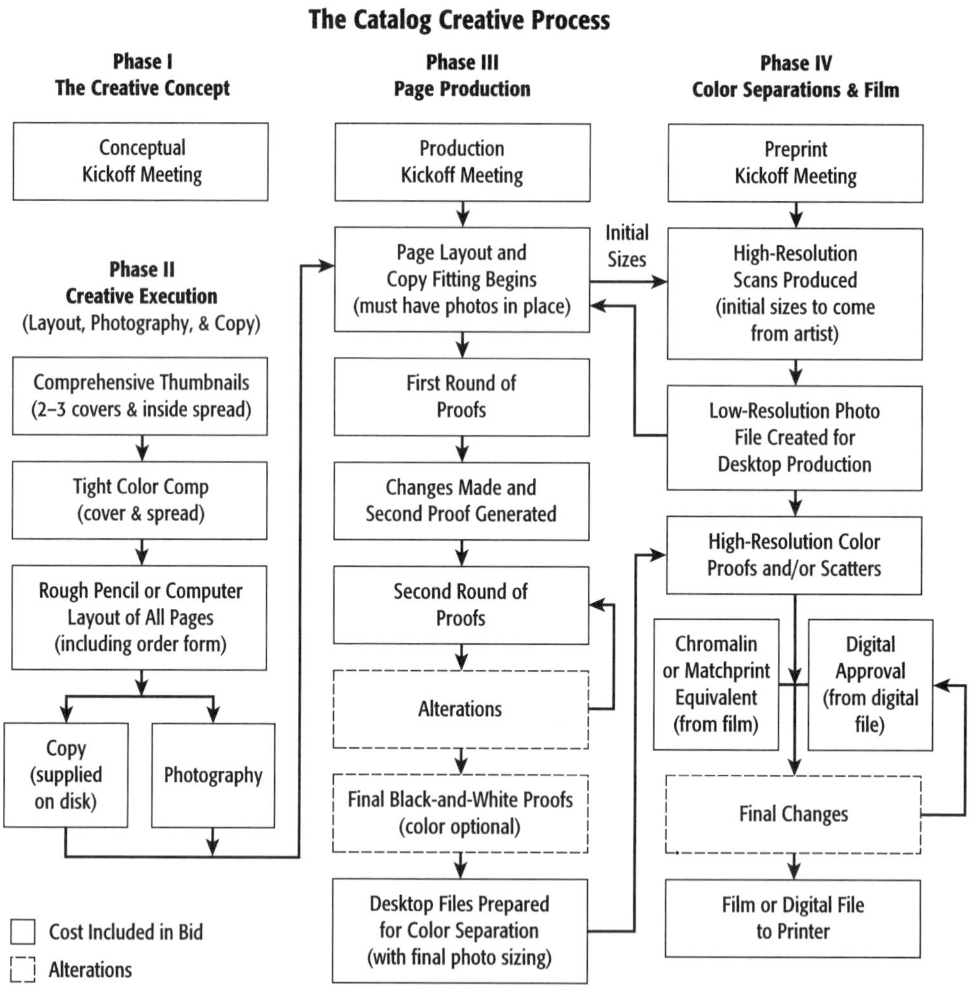

The Catalog Creative Process

Phase I
The Creative Concept

Conceptual
Kickoff Meeting

Phase II
Creative Execution
(Layout, Photography, & Copy)

Comprehensive Thumbnails
(2–3 covers & inside spread)

↓

Tight Color Comp
(cover & spread)

↓

Rough Pencil or Computer
Layout of All Pages
(including order form)

↓

Copy
(supplied
on disk)   Photography

Phase III
Page Production

Production
Kickoff Meeting

↓

Page Layout and
Copy Fitting Begins
(must have photos in place)

↓

First Round of
Proofs

↓

Changes Made and
Second Proof Generated

↓

Second Round of
Proofs

Alterations

Final Black-and-White Proofs
(color optional)

↓

Desktop Files Prepared
for Color Separation
(with final photo sizing)

Phase IV
Color Separations & Film

Preprint
Kickoff Meeting

↓

Initial
Sizes

High-Resolution
Scans Produced
(initial sizes to come
from artist)

↓

Low-Resolution Photo
File Created for
Desktop Production

↓

High-Resolution Color
Proofs and/or Scatters

Chromalin
or Matchprint
Equivalent
(from film)   Digital
Approval
(from digital
file)

Final Changes

↓

Film or Digital File
to Printer

☐ Cost Included in Bid
⌐⌐ Alterations

EXHIBIT 5.1

- The owner and other key decision makers
- A catalog consultant or creative agency representative; someone who understands the process and pitfalls of creating new catalogs can be an asset to your team and may be able to facilitate the meeting
- The marketing or circulation person; someone who knows the target audience, as well as the marketing and mail strategy, can report on what is working and what isn't once the catalog is under way
- A merchandise person who presents the catalog product and describes why the items were chosen; at subsequent meetings after the catalog has been established,

---

Creative Kickoff Agenda for A New Catalog

1. Review of catalog's target audience

2. Review of catalog's proposed product line

3. Review of the competition

4. Discussion of the niche, positioning, and brand of the catalog

5. Establishing the creative platform
   • The product line and what is unique
   • Differentiation from other catalogs and the competition
   • Upscale or downscale?
   • Development of the creative formula

6. Review of the circulation plan for the season
   • Number of catalogs mailed
   • Timing of mailings
   • Mix of prospect versus customer or "house" names

7. Catalog specifications

8. Pagination of the catalog

9. Production schedule

10. Catalog budget review

11. "To do" assignments

EXHIBIT 5.2

---

he or she presents product sales history reports and new product specification
sheets
• The creative or art director, who will design the catalog and prepare for pagination and layout
• The copywriter, who will make notes and ask questions about specific products
presented at the meeting
• Anyone else who may have insight to your catalog's niche and positioning

Everyone who attends the meeting must thoroughly understand the catalog's unique
positioning, niche, and brand, as well as its competition. Notice that the agenda in the
exhibit sets aside time to review research information about the target audience, examine
competitive catalogs, and discuss how the catalog will set itself apart in the marketplace.

The primary goal of the meeting is to develop a *creative platform*, a simple document
that contains three to five statements that clearly and concisely describe the catalog's ambience and persona. Where the niche describes the uniqueness of the catalog brand, the creative platform uses descriptive words—"informative," "fun," "value," "wholesome"—to
describe the brand image. The creative platform for Wolferman's English Muffins promises
"the finest muffins and baked goods in the world" displayed in large, "bite off the page"
photos.

Plow & Hearth distributes its creative platform on a small laminated card to everyone involved in the catalog process (see Exhibit 5.3). When merchants select new products, they use the card to help keep them focused. When artists lay out the catalog, they refer back to this handy creative platform card.

Some catalogers create a "look book" to describe the platform—a collection of images that reflect the audience and its lifestyle and that typify the images to be presented in the catalog. Some add pictures that emulate the type of photography and other graphic treatments they feel support their unique positioning. This is an especially helpful technique for people who aren't familiar with the vocabulary of design but want to convey a certain look to the art director. A related tool is the "swipe book," a collection of catalogs from other companies with layouts, offers, photography, or copy that you think, or that the art director thinks, are effective.

Don't rush this discussion. There are many points to cover concerning merchandising, creative, and marketing. The merchandiser will want to review the product line and explain how it was selected and why it is unique. He or she should bring product samples and specification sheets to turn over to the creative staff responsible for describing the products in words and pictures. The designer will want time to absorb information about the audience and products in order to create a look that meets customers' aesthetic expectations. Again, a "look book" or "swipe book" will be helpful in identifying these creative elements. Finally, the circulation manager will want to explain the mailing strategy that will deliver the new catalog into customers' hands.

It's easy to lose focus during the design process. A well-articulated creative platform or formula gives designers a benchmark against which to measure creative decisions. What typeface should be used? What color accents? How dense should the catalog be? The creative platform answers those questions and should be used to drive decisions about design, layout, copy, photography, and production.

When the creative platform has been pinned down, the discussion can shift to paginating, or organizing the catalog, a detailed process that is discussed later in the chapter.

EXHIBIT 5.3
Plow & Hearth Creative Platform

The production schedule and budget are reviewed, and everyone leaves the meeting with firm assignments.

ASSEMBLING YOUR CREATIVE TEAM

Take time to gather the right creative team. You certainly wouldn't use an orthopedic surgeon to do heart surgery, so why should you hire an art director or photographer with no catalog experience?

If you are looking outside the company for expertise, review portfolios of all potential creative team members, and ask about their specific catalog experience. You want a catalog creative team that understands the creative process and knows how to use analytical tools and statistical reports.

Don't make price an issue. If you try to shave costs by hiring inexperienced or inappropriate people, you will spend more time, money, and effort trying to get the job done right!

Creative Kickoff Meetings for Existing Catalogs

A creative kickoff should take place every time a new catalog is planned. Instead of "blue-skying" a new look, subsequent meetings will review the presentation and performance of previous catalogs with an eye to implementing improvements in the next edition. Exhibit 5.4 shows a sample agenda.

A good kickoff meeting integrates marketing and merchandising in order to achieve and maximize the end results. The marketing team shares the following information:

- Results from previous promotions, summarized by customer and prospect segments. Any test results—for example, from offers—are presented.
- A synopsis of the results and what they mean for future catalog efforts.
- A proposed circulation plan by house and prospect segments that includes drop dates, offers, and any tests.
- An outline of marketing objectives and goals.
- Any updated information about customers and the target audience (modeling information, research, etc.)

Before new merchandise is presented, the previous catalog's merchandise is throughly reviewed. The "squinch" analysis of the previous season's results introduced in Chapter 2 can be used to analyze the success of specific products, categories, and price points as well as the "pulling power" of specific graphic treatments. Apparel catalogs analyze apparel products by how well they did on a model versus off a model. Home furnishings catalogs might compare products illustrated with a lifestyle shot against products shown individually.

Creative Kickoff Agenda for an Existing Catalog

1. Review of merchandise sales by item and page from the last catalog
   - Square-inch analysis
   - Conclusions—merchandise and creative

2. Critique of last catalog's creative presentation
   - What worked?
   - What can be improved?
   - Suggested creative changes

3. Review of competitive catalogs

4. Establishing next catalog's format, specifications, and offers

5. Review of the circulation plan for the season
   - Number of catalogs mailed
   - Timing of mailings
   - Prospect mail plan
   - Customer mail plan
   - Planned testing—timing, offers, reactivation, etc.

6. Presentation of new products

7. Pagination of the catalog

8. Production schedule

9. Catalog budget review

10. "To do" assignments

EXHIBIT 5.4

After previous merchandise has been analyzed, the merchandise staff presents each new product, outlines its specifications and benefits, and describes why it was selected for the catalog. Other supervisory people are often present to have a final review of product. Product specification sheets, samples, and photos are handed over to the copywriter and designer. The more information the merchandiser can provide up front, the less the need to add or change item codes, prices, and so forth later in the production cycle, when the cost to do so can be steep.

The next step is paginating the catalog, or deciding what product goes where. Previous catalog sales information helps determine the optimum place to position bestsellers or products with the highest margins.

Other components reviewed during the meeting include:

- Catalog specifications: number of pages, trim size, number of colors, type of order form, special bind-ins, and the like
- Identification of the color separator, catalog printer, and order form printer for the project
- Production schedule
- Circulation plan and mail date, expected in-home date, mail quantity, and expected results

With each subsequent catalog, this process becomes easier. Repeated items need not be given the same attention as new items. When the meeting is finished, schedules should be confirmed and a "to do" task list created. Have someone recap the meeting and circulate the document to others in your organization as a reference tool.

Basic Design Decisions

In order to develop a creative platform and concept, you need to make some basic decisions about the catalog's size, length, and colors and whether a table of contents or an index is required.

What Size Should Your Catalog Be?

Will you use the "standard" size (a variation of 8½″ × 11″), or will you produce a catalog that looks and "feels" different?

Your decision depends on a number of factors. First, you want to select a size that best reflects your creative platform. Next, you need to examine the catalog size used by your competition and consider whether you should match it or look different. Printing and postage considerations will also drive your decision. Before you select an odd size, make sure your printer can produce it cost effectively. Find out what size fits the press best to minimize paper waste. Before choosing, check with the post office to find out how much it will cost to mail your catalog. A slightly different size may have better postal efficiencies.

Can catalog size make a difference on the bottom line? Absolutely. If you are printing a business-to-business catalog, you certainly wouldn't print an oversize catalog that won't fit on a bookshelf or into a file. Format made a 600 percent difference in results for a company called Construction Bookstore, which changed from an oversize newspaper format (tabloid) to a regular, more efficient size (8⅜″ × 10⅞″). The smaller size was easier for customers to use and was a more organized effort.

How Many Pages?

The length of the catalog is usually determined by how many products will be displayed on a page. The more upscale the niche, the less dense the catalog. If your catalog and niche emphasize price and value, more products can appear on a page. An upscale catalog may feature only a few products per page—in some cases, even a single product.

How Many Colors?

Should you print a four-color catalog, or will one or two colors work? What is best for your creative platform? If color is critical as in apparel, full color is imperative. Three Dog Bakery, which has a monochromatic product, prints in two colors using a process called

---

CATALOG SIZE OPTIONS

- **Standard, full-size format (8⅜″ × 10⅞″).** This is the format used by most business catalogs and consumer catalogs that desire an upscale look and need room to show product.
- **Digest size (5½″ × 8½″).** Roughly half the size of the standard format, digests are used for jewelry and cosmetics catalogs such as Tiffany as well as catalogs with smaller, lower-ticket items. For many years Paragon and Lillian Vernon used the digest size.
- **Slim Jim (6½″ × up to 11″).** Created to provide more space at digest mailing rates, this format is used by some consumer titles but not by business catalogs. Many companies that tried this size have switched back to the standard-size format.
- **Square (9″ × 9″).** A unique format that grabs attention, the square is used by consumer catalogers such as L. L. Bean, Lillian Vernon, and Plow & Hearth.
- **Tabloid (11″ × 17″).** Folded in half to be mailed, the tabloid stands out but can be difficult to organize. Quill occasionally uses this format, printing on newsprint.
- **Oversize (9″ × 12″ or larger).** This very upscale format is often used by home decoration catalogs and was previously used by Patagonia.

---

duotones. This monochromatic look fits the catalog's creative platform because the products are all natural and the company wants to project an "earthy" look.

Is a Table of Contents or an Index Necessary?

Decide early if the catalog will include a table of contents or an index. Customers are accustomed to looking for a table of contents at the beginning of a book and an index at the end. Make it easy to use. A rule of thumb is that you don't need a table of contents if your catalog is forty-eight pages or less. An index is needed when the catalog has a large number of pages or is of a more technical nature. Many business catalogs have both.

Organizing the Catalog

One of the most tedious tasks of the conceptual kickoff meeting is to organize the way products are placed in the catalog, also called pagination. Tedious though it may be, pagination directly influences a catalog's success. I believe there is a lot of magic in pagination. A well-paginated catalog that really flows will naturally be easier to read and more interesting, and will produce good results. A poorly paginated catalog that is boring or hard to read will depress response.

The most important rule of organization is: Make your catalog easy to use and easy to order from! Organize the catalog the way customers will use it. Will customers seek out certain product categories, or will they read every page? Is the catalog a reference tool to be kept in a file or on the shelf? With accurate customer, marketing, and merchandising information, products can be placed in positions that enhance their sales and boost their profitability.

Business catalogs are often organized by product category or product information or application. Medical catalogs often organize items alphabetically. Sometimes catalogs are even organized by price point or color. The most common approach to consumer catalogs is free-form. Products of all varieties are mixed and presented in an intuitive manner that encourages customers to read every single page. Sometimes products are organized around a theme or a section—Hold Everything, for example, includes sections on tools for organizing kitchens, closets, offices, and bathrooms—but otherwise are organized to stimulate consumer interest.

Most catalogs are paginated with natural "hot spots" in mind—positions within the catalog that get higher readership and lend greater emphasis to a product—as the following section explains.

Take Advantage of Catalog Hot Spots

Retail store experts know and appreciate a store's "hot spots"—places where products just naturally seem to attract attention and sales. They understand how to design the store to direct traffic to these areas in order to effectively showcase bestsellers, slow sellers, and low-ticket, impulse items.

Catalogs also have hot spots: the front and back covers, and the beginning, end, and middle of the catalog. Customers are trained to go to these spots in order to get questions answered. Use catalog hot spots to:

- Emphasize products and sell, especially bestsellers and highest-margin products
- Emphasize your catalog's niche and set yourself apart from the competition
- Establish credibility in the marketplace, especially for prospects
- Provide reader involvement
- List customer service information such as ordering guidelines, special services, or the guarantee

The bigger the catalog, the more hot spots you will have. (Chapter 6 explains how to use color, graphics, and bind-ins to create hot spots in the valleys, or "dead spots," that fall between standard hot spots.) Let's look at the role of the major hot spots.

Front Cover

The role of the front cover varies depending on whether you are mailing to a prospect or a customer. Customers who have purchased from a catalog look forward to getting another. They view their favorite catalog like receiving a letter from an old friend or getting a special magazine, and they want to know what new products are being offered. Prospect covers, on the other hand, need to work harder at grabbing attention and quickly describing the catalog's niche.

The front cover has six roles:

1. **It attracts attention.** Catalogs compete with many items in the mailbox or the business in-box, and the front cover must stand out in order to keep the catalog out of the trash can.
2. **It tells customers and prospects who you are and what the catalog is selling.** Customers must be able to recognize the catalog's consistent graphics and a masthead. Prospects must be able to see your name in an easy-to-read typeface.
3. **It reinforces your niche.** The cover tells readers who you are and how you are different from the competition. The easiest way to describe your niche is with a tag line, or positioning line, a simple statement of descriptive words usually placed beneath the masthead.
4. **It can present an offer.** If you want to motivate your customers or prospects to action, present the offer on the front cover, and reference an inside page for a detailed explanation.
5. **It gets the reader inside.** If the cover can get readers inside the book before they place the catalog aside, your chance for an immediate sale is much greater. Compelling graphics or a photograph, copy, or a simple page reference to one of your more interesting or newer products will help.
6. **It sells a product.** Business catalogs often sell products on the front cover; consumer catalogs do so less often. Any product or image placed on the cover needs to support your niche or brand.

(See pp. 3 & 4 of the four-color insert for visual examples of front covers.)

Back Cover

Because the back cover may be the first thing seen when a catalog arrives in the mail, it must work just as hard as the front cover. The roles of a back cover are:

1. **Get the catalog mailed.** Work with your printer and the post office to make sure that the catalog is mailed cost efficiently and arrives in good condition. Find out the minimum space required for the address, and devote the balance of the cover to selling.
2. **Sell, sell, sell.** The back cover is the number-one selling page in the catalog! Place proven winners with best margins here. Add personalized messages and special offers when you ink-jet or laser-print customer names and addresses.
3. **Reinforce your niche, and tell what the catalog is selling.** Both the front and back covers should support the catalog's uniqueness. The logo and tag line should be prominently displayed on the back cover. Featured products should be representative of your niche and the price points inside the catalog.

4. **Get the reader inside.** If you sell products on the back cover, consider referencing other similar products that can be found inside. Repeat any special offers that might compel the recipient to buy. Do anything you can to get the reader inside.

5. **Present customer service information.** This is an obvious place for customers to seek your telephone number, fax number, phone hours, guarantee, or credit card policy.

(See p. 5 of the four-color insert for visual examples of back covers.)

The Inside Front Cover Spread (Pages 2–3)

The important opening spread must be organized and easy to read. Use color and graphics to make it visually appealing. Use this spread for:

- **The welcome letter or reason for the catalog's existence.** The welcome letter can help new catalogs carefully describe their niche and build credibility. Including a photo of the company spokesperson adds credibility and personalizes the company.
- **The guarantee.** Remember, catalog consumers cannot touch, feel, or try on your product. The guarantee helps remove the hesitant consumer's fears.
- **An explanation of the offer.**
- **Customer service information.** Many catalogs (especially business-to-business) list the different methods of ordering, or draw attention to their customer or technical service departments.
- **Bestselling products and products with high margins.**
- **Table of contents.** Smaller catalogs can use a "visual" table of contents that highlights products by category and provides an inside page reference.

(See p. 6 of the four-color insert for visual examples of inside front cover spreads.)

The Inside Back Spread

Because research indicates that about one-third of readers open a catalog somewhere other than the front cover, the inside back spread should be regarded as an important hot spot. This is a good place to print an index, but try to keep it to one page so that product can be sold on the facing page.

The Center Spread or the Pages Surrounding the Center Order Form

The most common type of binding, a saddle-stitched catalog, will open naturally to the center spread, especially when the order form is bound in the center. However, a bound-in order form makes the pages on either side individual pages, not a spread. Center pages are often likened to the retail store checkout stand, where low-ticket, impulse items are sold. With a perfect bound catalog, there is not the same natural center opening. Special bind-in cards or pages can help create natural places for the catalog to open.

The Order Form

The order form offers high visibility for answers to often-asked questions and for low-priced and sale items. In some cases, products placed on the "outside" of an order form will do better than they would inside the catalog! Many catalogers print the outside of the order form in four-color to better present products. A black-and-white order form can be used for products that are not color sensitive.

❖ KEY POINTS

- Follow the four-part catalog creative process in Exhibit 5.1 to keep the catalog on track and under budget.
- Include all key members of the creative team in the creative kickoff meeting, whether you are designing a new or an existing catalog. Don't give the meeting short shrift after you've been in business a year or two. It's still important.
- When you go outside for creative help, look for experienced catalog professionals.
- Make design decisions—format, number of pages, catalog organization, typography, and so forth—that help differentiate your catalog from the competition.
- Understand and maximize catalog "hot spots" to increase sales and profitability.

CHAPTER 6

Design, Photography, and Copy

When it comes to design, remember that a catalog is essentially, as Chapter 2 noted, "a store without walls."

The catalog store goes to the consumer's home or office and competes with other mail, while a retail store competes with other stores for traffic.

The consumer is allowed to go in through the "back door" or drop into the middle of the catalog store. Retail store customers generally enter a store only via the front.

Catalog customers can only see and read about a product. They cannot touch, feel, or try on a product, or ask a salesperson about it. And they must wait to get their purchase instead of taking it home immediately.

Just as there is a logic to designing retail stores, there is a logic to designing a catalog. A good catalog designer takes advantage of catalog "traffic flow" to create an attractive publication that stands out in the mailbox and is easy to use whether the customer comes in through the front, the back, or a side door. Together, the photographer, copywriter, and designer will present products in a manner that entices customers to place an order.

Half the battle of designing catalogs is developing the creative platform. The other half is knowing and understanding the rules that enable a catalog to attract attention, tell your product's story, and sell. These rules are not subjective; they represent years of research and tests that demonstrate how consumers read and process information in catalogs. These studies have been published by reputable companies such as the Gallup Research organization and reflect independent focus group research and years of industry observation and measurement.

The rules are broken, and often very successfully, by catalog design experts who have mastered the rules and begun testing "outside the box" to differentiate or improve the creative presentation. But new and smaller catalogs need to know the rules before they break them.

The Elements of Catalog Design

Catalogs are a visual medium. Appreciating this fact will help you realize why the images placed on a page matter so much. The visual images must tell the catalog's story and enable customers to understand what is being sold. Most catalog buyers browse a catalog and look at the pictures first. If they are interested in a particular product, they look at the price next. Following the price, they read the headlines, subheads, captions, or descriptive copy before proceeding to the body copy and details about color and size.

Design elements must support your creative platform. (Your creative platform, in turn, should support your catalog's niche, position, and brand.) If you're not sure what typeface to use, check the creative platform and make a font decision based on what best supports your desired image.

Design elements also need to be consistent so that catalog customers can quickly identify your catalog and easily find the information they need. Sharper Image and Lands' End are instantly recognizable because they use consistent design elements and place common elements such as page numbers, toll-free number, fax number, and website address in the same easy-to-find place on every page or spread. Once you arrive at a workable design, stick with it. Consistency of a catalog's design elements (layout, typography, photography, and copy style) enhances reader comfort and readabiliy.

Eye Flow

Most readers look first at the top right-hand corner of a catalog spread, then travel in a "sideways **U**" across the top of the page to the upper left-hand corner, down the far left-hand side of the page and across the bottom of the spread, and end up in the lower right-hand corner.

A good page layout directs eye flow. Many successful catalogs take advantage of this "sideways **U**" pattern by placing an interesting photo or product in the upper right-hand corner. Others place an interesting photo or headline in the middle of the left-hand page to entice the eye into a "sideways **V**." The "sideways **U**" and the "sideways **V**" are shown in Exhibit 6.1. Small products placed in the middle of the spread or the corners of the left-hand page will not be noticed as often unless the photography is eye-catching. If the best-selling product on the page is not visually interesting—a white shirt, for example—add a crazy-looking tie to be sure it will be noticed. Photographs can also help lead the eye to important copy. Images or people should always face into the page, not off the page or into the gutter. Likewise, products should face the copy whenever possible.

Color

Color can be a great way to grab attention, but it must be used wisely. Too much color can be confusing and can overpower the product. Some companies wrap up their entire identity with a single color. Tiffany & Company is known for its aqua color, used in the store, on its bags and boxes, and on catalog covers.

Eye Flow Chart

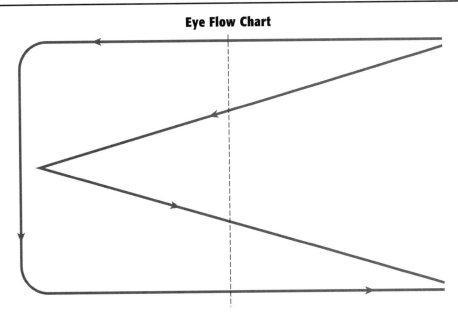

EXHIBIT 6.1

The eye usually starts in the upper right-hand corner and follows one of two paths before exiting the two-page spread.

Illustrations and Graphs

Sometimes a photograph is not enough to tell a product's story. Charts, graphs, and illustrations get high readership and help support the benefits of a product or explain technical features. The TravelSmith catalog uses illustrations to explain the hidden features of garments. Catalogs such as Gooseberry Patch and Vermont Country Store use illustrations instead of photographs to differentiate themselves from the competition. Others, such as Three Dog Bakery, use illustrations to add fun to catalog spreads. Often, illustrative art can help explain a product's features and benefit where photgraphy can't.

Be sure to include a variety of visual images to enhance eye flow. Vary the size of illustrations as well. The eye is bored when all the photographs or images on a spread are the same size.

Typography

Typography is abused more than any other design element. Catalog designers are hired to sell product, not win creative awards for fancy approaches to type. Type should be easy to read and in keeping with the catalog's positioning.

Type size should be compatible with your target audience: not too big, not too small, and comfortable and easy-to-read. Most catalogs use 9-point type with 10 or 11 points of leading, or white space (written "9/11"). Catalogs for mature audiences may want to use

10- or 11-point type. Avoid cluttering the catalog with too many kinds of type. Use one family of type fonts per catalog; a second font may be used sparingly.

Ragged-right type is by far the easiest to read, while justified-left-and-right is easier to read than ragged-left (or justified-right). Centered copy is difficult to read. Compare the readability of the examples in Exhibit 6.2.

Copy is easier to read in narrow columns. Keep the length of the copy line no longer than half of the page width.

Avoid placing copy over graphics. Unless your image is screened back (almost to a ghost), type will be difficult to read. Likewise, avoid white or light-color copy that is reversed out of a dark-color background. Use reverse type sparingly for headlines, graphic elements, or short clips of copy. Also, don't use a small type size when reversing because it is hard to keep the colors in register. Studies have shown that reverse type cuts readability by as much as 80 percent.

Wrapping copy around photographs or drawings of products (as in Exhibit 6.3) is a great technique for saving space on the page, and it helps to tie the image to the copy. Avoid getting the copy too close to the art element. A little white space helps eye flow.

Copy: Choices in Type Justification

Ragged Right

It's the unmistakable deep rumble of a Harley-Davidson Motorcycle captured in a mug. Lift the lid and the hidden sound chip sounds like you're ready to ride! And whether the guy (or gal) you give it to owns a Harley—or just wishes they did—it's sure to be a hit. The handle looks like a motorcycle handlebar, and the chrome-look lid sports the famous emblem. Unbreakable plastic. Batteries included.

Ragged Left

It's the unmistakable deep rumble of a Harley-Davidson Motorcycle captured in a mug. Lift the lid and the hidden sound chip sounds like you're ready to ride! And whether the guy (or gal) you give it to owns a Harley—or just wishes they did—it's sure to be a hit. The handle looks like a motorcycle handlebar, and the chrome-look lid sports the famous emblem. Unbreakable plastic. Batteries included.

Centered

It's the unmistakable deep rumble of a Harley-Davidson Motorcycle captured in a mug. Lift the lid and the hidden sound chip sounds like you're ready to ride! And whether the guy (or gal) you give it to owns a Harley—or just wishes they did—it's sure to be a hit. The handle looks like a motorcycle handlebar, and the chrome-look lid sports the famous emblem. Unbreakable plastic. Batteries included.

Justified

It's the unmistakable deep rumble of a Harley-Davidson Motorcycle captured in a mug. Lift the lid and the hidden sound chip sounds like you're ready to ride! And whether the guy (or gal) you give it to owns a Harley—or just wishes they did—it's sure to be a hit. The handle looks like a motorcycle handlebar, and the chrome-look lid sports the famous emblem. Unbreakable plastic. Batteries included.

EXHIBIT 6.2

Wrapped Copy

A Sound So Unique It's Patented!

It's the unmistakable rumble of a Harley-Davidson Motorcycle captured in a mug. Lift the lid and the hidden sound chip sounds like you're ready to ride! And whether the guy (or gal) you give it to owns a Harley—or wishes they did—it's sure to be a hit. The handle looks like a motorcycle handle bar, and the chrome-look lid sports the famous emblem. Mug is 11" high and made of unbreakable plastic. (Batteries included.)

Item #0505 Harley-Davidson Mug $11.95

NEW

EXHIBIT 6.3
Electric Outlet

Nonselling Space

White space, or "negative" space, is a design element and can be used to rest the eye. White space should not be trapped in the middle of several objects, as it draws too much attention. It is frequently used in upscale catalogs that can afford to have fewer items per page.

Layout Options

Too many similar pages makes a catalog look boring. To organize your pages, build a series of layout templates—each illustrating a different type of page design—and alternate the templates throughout the catalog. Don't create too many, however. Stick to three or four layout templates; ten or twelve alternating layouts will only confuse readers.

There are many kinds of layouts from which to choose:

- **The symmetrical, or grid, layout.** This layout divides the page into a series of grids. Grid spaces need not be equal, and it is fine to "break" the grid lines with a product.

- **The asymmetrical, or free-flow, approach.** This popular approach gives the designer the most flexibility. Mixing this technique with more-structured layouts helps traverse the "valleys" of the catalog.
- **Art and copy separation.** Some layouts separate art and copy, grouping pictures of products in one location and copy elsewhere on the spread. A letter or number keying system makes it easy for the reader to match products with copy blocks.
- **Product grouping layouts.** Product grouping layouts are appropriate for furniture or sets of products such as books, videos, and greeting cards, as long as every product is keyed to its copy and is easy to see. Show hard-to-see products in a close-up or an inset.
- **Hero product layout.** If your product line is expensive or you can afford to have a less dense page, you can place one product on a page or spread to grab attention and to show the product in finer detail.

(See p. 7 of the four-color insert for visual examples of layout options.)

Pacing the Catalog

Every catalog has hot spots and dreaded valleys. The bigger the catalog, the deeper the valleys and the more difficult it is to keep people browsing through the pages. To help pace the catalog:

- Mix layout templates to keep spreads interesting. Too much of the same thing will cause fatigue.
- Use color to stop the eye. Placing a background tint or a strong colored border will help create diversity.
- Add a bind-in within a valley. Inserts and bind-ins create a hot spot.
- Add something new, different, and out of the ordinary to make the eye pause and enhance browsing.

A variety of techniques can direct attention to a particular product or page. However, attention getters should be used with discrimination. Too many of them on a spread are confusing, and nothing gets attention. Common attention getters include:

- Special icons to announce a new, exclusive, or value-driven product.
- "Violators"—starbursts and other attention-getting graphic elements—that draw attention to a special feature or benefit.
- Testimonials or endorsements from customers, celebrities, or recognized experts. These are an effective way to deliver a sales message. Be sure to position this copy differently from product copy so that it stands out. Use pictures for celebrity endorsements and customer testimonials and profiles. One food-by-mail cataloger, Cushman Fruit Company, feels that its customers are so important that

the company runs an annual photo contest and uses pictures of customers throughout its catalog.

- Technical tips, product use suggestions, and recipes grab attention and make your catalog more valuable to customers, who may keep copies longer. Williams-Sonoma places recipes in a shaded box to set the element apart from product copy.
- Captions under photographs and call-outs that explain product benefits. These are among the first things readers notice on a page.
- Editorial copy. Company vignettes, customer testimonials, and how-tos can attract attention when they're set apart in shaded "sidebars."

What Happens During the Design Process

Creative execution—layout, photography, and copy— is Phase Two of the catalog creative process as shown in Exhibit 5.1 on page 74.

Once the overall catalog creative concept has been pinned down and the catalog has been paginated, the designer begins preparing cover and page concepts. First, "thumbnail sketches" are developed. These miniature sketches, usually in black-and-white, illustrate several alternative creative concepts and page layouts. When an approach has been agreed on, the designer prepares detailed, full-size, color comprehensives, or "comps," of the cover and page spreads, showing such graphic elements as the logo; headlines and body copy; call-outs, captions, and sidebars; photography and illustrations; and color and white space. Generally, the designer produces tight color comps of the final cover idea and three or four two-page spreads.

Comprehensives are then approved by the catalog design manager and someone who is responsible for profit and loss and the budget. Consensus must be reached before page layout begins! When comprehensives are approved, the designer uses a pencil or computer to design every page of the catalog and the order form. Each two-page spread shows all details needed for the photographer and writer to be able to complete their jobs. The end product is a set of detailed black-and-white page layouts. Layouts may be revised several times before being approved and turned over to the photographer and copywriter.

Precise layouts tell the copywriter how much space is available for body copy and whether sidebars, captions, and such are needed. They tell the photographer the size of the final shot and what kind of shot is desired.

Catalog Photography

In catalogs, a picture is definitely worth a thousand words. The number one rule in catalog photography is that the product is the "hero." Many art directors and photographers want to add props and accessories that convey a lifestyle or a beautiful image. The truth is that overpropping takes away attention from the products you are selling. The product is the hero. Propping, including models, should be used only to explain a benefit or demonstrate the size and scale, fit, and product use.

Many types of shots are used in catalogs. A product displayed in a natural environment is called a framed shot. The background is left in the photograph but is cropped tightly enough so that the product remains the hero. Silhouettes (called "silos" or "COBs" for "cut out the background"), which show the product without background ambience or props, allow the product photo to be as large as possible. Adding a drop shadow where the product would normally touch a surface helps prevent the product from appearing to "float" on the page. Color separators can prepare both silhouettes and shadows when scanning the original transparencies. Be sure to specify what you want when handing over transparencies.

An in-use shot, which shows a product being used, helps explain features and benefits. "Before-and-after" shots attract attention by dramatizing the end benefit.

When your creative platform calls for a specific ambience or setting, location photography might be necessary. However, I've seen catalogers spend thousands of dollars sending people to exotic locations and then end up cropping out much of the background. Many locations can be re-created closer to home or built in the photo studio. Catalogers often rent empty homes to create room settings at affordable prices.

Model shots are appropriate for categories such as apparel, but they can be distracting when they do not enhance the product. Choose models who are appropriate to your target audience. An outdoor-apparel catalog should use "outdoorsy" people; a sports catalog for women should use women athletes. While using real customers has succeeded for some catalogs, trying to save money by using friends and family instead of professional models can look amateurish. Models are trained to look natural in front of the camera. If your budget permits, pay the extra to hire a model and a hair and makeup stylist to get the required look.

Some products, such as a suite of furniture or a set of dishes, work well in group shots. If the shot includes a product that is hard to see, such as a lamp or a throw pillow, pull the item out of the photograph as a silhouette, or present it in a close-up shot. Be careful with group shots: when they are too busy, nothing stands out.

It isn't always easy for a photo to tell the whole product story, especially when the product features are hidden. A photo can't demonstrate how good something tastes or how wonderful a stereo system sounds. In these cases, a photograph must be augmented with captions, call-outs, and inset photos that explain the whole story.

(See p. 8 of the four-color insert for visual examples of photography.)

The Elements of Good Copy

The photograph may grab attention, but it's the copy that tells the rest of the story and closes the sale. Whatever the photograph cannot "say," the copy should. A bottle of skin care lotion can't say that it will make your skin softer in ten days, but the copy block can. However, copy should be only long enough to get the full message across, and no longer.

Copy is extremely important in creating and reinforcing brand image, and it needs to support the creative platform. Business catalogs tend to be more to the point and less flowery than consumer catalogs. If your company is perceived as the expert in your industry, then catalog copy should be authoritative. If there is a personality behind the catalog, then copy should be written in first person as if that person is having a "chat" with the consumer. When deciding what your copy "voice" or "persona" will be, refer to your niche and the creative platform that you previously developed. In the beginning, trying different styles and copywriters is helpful in determining what copy works best, but once you settle on a voice, stick with it.

Good copy grabs attention, entertains, educates or informs the reader of specific features and benefits, and builds confidence that products will do as they promise. For each product, a copy block should include:

- A descriptive or benefit headline, sometimes accompanied by a subhead
- Benefit statements that sell the end benefit
- Specific product features such as content, size, dimensions and weight, color, and shipping instructions, e.g., is over-sized and will be shipped by truck instead of UPS or USPS
- In spreads with group shots, key codes that match the photo to the copy
- Item codes and prices

Copy blocks need to be consistent in their presentation and to look the same throughout the catalog. Information should be organized to facilitate decision making. Usually, the headline, item number, and price are presented in boldface to make them easy to locate and read.

Product copy isn't the only place where you can position yourself in the marketplace and grab attention. An opening or welcome letter can include information about new and interesting products, customer service facts, special offers, gift-giving opportunities, and other benefits. Focus the letter on what the catalog offers customers, not on the company. Also, page or spread headlines can grab attention and describe what is offered on the pages. Editorial sidebars such as question-and-answer blocks, technical tips, recipes, and customer testimonials are effective as well. The guarantee copy can reassure customers, and service information can reinforce the convenience of purchasing from your catalog.

It's the copywriter's job to draft copy to fit the layouts, which specify the number of lines and characters per line in each copy block. The writer also creates headlines, photo captions, call-outs, charts, editorial sidebars, welcome letters, and product headlines, and enters product numbers, prices, and other descriptive copy in the copy block.

Great catalog copywriters are hard to find. Sometimes it takes several attempts before copy melds with your niche or creative platform. Even though catalogs are more visually oriented than copy driven, copy should not be treated as an evil stepsister. After all, copy is what closes the sale.

Designing the Order Form

Of all the sections in the catalog, the order form requires the most planning. Unfortunately, too many catalog designers put off order form design until the last minute, triggering a crisis at the printer. Design and print your order form so that it is ready when your catalog goes to press. Otherwise, you may lose your place in the bindery line.

Every catalog needs an order form. Even if you're a business-to-business cataloger whose orders arrive by phone or the Internet, the order form is critical. Both business and consumer customers use the order form as a work sheet in planning their orders, because it guides them through the ordering process, answers customer service questions, and presents ordering information such as shipping, taxes, and return policies.

Before you begin designing your order form, collect and examine examples of well-organized, easy-to-use order forms. I recommend emulating the best. If you are a gift catalog, adopt the approach of a catalog such as Omaha Steaks, which provides space to list five or six gift recipients. If your catalog will emphasize Internet ordering, model your order form on one that encourages Internet orders. Make sure your form fits the needs and service proposition of your catalog. Free shipping with any order, quantity discounts—whatever is unique about your offer and reflective of your brand—should be prominently featured on the form.

ORDER FORM CHECKLIST

Don't leave important information off the order form! Use this checklist to make sure the basics are included.

- Customer's name and source code—ink-jetted or lasered
- Space for an address correction
- Space to fill in an E-mail address and a place to "opt-in" to any future Internet offers
- Space for two or more gift recipient names and addresses
- How-to-order information, including phone, fax, address, and website
- Hours for phone ordering
- Customer service phone number and hours
- Shipping information, including costs and special delivery options
- Offers
- Product return information
- Guarantee
- Any required legal information
- Size charts or personalization information
- Mailing "opt-out" information, giving customers the opportunity to tell you that they prefer that you don't rent their names
- State tax chart

Use graphics and icons to organize information, increase readability, and add interest to a potentially boring form. Color can also help. In a two-color order form that presents only ordering information, the second color can differentiate sections. If the order form is used to sell products that are color sensitive, one side of the order form will need to be printed in four colors.

If you are ink-jetting the name, address, and source code on the order form, your placement options are limited. Most printers can ink-jet only order forms that are placed in the center of the catalog. An affordable option is to print the order form on inexpensive, noncoated paper and bind it into the center of the catalog; another is to print the form on an actual catalog page. Whatever your choice, be sure to place the form where the customer expects to find it—the center spread or the back inside spread.

As noted earlier, a wide range of order form formats is available. Talk to an order form printer about the options, and be sure to request a design template that shows where type can be placed. The template should include ink-jet locations and space requirements, trim and bleed designations, position of staples or glue strips, paper and color options, and the exact dimensions of the form.

A detachable order form envelope has traditionally been included as a courtesy and convenience to customers, but as telephone and Internet orders increase, many catalogers are opting to eliminate it. The most expensive part of the order form, the envelope requires a specialty printer as well as a longer lead time to produce. Consider whether your target audience needs an envelope, and whether the envelope will be postage-paid (business reply envelope) or not (reply envelope), and spend the time to cost out your options.

❖ KEY POINTS

- Establish a creative platform that supports your brand before you begin the creative execution.
- Make sure your overall design treats every element: layout, photography and illustrations, graphs, charts, typography, color, and white space.
- Use the principles of good eye flow to direct readers through catalog pages and spreads.
- Use a variety of layouts to enhance interest, pacing, and eye flow throughout the catalog.
- Don't stint on photography. In the visual medium of catalogs, good photography and illustrations will improve response rates and sales, while poor photography will hurt sales.
- Every catalog needs some type of order form, although as more orders come in via telephone or the Internet, smart catalogers are reducing the size and expense of order forms.

Offers

Offers

3 FREE GIFTS
with your order from this catalog

Sorry, no Fingerhut Express Deliveries to P.O. boxes, APO/FPO addresses, or to AK, HI, PR, GU or VI. See each catalog page to find out which products can be shipped by Fingerhut Express.

Eyeglass Repair Kit
Small enough to fit in any pocket, purse or bag, this repair kit is an absolute necessity for eyeglasses and sunglasses wearers! Contains: mini-screwdriver, hinge screws, hinge rings, nose pads and a convenient plastic carry case. Case measures approx. 2 ¾"L x 1 ⅛"W x ½"H.

Jar Opener
Get a tight grip on stubborn jar lids and see how easily they open with this 6" jar opener. Keep it handy in your utility drawer the next time you need to open a new jar.

Surprise Free Gift
We can't tell you what it is, but we [...] you it's something nice for you, yo[...] or your family. And it's yours whe[...] any product in this catalog.

We reserve the right to substitute similar merchandise of equal or better quality. If substitut[...] is not acceptable, you can retu[...] [...]ring your free trial period without further obli[...]

c.

Gifts of Sunshine, Health & Good Taste

Free Shipping Offer!

To: Very Small Group (of important Cushman Customers we didn't hear from last year).

What: Very Big...Special Offer.

Why: We really miss you (and would do almost anything to get you back, including bribery).

Free Shipping

on every single gift you send anywhere in the continental U.S.A. and Canada. Yes, FREE SHIPPING when your order totals just $50.00 or more...I'm serious, please come back.

d.

BAKER'S CHOICE
Wolferman's Gift of the Month Club

Order once and have your thoughtfulness delivered all year long. With this gift-giving option you can choose to send a gift of Wolferman's baked goods every (1) every month or (3) every season. Each delivery is a reminder of your thoughtfulness. A generous gift for special customers and clients, good friends and family members.

Starting in December, we'll send a personalized card to announce your very special gift. You can choose to begin your gift by sending our **Grand Sunday Brunch Basket**, **Bountiful Breakfast Basket**, or **Best of Wolferman's Tin**.

Then throughout the year, Wolferman's will send the selection pictured on page 37 at the intervals you've chosen for refilling the gift basket.

To order, simply select the item number for the 12, 6 or 3 month **Grand Baker's Choice**, **Bountiful Baker's Choice** or **Baker's Choice**. A card announcing your gift arrives in December, followed by the first delivery before Christmas – please order by December 10th.

(Custom Ribbon Creations not available.)

Grand Baker's Choice
Begins in December with Grand Sunday Brunch (see page 27).
#9156 12 Month Grand Baker's Choice $324.95
Every month December through November
#9157 6 month Grand Baker's Choice $199.95
December, March, May, July, September, and November
#9158 3 month Grand Baker's Choice $169.95
December, March, June, and September

July: Tea Bread Sampler (pg. 15)

February: Tiny Scone Sampler (pg. 10)

August: Miniature Sampler (pg. 12)

March: Sweet Sampler (pg. 5)

September: Classic Cinnamon Rolls (pg. 10)

e.

a. Guarantee
b. Guarantee
c. Free gifts
d. Free shipping
e. Clubs
f. Drive store traffic

Front Covers

a. Luminescence
b. Garfield
c. Cushman Fruit
d. Lietz-Sokkia

Front Covers

a.

b.

c.

d.

a. Austad's **c.** Breck's
b. Hello Direct **d.** King Catalog

Back Covers

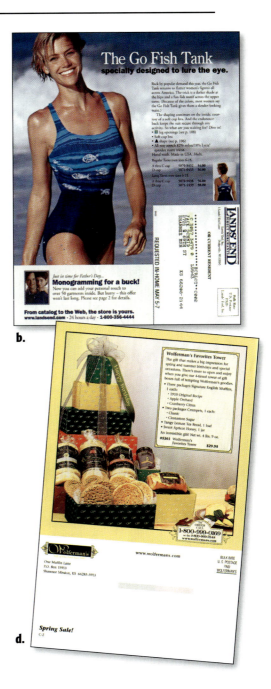

a. Christine Columbus   **c.** Pierce Chemical
b. Lands' End   **d.** Wolferman's

Inside Front Cover Spreads

a. Garfield
b. Doctors Foster & Smith
c. Cushman Fruit
d. A. M. Leonard

a.

b.

c.

d.

Page Layout Examples

a.

a. Art and copy separation
b. Hero product
c. Grid or symmetrical
d. Product grouping
e. Assymetrical layout

b.

c.

d.

e.

Photography

a.

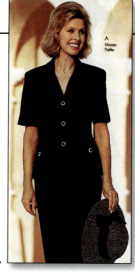

b.

a. In-use shot
b. Model shot
c. Silhouetted shot
d. Framed shot
e. Illustrative art
f. Photo styling
g. Product grouping

c.

d.

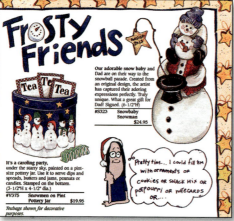

e.

f.

g.

CHAPTER 7

Managing Page Production, Color Separations, and Printing

In catalog design and production, the catalog designer serves as architect/general contractor to the rest of the creative team, which "subcontracts" specialized tasks. The designer develops the master plan, budget, and schedule. He or she also prepares elaborate cover designs and page layouts from which the photographer will shoot, the copy person will write, and the page production person will actually build catalog pages.

Page production can be handled internally or outsourced. Larger mailers that produce six or eight or a dozen catalogs annually usually develop an in-house page production capability. Start-up and medium-size catalogs more readily outsource production to companies or agencies that specialize in, and have a strong history of, creating successful catalogs. Not every advertising agency or sales promotion group is capable of producing wonderful, productive catalogs. Award-winning graphics? Sure! But knowledge of eye flow, catalog hot spots, response-generating copy, quality layouts, and product-enhancing photography may be missing if the creative staff doesn't know the basics of catalog design and production.

Understanding the page production process will help you determine whether it makes sense to "do it inside" or to hire a qualified outside catalog group.

Managing Page Production

The blueprint for the catalog is a set of detailed page or spread layouts. By the time the page production person prepares to start on page development, layouts are complete, and photography, illustrations, and copywriting are complete and approved.

Page production for a thirty-two-page catalog should take fifteen to twenty working days. The complexity of pages, number of pages that can be picked up from previous catalogs, special art techniques required, and other variables will have an impact on the schedule. Page production is not a stage of the creative development that can be rushed. If it is, errors may result, or pages may look inconsistent or unrelated.

Catalog design flows into page production in Phase Three of the catalog creative process, shown in Exhibit 5.1 on page 74. As you go through the steps, keep in mind an old rule of thumb: The earlier you make changes in the creative production process, the less it costs. To wit:

- It costs about $5 to make a change in layout or copy at the rough stage.
- It costs about $50 to make a change at the finished layout stage.
- It costs about $500 to make a change at the color separation stage.
- It costs about $5,000 to make a change at the printing stage.

It doesn't take a rocket scientist to figure out that the best time to make any change in price, item number, copy design, or photography is early in the creative process.

Step 1: Production Kickoff Meeting

The page production process begins with a kickoff meeting in which the production team reviews every detail of page construction. The catalog designer who has done the detailed layouts is present, as is the artist who will produce the catalog on computer. I recommend that the color separator and even the printer also attend.

At the meeting, participants construct the schedule, review the budget, and determine who is responsible for each task. Specifications from the color separator and printer are checked to make sure that pages will be laid out correctly. An overlooked printer specification caused one catalog team I know to produce film that was an eighth of an inch off—and the whole thing had to be chucked and redone. It's a good idea to review the designer's layouts for special features, colors, and graphic elements.

Step 2A: Photo Scanning and Input

There are two ways to incorporate photography into page production. In **automatic picture replacement** (APR), the more widely used, the color separator provides the production artist a low-resolution scan of each photo for size and position. Photos need to be scanned only once. The FPO, or **for position only**, method entails two scannings. The artist hand-scans each image for placement; the color separator uses FPO images as a guide, deleting them from the file and replacing them with high-resolution scans. The APR approach saves both time and money.

Step 2B: Page Layout and Copy Fitting

Final approved copy, written to fit the number of lines and character count indicated in the layouts, is supplied on disk. Copyediting should already have taken place. The only changes made during this phase are those required to fit copy, such as adding or cutting a word or eliminating a "widow."

Step 3: First Round of Proofing

This step is the first opportunity to review the spreads with copy and visuals in place. Final changes must be made here! Wholesale redesign of catalog pages at this point is costly. Every person in the company who needs to see, review, and approve the spreads must participate at this stage—no opting for review at a later date.

Step 4: Changes Made and Second Proof Generated

Corrections and minor changes may be made to enhance the design, make the copy more readable, and ultimately sell more product. If a catalog is buying page production on the outside, the second round of proofs is normally included in the cost. Make certain that you know how many proofs are included in your budget. Any changes made after this step usually are considered alterations, for which you will be charged.

Step 5: Final Proofreading

Embarrassing errors can be avoided if the catalog is carefully proofed one last time. The catalog production house and the client have a shared responsibility for final proofreading. It's a good idea to develop a checklist of "fatal error" elements to subject to a final review, such as:

- Phone number
- Customer service number
- Street address, city, state, and zip code
- Item numbers
- Item coding on each page

- Fax number
- Website address
- Prices
- Inside page references
- All copy spelling

Step 6: Final Alterations

Last-minute changes are inevitable: prices change, a product is dropped and replaced, or the company president doesn't like a word or two. These final changes are called "AAs" (for author's alterations), and the page production artist makes them to the final layouts. Some companies insist on a set of inexpensive color proofs at this stage to see everything in laser-printed color. More often, however, proofing is done in black-and-white.

Step 7: Desktop (Electronic) Files Are Prepared for the Color Separator

The production artist prepares electronic files of all pages for the separator, along with a hard-copy memo that documents standardized printing colors (PMS colors), fonts and type sizes, line screen, file formats, and other information that enables the separator to open and use the files correctly.

Managing Color Separations

As with page production, color separations for a thirty-two-page catalog should take about fifteen to twenty working days. Quite a bit of time can be gained if the separator begins photo scans as soon as photography is complete and photos have been selected by the art director or production artist. Final assembly and production of color proofs can be done in five to ten workdays. Film, if required, takes another two to three days.

Ask for bids from two or three color separators with catalog experience. Developing long-term contracts or relationships with qualified color houses will not only help ensure consistent quality and budgets but also allow you to archive photo images for reuse in future catalogs. Exhibit 7.1 provides a checklist for working with color separators.

Step 1: Prepress Kickoff Meeting

It's a good idea to hand transparencies over to the color separator at a formal meeting with the art director, the production artist, and the color separator's representative, who will supervise the color work and understands the scope, timing, color requirements, and quality of work required. In the handoff session, each transparency should be reviewed and color expectations discussed (e.g., "match the transparency," or "match the actual product sample for color," or "lighten the background"). Good communication at this stage saves money and effort further down the road.

Step 2: High-Resolution Scans Produced

The color separator scans each image at high resolution and stores the image in a digital file. Color "scatters," the first round of color proofs, are prepared for the catalog agency and/or client to review. Proofs may show individual images or entire pages that have been

---

Color Separation Checklist

1. Get a minimum of three bids for separations *in writing*.
2. Ask to see samples of the color separator's work. Check color sensitivity—for example, skin tones, apparel, food.
3. Visit the plant. Is it a modern facility with state-of-the-art equipment? Is it clean and organized?
4. Ask if the firm separates by individual transparency or by page or spread.
5. Ask what method of color proofing is used.
6. Furnish the separator clean and complete electronic files.
7. Furnish artwork to size.
8. Identify special effects desired.
9. Have the printer in on meetings with the color separator.
10. Ask who is paying for corrections!

EXHIBIT 7.1

"gang scanned," or scanned at one time. Although gang-scanned images save money for low-budget catalogs, they cannot be changed by the artist. Only individual images can be enlarged, shrunk, or otherwise manipulated.

Step 3: Low-Resolution Photo File Created for Desktop Page Production

The color separator provides the page production artist with a low-resolution photo or image file to include in the page layout along with the copy. Digitized images can be enlarged or reduced up to as much as 120 percent without rescanning the original transparency, making it easier for the production artist to make minor size adjustments during page production.

Step 4: High-Resolution Color Proofing

While the page or spread layout is being finalized by the page production artist, the color separator shows initial proofs, or scatters, to the designer, art director, or catalog manager responsible for approving color. If color is critical, as in the case of apparel or food, proofs may be compared with actual product samples. Color corrections are suggested, and the color separator makes a second round of proofs.

Step 5: Integrating Production Files and Color Separations, and Producing Film

This stage begins when the page production artist gives the color separator a disk containing the electronic layout of the catalog, including all support files such as logos, graphics, and fonts. (Because digital graphics files are large, this is usually an electronic file, e.g., Zip disk or a writable CD.) The separator then marries the electronic file and the high-resolution photo images to produce final pages. The entire page makeup of the catalog is now complete. Inexpensive color proofs (called Iris, Rainbow, or Xerox Approved) are generated for customer review.

Step 6: Final Color Proof

Before composite film is created or a plate is burned from a digital file, the color separator produces a high-resolution proof (sometimes called a Chromalin or Matchprint) of the entire catalog for all to review and approve.

Step 7: Film or an Electronic File to Printer

The color separator prepares final composite film or an electronic file for direct-to-plate printers. An approved hard copy of the high-resolution file is also sent to the printer for use in print proofing.

Managing the Printing Process

The final phase of catalog production is printing, an activity that continually changes dramatically. Instead of merely applying ink to paper and binding the catalog, most printers serve as a partner in the entire "back-end" production and mailing of the catalog. Today's catalog printers can perform all or most of the following functions:

- Print and bind catalogs, order forms, bind-in and blow-in cards, and other inserts
- Handle color separations
- Use ink-jet labeling on the back cover and order form
- Affix special-message "dot whacks" to covers for targeted customers
- Merge-purge and sort mailing lists down to the carrier-route level to obtain maximum postal discounts
- Commingle catalogs from other mailers to reduce postal costs; three cents a catalog saved by mailing a catalog with others printed the same week can add up
- Bar-code catalog address blocks to obtain postal discounts
- Bag, tag, and deliver catalogs to postal facilities
- Plan trim size and paper stock to reduce weight and cost of the catalog in the mail while reinforcing the catalog's brand and positioning
- Selectively bind different signatures for different customer and prospect lists, in order to showcase certain products to certain markets
- Provide environmentally acceptable paper and ink options
- Determine the most efficient method of printing based on quantities mailed
- Personalize covers, opening spreads, and selective positions in the catalog

In effect, the printer is becoming the cataloger's partner in reaching customers on time, with the most efficient, most cost-effective, and best-looking catalog possible for the dollars the cataloger is willing to spend.

The length of time required to print depends on the print run, number of pages, and complexity of the job. Typically, a four-color, thirty-two-page, full-size catalog with a run from 500,000 to 1 million will take about seven to ten days to complete, including platemaking, actual printing, binding, ink-jetting, and mail preparation. The art director should check the color match print or blue lines provided by the printer and also be present when the job goes on press along with the press operator and the printer's sales representative to approve color. Exhibit 7.2 provides a checklist for working with printers, while Exhibit 7.3 on pages 104–105 shows a detailed specification list that will help you secure accurate bids.

Managing the Creative Schedule and Budget

Launching and building a catalog is expensive, and creative costs represent a major investment. Successful catalogers who value cost containment understand the creative budget and work hard to control it. Overruns in the creative area can have serious consequences for a catalog's profitability, as Chapter 13 will demonstrate.

Printer Checklist

1. Prepare a detailed bid/specification sheet.
2. Define the quality of printing desired.
3. Ask for printed samples on a comparable type of paper.
4. Always get three or four competitive bids *in writing*.
5. Select paper to match your catalog's image/identity and products:
   • Weight
   • House paper
   • Best-results paper
6. Discuss addressing and mailing with your printer:
   • Letter shop
   • In-house
7. Determine who will produce the order form.
8. Visit the printing plant before committing to print.
9. Be on-site as the catalog is printed.

EXHIBIT 7.2

There are two types of creative costs: fixed and variable. ***Fixed costs*** are those tasks that do not vary by volume or quantity of catalogs mailed, including:

• Creative concept
• Catalog design and layout
• Copywriting
• Photography
• Illustrative art
• Computer page production
• Color separations

Fixed creative costs are an investment. When you take 200 photos for a new catalog, chances are good you can reuse quite a number in future catalogs, unless you are producing a totally new catalog every issue, as in high-fashion apparel.

Variable costs are measured by the unit or by the thousand and change as the quantity of mailings goes up or down. In direct marketing terms, variable costs such as printing, postage, and mailing lists are charged on a per-thousand basis. For example:

• A cataloger rents a mailing list for $120 per thousand (or 12¢ each)
• Printing of a catalog is charged at $350 per thousand (or 35¢ each)
• Postage to mail a catalog under 3.3 ounces, non-letter size, with no automation is $304 per thousand (or 30.4¢ each)

Most variable costs decline as volume increases. The per-unit cost of printing 10,000 copies of a thirty-two-page catalog is considerably higher than printing 1 million catalogs. While postage doesn't decline with volume, catalogers can sort larger quantities and take advantage of postal discounts based on three- and five-digit automation, bar-coding, and carrier-route mail preparation. By far the two largest budget items in creating and mailing a new catalog are printing and postage.

Production (Print, Laser, Mail) Estimate Form

Client _____   Today's Date _____

Project Name/Job # _____   Date Needed _____ ☐ A.M. ☐ P.M.

Mail Date _____   ☐ Estimate   ☐ Actual job

Mail Quantity _____   Quantity to Produce _____

Project: ☐ Catalog   ☐ Self-mailer   ☐ Solo package   ☐ Other _____

Component #1:

☐ Catalog   ☐ Catalog OF   ☐ Bind-in   ☐ Letter   ☐ Envelope   ☐ Self-mailer   ☐ Other

Size: _____   Folded/Finish: _____

Stock: _____

Prints:
   ☐ PMS   ☐ Process   ☐ Side 1:   ☐ Side 2:

      ☐ Full bleed   ☐ Die cut   ☐ Perforated   ☐ Glue strip   ☐ ¼ margin included

Artwork: ☐ Camera-ready   ☐ Film with: blue line   color key   match print

        ☐ Direct to plate (digital) with: Fugi proof   DuPont proof   Kodak approvals

Color separations: Separations (#)   # New   # Pickup   # Resized

                Halftones (#)   Duotones (#)

                Screens (#)   Drop shadows   Other special effects

Bindery: ☐ Saddle stitch   Bind-ins (#)

        ☐ Perfect bind

        ☐ Z-fold   Copy in   Copy out

        ☐ Barrel fold   Copy in   Copy out

        ☐ Accordion
        Other fold–show dummy

        Bind to component? Which component: _____   What page spread: _____

        Versioning in bindery? _____

        Quantity of drops: _____   Date(s): _____

Additional Comments:

EXHIBIT 7.3

Lasering and Mailing Estimate Form

Client _____

Quantity to mail _____

Date materials are due to production _____

List Work:

List source: ☐ Client provided ☐ Rented list ☐ House list ☐ Ordered by JSA

How many different files? _____

List format: ☐ Magnetic tape ☐ Diskette ☐ E-mail ☐ Labels
☐ Cheshire 4-up 2-up
☐ Press sensitive 4-up 2-up

Variables: ☐ Locations/dealers ☐ Text ☐ Offers ☐ Response form ☐ Variable instructions attached

Tape Work:

Tape work required: ☐ Dup/elim ☐ Merge-purge ☐ Gender ☐ Upper/lower case
☐ Zip + 4 ☐ Carrier route ☐ Postal presort ☐ NCOA ☐ Key codes

Laser Work:

Components to laser: Letter copy _____ Name/address only_____ Name/address + letter_____

If salutation, specify format— "Dear FN" etc. _____ No Name–default to _____

Lettershop/Fulfillment:

# of pieces total _____ # of pieces that match insert into envelope? ☐ Yes ☐ No

Size of carrier_____ What drives envelope_____

Special instructions: Tabbing Packaging (to ship) Other _____

Mailing:

Postage: ☐ First class ☐ Bulk rate ☐ Other

Method of postage: ☐ Preprinted indicia ☐ Live stamp ☐ Meter

Client permit–how it should read exactly_____

Number of samples Live John Q Address to deliver samples:

Additional Comments:

EXHIBIT 7.3 (continued)

Fixed Creative Costs

The preliminary creative budget outline in Exhibit 7.4 is a fairly accurate representation of the types of fixed costs that go into each catalog. Let's look at each cost separately.

Creative Concept

This one-time meeting helps the start-up catalog develop and refine its initial creative concept.

Estimated time: one to two days
Estimated budget: $2,000 ranging to $20,000 for high-end fashion catalogs

Creative Kickoff

In the formal creative kickoff or handoff meeting, new products are introduced, catalog specifications and mailing strategy are reviewed, the catalog is paginated, the schedule is established, and responsibilities are assigned.

Estimated time: one to three days, depending on the number of items
Estimated budget: $3,000 and up

Design Concept

Cover and page concepts are prepared and reviewed. For new catalogs, key design elements are established, including logo; text, headline, and caption typeface; and use of color and white space. Generally, two or three new cover ideas and three or four two-page spreads are mocked up at this time.

Estimated time: one to two weeks
Estimated budget: $5,000 and up

Page Layout

A detailed blueprint or layout of catalog pages and the order form is created, approved, and turned over to the photographer and copywriter for the next steps.

Estimated time: two to three weeks, depending on the total number of pages
Estimated budget: $150 to $250 per page

Copywriting

Writers draft copy to fit the layouts. Copy, including product numbers and prices, is edited and approved.

Preliminary Creative Budget

Components: Number of pages
Number of colors
Number of products
• New products
• Pickup products
Number of new photographs

Creative concept
Conceptual development, including pagination, positioning, and offers $_____

Conference and travel time
Time spent with copywriter, artist, and others to define the project $_____
and target audience

Layout and design
Design concept, color comps of covers and spreads $_____
Page layouts—entire catalog $_____
Order form design $_____

Copy
Copywriting, editing, and fitting $_____

Production art
Page production via desktop electronic publishing $_____
Stats, disks, prints, and art materials $_____
Alterations allowance $_____

Project supervision
Supervision of project up to color separations $_____

Miscellaneous
Federal Express, messenger, fax, etc. $_____

Total Creative Without Photography* $_____

Photography/Illustration
Photography, including film and processing $_____
Cover/large set photo, per shot $_____
Complex photo, extensive propping, per shot $_____
Simple hard goods, minimum propping, per shot $_____
Photo art direction, per hour $_____
Illustrative art $_____

Estimated Total Photography—based on [X] products per page $_____

Please note: All client alterations are additional.

Accepted by: _____   Date: _____

*Travel and miscellaneous expenses relating to travel are in addition to this budget.

EXHIBIT 7.4

Estimated time: two to four weeks, depending on the number of items and pages

Estimated budget: $5,000 to $15,000, depending on the number of items and pages

Photography

The photo budget varies with the complexity of the shots to be taken. (See Exhibit 7.5 for the price range.) The more difficult the shot, the fewer can be taken in a day, and the more expensive they become. The budget should include charges for film and processing, including Polaroid preshots; art direction and styling; procuring props, accessories, and building sets; model fees; and location rental. The photographer's bid should include a waiver that confirms that the catalog owns all photo rights. In addition, it is common practice in catalog photography to make sure that there are no residual fees of any kind.

Estimated time: eight to fifteen shots per day, depending on the complexity

Estimated budget: $100 to $1,000 per photo, depending on the complexity and styling required

CONTROLLING COSTS THROUGH VISUAL ASSET MANAGEMENT

Visual asset management is a fancy term for getting the most from your photography budget. Catalogs that practice visual asset management store all photography and illustrations in a digital data bank where they can be retrieved easily by different users within the company. A digital storage system lets the Honey Baked Ham catalog share its wonderful images with its retail, corporate, and Internet divisions and use them for its own space ads as well.

Many color separators and printers will maintain your visual images in a central database that can be accessed by anyone in need of high- or low-resolution images from your catalog. It's a cost-effective practice that can make a significant difference on the creative bottom line.

Photography Budget

Photography Fee Schedule	Range of costs
Cover shots	$350 to $700 each
Difficult, ambience shots	$250 to $500 each
Propped, complicated shot	$175 to $300 each
Tabletop–lightly propped	$125 to $150 each
Simple silhouette	$75 to $125 each
Film and processing	$20 per shot
Photo art direction	$600 to $800 per day
Product styling	$300 to $500 per day per stylist
Product handling and management	$400 to $500 per day
Props and set building	$400 to $500 per day
Model fees	$125 to $300 per shot

EXHIBIT 7.5

Computer Page Production

The budget for computer page production includes production of each catalog page and the order form; proofreading; prints, disks, and art materials; delivery or messenger charges; and art director supervision. Two or three sets of revisions should also be built into the budget. Most catalog production agencies charge on a "per page" basis, plus materials.

Estimated time:	two to three weeks	
Estimated budget:	New catalog pages	$125 to $250 per page
	Revised pages (simple design or photo changes)	$75 to $195 per page
	Pickup pages (minor changes)	$50 to $95 per page
	Selection and sizing of photography	$50 to $75 per hour
	Proofs (b&w)	$50 per thirty-two-page set

Alterations

Any changes by the cataloger to amend prices, products, item numbers, or other content are considered alterations and will be charged accordingly, depending on the stage at which the alteration takes place.

Color Separations

Color separation budgets can vary widely, depending on the quality level desired and the type of merchandise being offered. In apparel, jewelry, and food catalogs, color is critical, and catalogers typically pay more for separations. Costs are lower for business, industrial, and consumer catalogs in which color plays less of a role.

Estimated time:	two to three weeks	
Estimated budget:	Industry average	$650 per page
	Least expensive—ganging all photos by page	$200 to $350 per page
	Middle-range quality (e.g., tabletop products or hard goods)	$500 to $700 per page
	High quality (apparel, food, etc.)	$1,000 and more per page

❖ KEY POINTS

- Hold a prepress kickoff meeting, and establish a formal flowchart or process chart to follow during page production, color separations, and print management.
- Make changes as early in the production process as possible. The "$5, $50, $500, $5,000" rule will save you money.

- Build in time to proofread. You can live with minor mistakes, but major ones can be costly. Create a proofreader's checklist to make sure you are checking all important elements.
- Build a strong partnership with your color separator and printer, and they will help you find ways to improve efficiency and save money. Longer-term contracts may be worthwhile.
- The creative budget can have a big impact on your catalog's bottom line. Benchmark your creative costs to save money.

PART 3

Catalog Marketing

Several years ago, I had the opportunity to work with a fledgling company in the spill control and cleanup business. The company, strangely called the New Pig Corporation, sold an expanding line of "pig tails" that looked like one leg of a pair of panty hose filled with an absorbent material. Machining companies used the tails to absorb oil spillage around cutting tools. The company's direct selling methods and expanding product line demanded that it look at how to promote multiple products. A catalog was one format being considered.

When I asked the president how New Pig Corporation was organized, he responded with a classic description of a direct marketing organization. "We have two main divisions," he said. "One group's job is to get new customers. The other's is to keep the customers coming back. It's really get 'em and keep 'em."

In formal marketing terms, "get 'em and keep 'em" represents the front end and back end of marketing. **Front-end marketing** is the process of prospecting for and acquiring new customers, an activity that costs money. **Back-end marketing** is the process of converting one-time buyers into two-time and longer-term loyal customers, an activity that yields the profits needed to sustain and grow the company. Exhibit 8.1 capsulizes the objectives of the front and back ends as well as how their results are measured.

Front-End/Back-End Concept of Marketing

| Prospects = Costs |
| Customers = Profits |

Objective	How Results Are Measured

| Front-End Marketing |

Objective	How Results Are Measured
Acquire first-time customers	Cost per customer
Acquire new leads	Cost per lead
Acquire new inquiries	Cost per name
Convert leads and inquiries to customers	Cost of conversion
Minimize cost of building the customer file	

| Back-End Marketing |

Objective	How Results Are Measured
Convert one-time buyers into two-time buyers	Growth of multibuyer file
Maximize number of mailings to customer list	Number of customer mailings/year
Make a profit	Return on investment
	Return on sales
	Lifetime value of a customer

EXHIBIT 8.1

Both front-end and back-end marketing are important. New names are needed to replenish customers who have dropped away; loyal customers are needed to ensure sales and profitability. Prospecting for new customers and nurturing them is important to the long-term health of the catalog company. The following chapters describe both processes in detail.

CHAPTER 8

Acquiring New Customers

My first job at Fingerhut Corporation was to manage its front-end marketing. No sweat, I thought. After all, I knew a lot about marketing and new customer acquisition from my days as Publisher of the Book Division of *My Weekly Reader*. But when my boss told me that in the new budget year, my group was to bring in one million first-time buyers at a cost of no more than $2.50 per name, I looked for a place to hide. The task seemed insurmountable, until I examined the prospecting programs already under way and realized that nearly three-fourths of the names were "in the bank." All we had to do was develop innovative programs in list rentals, space advertising, freestanding inserts, and even television to obtain the other 250,000 names. A challenge, but not impossible.

There are dozens of ways to build a customer list. Traditionally, catalogs have built their buyer files through list rentals—a good source of quality buyers with significant long-term value. But response rates are declining as the catalog industry matures and consumers are overwhelmed with catalogs they never requested. Almost every type of rental list (response, subscription, compiled, or co-op) has lower response than it did five or ten years ago. A 2 percent response was once the standard by which catalogers judged their prospect mailings. This is no longer true.

Decreased response and increases in charges for postage, paper, and printing make the cost of obtaining a new buyer two or three times what it was fifteen years ago. To maximize profits, catalogers in today's environment must determine how much it costs to acquire a new customer and how long, on average, it takes for a buyer to pay back—and plan the program accordingly. As response rates fall, mailers are examining other alternatives. Prospecting exclusively through list rentals seems to be a passé strategy. Today, most catalogers make list rentals part of the new customer strategy but also use alternative media to find responsive new names.

Prospecting Through List Rentals

Despite their problems, list rentals are still a valid source of new customer and prospect names. List rentals come in four varieties: response lists, subscription lists, compiled lists, and co-op lists.

Response Lists

A response list is a list of customers who have either made a purchase or requested information from another company. Typically rented for one-time use, response lists can be very effective, because they contain known buyers or responders. Many offer huge universes for consumer and business-to-business offers. While expensive, these lists are a good investment.

Information about the types of buyers on the list, what they bought, and where they bought (in-store, catalog, magazine ad, etc.) is provided on a rate or data card. (An example is shown in Exhibit 8.2.) A data card tells how many names are available, the rental cost per 1,000 names, the selections available, and the cost for each selection. The list broker can tell you when the list was last updated (very important) and which other companies are renting the list on a regular basis.

Targeting prospects through these lists is a matter of matching up demographic and buying profiles as well as method of purchase. A list of forty-five- to fifty-five-year-old women who buy gardening tools may not work if you're selling tennis equipment. Likewise, people on a list of retail buyers may not be willing to purchase by mail. If you are selling a $500 item, customers whose average order value is $25 may not be willing to spend such a large amount.

Look for lists used successfully by companies selling similar products. A list that has been used more than once by a particular company will be shown as a **continuation**, meaning the company was pleased enough with the results to use the list a second time.

The best way to select response lists is to work with a list broker. List brokers can help you find lists that match the profile of your buyers. They can furnish you with data cards that describe each list, and help you understand the list's demographics and "selects," or segmented selections of a list of mail-order buyers, such as all female names, most recent buyers, and purchase level.

Keep a library of competitors' data cards if their lists are on the market. You can find out what their customers are like, whether their lists are growing or shrinking, and what their sales are likely to be. This research is easy and free and should be done once or twice a year.

Subscription Lists

Subscription names come from people who subscribe to magazines, newspapers, or newsletters for gardeners, chefs, runners, scuba divers, and other distinct markets.

Williams-Sonoma
Catalog for Cooks

44,843	February 1999 Buyers	+$21	$100/M
95,594	60 Day Buyers	+$19.50	$100/M
308,825	3 Month Buyers	+$16	$100/M
511,186	6 Month Buyers	+$11	$100/M
679,578	12 Month Buyers		$100/M
512,573	13–24 Month Buyers		$100/M
66,113	30 Day Inquiries		$50/M
112,914	60 Day Inquiries		$50/M
144,559	3 Month Inquiries		$50/M
228,777	6 Month Inquiries		$50/M
	Fund-raisers/Publishers		$65/M
	Counts Thru 02/99		

Williams-Sonoma is recognized as the authoritative source for the cooking enthusiast and home entertainer. These upscale mail-order customers look to the catalog for cooks to supply their homes with the latest gourmet "essentials" and for distinctive gifts. Products include high-quality cookware and kitchen tools, informal tableware and linens, and food specialities from around the world.

Additional Selections:
  Last Purchase @ $6/M
  $150+ @ $46/M

Demographics: Average age 45; $75,000+ average income

Updated by 10th of every month.

Last Update: 03/99
Next Update: 04/99

——— DATE ———
3/01/99 Updated
4/02/99 Confirmed

——— UNIT OF SALE ———
$91.00 Average

——— GENDER ———
67% Female   23% Male
Can Select

——— MEDIA ———
100% Direct Mail
  (Catalog)

——— ADDRESSING ———
4-Up Cheshire or Mag Tape

——— SELECTIONS ———
$21.00   50+ Buyers
$31.00 $100+ Buyers
$26.00 $75+ Buyers
$6.00   SCF
$6.00   State
$6.00   Zip
$1.50   Keying
$25.00   Mag Tape
$7.50   P/S Labels
$8.00   Run Charges
$11.00   Credit Cards
$6.00   Gender/Sex
$6.00   Multibuyers
$6.00   Single Buyers

——— MINIMUM ORDER ———
8,000

EXHIBIT 8.2
Williams-Sonoma Catalog for Cooks Response List

Subscription lists are highly targeted, offer large universes of names, and are somewhat less expensive than response lists. However, not all names are paid subscribers—especially true of so-called controlled-circulation subscriptions, publications offered free to people working in the field. And because subscriber lists contain no purchase history, names may or may not be mail-order buyers and are generally considered less qualified.

Research subscription lists by requesting media kits that describe the demographic and buying patterns of magazine readers—who read the magazine, their age ranges, other interests, and so on. A data card for a subscription list is shown in Exhibit 8.3. Remember, however, you can't assume that because a certain group of golfers subscribe to *Golf Digest*, they will buy golf equipment by mail.

Subscription lists are important for business-to-business catalogs but generally do not work for consumer catalogs. Test them carefully. Instead of mailing subscribers a catalog, try running a small direct-response ad in the magazine, offering potential buyers a free catalog, or even advertising a bestselling product.

Geographical modeling can improve the chances of making some portion of a subscription list work. For example, the *Better Homes and Gardens* subscriber list in Exhibit 8.3 has almost 8 million names—too many to rent! By using your own list to identify characteristics of buyers versus those who did not respond to a particular mailing, it is possible to identify portions of a rented list that will work better. Exhibit 8.4 on page 119 shows a sample of a geographical or postal-code modeling constructed using a chi-square statistical analysis (CHAID) that evaluated more than 100 demographic variables (household income, number and ages of children in home, type and number of automobiles, home value, etc.) to determine which characteristic is the most reliable in differentiating this catalog's buyers from nonbuyers. This information could be used to rent only the zip segments of the *Better Homes and Gardens* list that match your criteria.

Compiled Lists

Compiled lists contain publicly available information compiled from government records, censuses, telephone directories, warranty cards, and similar sources. Examples of compiled lists are high school or college students, senior citizens, affluent Americans, residents of Missouri, people who bought new automobiles in 1997, and Black & Decker warranty cards. Business compiled lists may include attorneys, accountants, teachers of reading, company presidents or other executives by name or title, engineers, businesses with fewer than ten employees, or many other categories.

Both business and consumer lists offer extensive selects. Business compiled lists can be selected by type of business, SIC code, geographic location, size and sales of company, telephone number, company headquarters or branches, even company officers. Consumer lists can be selected by almost any demographic and even some lifestyle factors, including household income, number and age of residents in a dwelling, and number and age of children. A sample data card for a compiled list is shown in Exhibit 8.5 on page 120.

Better Homes and Gardens
Subscribers

7,600,000	Total Circulation	
5,900,000	Active Subscribers	$75/M
41,000	Canadian Archives	$90/M
	Fund-raising Discount	$65/M
	Reuse	Inquire
	Counts Thru 12/98	

Prices are in U.S. Funds

* Excludes merchandise, magazines, etc. offers

Published by Meredith Corporation.

Better Homes and Gardens magazine readers hunger for the expert how-to information provided in this 75-year-old giant. Monthly editorial features recipes from the Better Homes and Gardens Test Kitchens; advice on family, children, health, and finances; features on home remodeling and decorating, gardening, pets, and crafts; and tastes of family-oriented travel destinations.

Additional Selections:
  Status–Please inquire
  Income–
    Index @ $5/M
    Household @ $5/M
Special Composite Interest @ $5/M
Home Value Index @ $5/M

Status: 1) Ordered (ordered in the month and are paid and unpaid)
2) Paid In (payment was received in the month)

Demographics (MRI 1998 Fall):
  Median age 44
  Average age 46.1
    $47,486 Median household income
    $55,651 Average household income
    $113,714 Median home value
    $119,342 Average home value
    65.0% Married
    78.0% Own home
    54.0% Attended college plus
    65.0% Employed
    47.9% Working women
    68.0% Reside in A or B county

——— DATE ———
1/01/99   Updated
2/04/99   Confirmed

——— UNIT OF SALE ———
$19.00/Year (12 Issues)

——— GENDER ———
78% Female 22% Male
Can select

——— MEDIA ———
100% Direct Mail (DTP/Agent/Insert/Renewals)

——— ADDRESSING ———
4-Up Cheshire or Mag Tape

——— SELECTIONS ———
$5.00   Age
$5.00   Contributors/Donors
$5.00   Home Owner
$5.00   Postal Code
$5.00   Length of Residence
$5.00   FSA
$10.00 Change of Address
$5.00   Province
$5.00   SCF
$5.00   State
$5.00   Zip
N/C   Keying
N/C   Mag Tape
N/C   Cartridge
$10.00 P/S Labels
$5.00   Run Charges
N/C   Diskette
$5.00   Hot Line
$5.00   Presence of Children
$5.00   Gender/Sex
$5.00   Source

——— MINIMUM ORDER ———
5,000

——— NET NAME POLICY ———
85% + $5.00
Run charges
100,000

EXHIBIT 8.3
Better Homes and Gardens Subscription List

Better Homes and Gardens
Subscribers

Special Composite Interests: Collectibles, Cooking, Crafts, Decorating, Gardening, Health, Needlework, Sewing, Quilting, Woodworking, Do It Yourself

Contributors: General, Health/Institutional, Political, Religious

100% Home address

List owner/manager cannot be named within the mail piece.

No telemarketing.

Upon request, previous orders on specific offers up to 12 months may be omitted.

Shipments into Canada will have an additional charge for 7% goods and service tax.

List owner eliminates business address, DMA mail preference service and list owner preference files, complimentary copies, and interfile dupes.

First-time orders must be prepaid.

Lists are prepared zipped and in sequence.

4–6 working days for order processing.

Cancellation within 10 days of mail date must be paid in full. $5/M run charges on orders canceled prior to 10 days before mail date.

Updated by the 15th of each month.

Last Update: 01/99
Next Update: 02/99

EXHIBIT 8.3 (continued)
Better Homes and Gardens Subscription List

Zip Code Modeling

	Zips	Mailed	Response	Resp Rate	% Sample	Estimated Lift
Group 1	**1,760**	**90,006**	**1,983**	**2.20**	**10.26**	**17.82**
Segment 7	396	27,563	624	2.26	3.14	21.06
Segment 12	901	21,817	480	2.20	2.49	17.65
Segment 21	463	40,626	879	2.16	4.63	15.70
Group 2	**1,596**	**91,211**	**1,936**	**2.12**	**10.39**	**13.51**
Segment 14	448	33,011	707	2.14	3.76	14.53
Segment 22	1,148	58,200	1,229	2.11	6.63	12.92
Group 3	**1,154**	**78,867**	**1,636**	**2.07**	**8.99**	**10.93**
Segment 16	604	45,201	947	2.10	5.15	12.04
Segment 20	550	33,666	689	2.05	3.84	9.44
Group 4	**1,214**	**87,202**	**1,734**	**1.99**	**9.94**	**6.34**
Segment 11	765	53,762	1,079	2.01	6.13	7.33
Segment 19	449	33,440	655	1.96	3.81	4.75
Group 5	**2,699**	**75,992**	**1,476**	**1.94**	**8.66**	**3.87**
Segment 15	1,998	35,990	701	1.95	4.10	4.16
Segment 8	701	40,002	775	1.94	4.56	3.60
Group 6	**1,999**	**93,004**	**1,789**	**1.92**	**10.60**	**2.86**
Segment 23	1,603	40,221	777	1.93	4.58	3.31
Segment 10	396	52,783	1,012	1.92	6.01	2.53
Group 7	**1,429**	**83,114**	**1,462**	**1.76**	**9.47**	**−5.93**
Segment 18	679	26,999	501	1.86	3.08	−0.77
Segment 13	299	28,003	484	1.73	3.19	−7.57
Segment 6	451	28,112	477	1.70	3.20	−9.26
Group 8	**3,207**	**115,486**	**1,934**	**1.67**	**13.16**	**−10.45**
Segment 17	612	75,611	1,275	1.69	8.61	−9.86
Segment 25	2,595	39,875	659	1.65	4.54	−11.62
Group 9	**4,959**	**87,137**	**1,407**	**1.61**	**9.93**	**−13.65**
Segment 4	662	34,311	561	1.64	3.91	−12.56
Segment 9	3,812	38,014	619	1.63	4.33	−12.92
Segment 5	485	14,812	227	1.53	1.69	−18.05
Group 10	**21,897**	**77,843**	**1,032**	**1.33**	**8.87**	**−29.10**
Segment 3	1,799	10,964	156	1.42	1.25	−23.91
Segment 2	999	9,009	116	1.29	1.03	−31.14
Segment 26	17,001	43,763	507	1.16	4.99	−38.05
Segment 1	1,786	12,907	133	1.03	1.47	−44.90
Segment 24	312	1,200	120	10.00	0.14	434.76
Overall				**2.14**	**100.00**	**0.00**

EXHIBIT 8.4

Lawyers at Law Firms Masterfile

Page 1

M32231

571,814 Lawyers Masterfile $60/M

This comprehensive compilation of lawyers provides you with complete coverage of the legal marketplace. It includes attorneys in every law firm from the solo practitioner to the largest legal firms in the country.

Additional Selections:
    Lawyers at Law Firms @ N/C
    Lawyers in Solo Practice @ N/C
    Senior Partners @ N/C
    Associate/Junior Partners @ N/C
    Law Firms @ N/C
    Lawyers by Specialty @ N/C
    A.B.A. Members @ N/C
    Non A.B.A. Members @ N/C
    Size of the Firms (numbers of lawyers per firm)—
      Please inquire
    Name of Senior Partner at Each Firm—Please
      inquire

Lawyers at Law Firms	262,580
Lawyers in Solo Practice	309,234
Senior Partners	228,179
Associate/Junior Partners	57,892
Law Firms (includes number of lawyers per firm)	83,567
Lawyers By Specialty	Inquire
A.B.A. Members	72,296
Non A.B.A. Members	214,952
Total Law Firms	63,336

Law Firms by Size:

2	32,426	8	905
3	8,072	9–14	2,711
4	4,232	15–24	1,285
5	2,681	25–49	774
6	1,825	50–99	316
7	1,200	100+	130

Approximately 99% have phone numbers

Updated quarterly.

DATE
6/01/00   Updated
7/10/99   Confirmed

N/A

GENDER
99,783 Female
417,525 Male/Can Select

MEDIA
100% Compiled

ADDRESSING
4-Up Cheshire or Mag Tape

SELECTIONS
$10.00	Phone Number
$5.00	Business Address
$5.00	Home Address
$5.00	SCF
$5.00	State
$5.00	Zip
$2.00	Keying
$25.00	Mag Tape
$8.00	P/S Labels
$5.00	Gender/Sex

Minimum Order
5,000

EXHIBIT 8.5
Lawyers at Law Firms Masterfile Compiled List

While compiled lists are the least expensive, you get what you pay for. They do not contain known mail-order buyers, nor have consumers on compiled lists shown an interest in a particular product. They can be helpful to retail stores seeking to reach all likely prospects living near their stores; using mapping software in conjunction, retailers can accurately identify potential customers within a five-mile radius.

Compiled lists make sense in business-to-business applications because fewer response lists are available. For many businesses, even the best lists are not specific enough to identify the right target within a company. Often a business will target all companies of certain types as prospects and call each company to verify or update the list, add new names, determine who makes which decision (buyer, influencer, decision maker), and obtain a phone number for each person. Even though it is possible to select names by job title, you may need to reach several people in the company who are not on any list. Only once these people have been identified do the marketers start the "selling" part of the marketing campaign.

A compiled list works well for this kind of multiple-contact, "mail-phone-mail" strategy because it can be purchased for unlimited use in a twelve-month period. Calling back prospect names on a response list would constitute another rental and would be quite expensive.

Compiled lists are less useful for consumer catalogs. Although they are huge—some of the big lists have 25 million names—and certain selections are available, some kind of database modeling is required to find bona fide mail-order buyers who may have an affinity for a catalog. It costs just as much for printing and postage to use a compiled list as it does a response list, so don't be penny-wise and pound-foolish.

Co-Op Databases

A fourth type of list comes from a *co-op database*, a massive database of known catalog buyers available only to participants. In exchange for providing confidential buyer lists and purchase histories to the companies in this field, list owners receive statistical modeling that reveals more about their customers. They may rent names of comparable buyers for 30 to 40 percent less than it costs to rent new response lists. Co-op databases for business segments are now available. Examples of co-op databases are Abacus and Z-24.

Alternative Media

With response down and postage and paper costs up, it is time to seek additional sources for new customers. I'm not suggesting that catalogers throw out list rentals. But I do think it's time to stop spending the bulk of prospect dollars on cold list rentals and start adopting a more balanced approach that incorporates testing new media and other growing, viable alternatives such as the following, listed in order of effectiveness.

Catalogs Offering Other Catalogs

Advertising a catalog in a "catalog of catalogs" is an effective way of generating new leads on a per-inquiry basis. Shop At Home and Publisher Inquiry Services (The Best Catalogs in the World), as shown in Exhibit 8.6, are the largest companies that offer this service. Advertisers pay nothing to include a photo and description of their catalog, and pay only for each inquiry that is generated. On the plus side, up-front costs are minimal, and as many

EXHIBIT 8.6
Catalog of Catalogs

as 25 percent of these names will convert into buyers. But hundreds, not thousands, of inquiries will be generated; strong, recognizable catalog brand names will fare better than lesser-known catalogs.

Magazine Advertising

Magazine advertising is an effective but expensive prospecting medium. Magazine space ads are the primary prospecting tool of Omaha Steaks, but the company has worked hard to develop a control ad and an offer that works. It takes time to formulate just the right combination of product and offer that will attract new buyers. You may need to test eight or ten products before you find a bestseller. Fortunately, it's possible to test in a classified or a one-sixth-page black-and-white ad, and then expand to a larger-size, two- or four-color ad as response permits. Exhibit 8.7 shows a one-sixth-page ad that uses a direct sale approach, while the full-page ad in Exhibit 8.8 uses a two-step catalog request.

EXHIBIT 8.7
Space Ad Using One-Step Direct Sale Approach

From a remote valley in Peru, 3° below the Equator, comes the Cashmere of cotton.

The story behind the Lands' End® Interlochen

It's as distant as Shangri-La. But in Peru's tropical Piura River valley, a combination of soil, climate and just plain luck has produced the world's *finest* cotton.

Peruvian pima cotton.

And when you snuggle into a Lands' End Interlochen™ Polo Shirt, and feel its softness next to your skin – well, you'll understand why we *had* to come here for it.

In this valley, they're picky...

They've cultivated pima cotton in the Piura Valley for centuries.

And long ago, local farmers knew they had a good thing growing.

They said their cotton was, "Suave como el pelo de un angel." *Soft as the hair of an angel.*™

So, they've always taken extra care with it.

Instead of using mechanical pickers, they pick each cotton boll by hand. To make sure it's ripe and ready.

When the extra long staple cotton is spun into yarn, it comes out with a *silkiness* all its own.

This yarn our Peruvian friends turn into a cushiony, interlock knit. A lofty fabric – 6.1 oz. per sq. yd. – that looks as heavenly as it feels.

Finally, our shirtmakers get their licks in.

Taking their good old time, they patiently add two-needle coverstitching at the armhole and sleeve cuffs. (Gives a crisper, dressier look.)

They stitch smooth jersey tape inside the collar. And finish the bottom with "tree top"

side vents, so it looks neat even untucked. They don't miss a trick.

Yet the price is –

Only $23.50! Surprised? The fact is, you'll find *everything* in our catalog is priced fairly.

It's not always the lowest price. But it's always a good *honest* price, considering the pains we take with fabric, construction and detail.

If you haven't shopped Lands' End, here's an invitation. Phone us any time and talk to one of our nice, neighborly people. They'll gladly answer your questions about size or anything else.

You can't go wrong. Everything is – "Guaranteed. Period.®"

Why not call for our catalog?

It's full of good things to wear, each with a story...

© 1999 Lands' End, Inc.

Guaranteed. Period.®

If you'd like a free catalog call

1-800-881-6899

Or visit us at

www.landsend.com

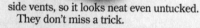

EXHIBIT 8.8
Two-Step Space Ad Generating Catalog Request

Space ads that offer catalogs instead of selling product also require testing. Ads may offer catalogs free or for a nominal price; include a toll-free phone number or ask the customer to place a regular call; and provide an address to request a catalog or include a reply card or coupon. Charging a modest amount for the catalog (e.g., $1.00 or $2.00) will produce fewer leads, as will making the prospect call or mail in a request, but those leads will be better qualified and more responsive. Given the trade-offs, a large cataloger that needs to generate tens of thousands of leads will probably opt for less-qualified names, while medium-size and smaller catalogers may find qualified leads or even direct sales of a winning product more productive.

Through magazine advertising, catalogers can reach a highly targeted audience, but it is an expensive medium that requires careful testing. Keep in mind that some publications are more mail-order oriented than others. When you review rate cards and talk to promotion managers about magazine buys, be sure to ask about other mail-order advertisers.

Newspaper, Sunday Supplements, and Newsstand Publications

Parade and other local Sunday magazine sections, *USA Weekend, Woman's Day, Family Circle*, freestanding inserts (FSIs), and the more sensational publications such as the *Globe* and *National Enquirer* represent a category of media that are sold predominantly on newsstands, not by subscription. They reach a huge slice of middle-class America—value-driven people who use coupons and are interested in collectibles, food, and fruit by mail, and similar offers. This is not the environment for an upscale or a business offer.

For catalogers targeting this segment, it's possible to keep costs down by testing specific regions or qualifying for a special mail-order page rate. Ask about remnant buys—bargain prices on space available after a publication closes. Remnant space brokers can help catalogers achieve savings of 40 percent, 50 percent, and more through remnant buys.

Package Inserts

Package inserts are promotions that ride along in a customer shipment. A Fingerhut package or book club shipments (e.g., Mystery Book Club) may contain 6 to 12 mail-order ads placed by participants in their package insert programs.

Package inserts offer several admirable traits. The promotion is going to a known mail-order buyer, and a recent one. The promotion can be targeted by type of product purchased, and it has the implied endorsement of the company in whose box the insert is riding. It can be as simple as a postcard or as elaborate as a minicatalog offering dozens of products, provided it meets the mailer's specifications. Just remember that the creative expenses are your responsibility, and the owner of the package-insert program has the right to refuse offers that it regards as competitive.

The advantages add up to a very viable option for new customer acquisition. List brokers can tell you about the wide variety of package-insert programs available to test.

Card Decks

Card decks—a collection of 3″ × 5″ cards shrink-wrapped into a "deck"—are produced by magazine publishers, who send them to their subscribers. Highly targeted but small, they work well in generating leads or catalog requests but seldom have enough room to present and sell a product. Cards can be targeted by audience and have proven highly effective for business mailers. Consumer card decks are harder to come by but, where available, are worthy of testing. A few examples are shown in Exhibit 8.9.

EXHIBIT 8.9
Card Decks

The Internet

For new and smaller catalogs, a website is an inexpensive and effective place to generate catalog requests or sell winning products with great margins . . . providing your prospects can find you among the millions of sites on the Internet. Ultimately, the Internet may be the number one source of leads and a significant selling vehicle, but it will take time to get there. Business catalogers have a head start, because more businesses use the Internet than consumers at home.

Other Alternative Media

There is a "second team" of media that merits discussion and testing.

Public relations is a great source of free editorial copy. Cultivate magazine editors, and alert them to new products that dovetail with readers' interests. The Gooseberry Patch catalog often is mentioned in *Victoria* because its products are a great match with *Victoria* readers. Items are featured with the catalog's phone number or mailing address . . . at no charge whatsoever.

Billing inserts that ride along in MasterCard or Visa bills offer big numbers for a reasonable price, because mailing costs are shared. Response can be low, however. Use them to generate catalog requests rather than trying to make a sale.

Trade shows are a great opportunity for business catalogers to get their catalogs into the hands of prospects. Code the catalogs so orders can be traced back to their source.

Because customer referrals, especially from loyal customers, are such an effective source of high-quality names, some catalogers build special referral programs for customers.

Television and radio are a low priority for catalogers, but it's worth looking into these media.

Two Key Analytical Media Benchmarks

Two measurement tools—cost to get a customer and lifetime value of that new customer—will help catalogers compare new prospecting media with list rentals. By knowing the cost of getting a customer and the value of that customer over time, you can compare the results of one list with another, or a list with a space ad, and select the combination of media that provides you with the best front-end cost and best back-end value. Let's look at each of these analytical tools.

Measuring the Cost of Acquiring a Customer

Exhibits 8.10 and 8.11 present a simple formula for measuring the cost of acquiring a new customer. The one-step direct sale shown in Exhibit 8.10 illustrates the cost of acquiring a new customer through a list rental and from a space ad, assuming three hypothetical

Measuring the Cost of Acquiring a Customer

One-Step Direct Sale–List Rental		Example A	Example B	Example C
	Variable Costs	Calculation	Calculation	Calculation
Total Mailings		1,000,000	1,000,000	1,000,000
Response Rate		2.00%	1.00%	2.00%
Total Responses–New Buyers		20,000	10,000	20,000
Average Order Value		$50	$50	$100
Gross Sales		$1,000,000	$500,000	$2,000,000
Margin Before Advertising*	35%	$350,000	$175,000	$700,000
Advertising Cost Including List Rental	$0.60	$600,000	$600,000	$600,000
Profit Contribution (Loss)		($250,000)	($425,000)	$100,000
Cost per Name–Profit (Loss)		($12.50)	($42.50)	$5.00

One-Step Direct Sale–Space Ad		Example A	Example B	Example C
	Variable Costs	Calculation	Calculation	Calculation
Total Circulation		1,000,000	1,000,000	1,000,000
Response Rate		0.10%	0.05%	0.05%
Total Responses–New Buyers		1,000	500	500
Average Order Value		$19.95	$19.95	$39.95
Gross Sales		$19,950	$9,975	$19,975
Margin Before Advertising*	35%	$6,983	$3,491	$6,991
Advertising Cost–Space Ad, per 1,000	$10.00	$10,000	$10,000	$10,000
Profit Contribution (Loss)		($3,018)	($6,509)	($3,009)
Cost per Name–Profit (Loss)		($3.02)	($13.02)	($6.02)

* = Sales less cost of goods and fulfillment

EXHIBIT 8.10

situations. To calculate the cost per name, multiply the response percentage by the number of catalogs mailed to estimate the number of buyers: in the first hypothetical example, 2 percent response times a million catalogs is 20,000 buyers. Next, multiply the number of buyers by the average order value (AOV) to arrive at gross sales—in the first example, it comes to $1 million. Multiply gross sales by the margin before advertising (here 35 percent) and subtract the cost of advertising including list rental, and in Example A, you arrive at a loss of $250,000. Divide that loss by the number of buyers, and it's clear that this company lost $12.50 acquiring every new name. Results of the third column are better; this company actually earned $5.00 on this name.

This tool makes clear the impact of average order value and response rate on earnings. While the AOV of the first two calculations remained the same, the higher response rate in the first example significantly lowered the cost of acquiring the name. In the third example, response remained 2 percent, but the average order value was twice as high, greatly benefiting the cost per name. Lists that yield high response rates and a high AOV

Measuring the Cost of Acquiring a Customer

Two-Step: Lead Generation Catalog Request and Lead Conversion

Step 1: Catalog Inquiry	Variable Costs	Example A Calculation	Example B Calculation	Example C Calculation
Total Circulation		1,000,000	1,000,000	1,000,000
Response Rate		0.05%	0.50%	1.00%
Total Responses–Catalog Inquiries		500	5,000	10,000
Average Order Value		$0.00	$0.00	$0.00
Gross Sales		$0	$0	$0
Advertising Cost–Space Ad, per 1,000	$10.00	$10,000	$10,000	$10,000
Profit Contribution (Loss)		($10,000)	($10,000)	($10,000)
Cost per Name–Profit (Loss)		($20.00)	($2.00)	($1.00)

Step 2: Catalog Mailing to Inquiries	Variable Costs	Example A Calculation	Example B Calculation	Example C Calculation
Mailings to Catalog Inquiries		500	5,000	10,000
Response Rate		1.50%	5.00%	7.50%
Total Responses–Catalog Orders		8	250	750
Average Order Value		$75.00	$75.00	$75.00
Gross Sales		$600	$18,750	$56,250
Margin Before Advertising*	35%	$210	$6,563	$19,688
Advertising Cost–Catalog in Mail	$0.50	$250	$2,500	$5,000
Advertising Cost–Step 1		$10,000	$10,000	$10,000
Profit Contribution (Loss)		($10,040)	($5,938)	$4,688
Cost per Name–Profit (Loss)		($1,255.00)	($23.75)	$6.25
Total Cost: Step 1 and Step 2–Profit (Loss)		($1,255.00)	($25.75)	$5.25

* = Sales less cost of goods and fulfillment

EXHIBIT 8.11

are gold mines. Although they are rare, the more niche-driven your catalog, the more likely you are to uncover one or two lists that always reach breakeven or better.

Calculating the cost of acquiring a customer through a space ad is somewhat different. Multiply the response percentage by the total circulation to determine the number of buyers—in the first example, 1,000. Multiply those thousand buyers by an average order value of $19.95, and you get gross sales of $19,950. Multiply $19,950 by the margin before advertising (again, 35 percent) and subtract the cost of the space advertising (here, $10,000), and it is clear that the space ad in Example A lost $3,018 and the company spent $3.02 to acquire each customer. Lead-generating space ads almost always lose money, even with a direct sale. All three of these examples could be acceptable, depending on the criteria of the company.

The two-step process shown in Exhibit 8.11 is a bit more complicated because it illustrates the cost of generating a lead or catalog request and then converting that lead to a customer. Using Example A, total circulation is multiplied by the response rate from the advertisement to indicate a total of 500 catalog inquiries. Because no sales were generated, the $10,000 cost of the advertising yields a $10,000 negative profit contribution; dividing that figure by the number of names reveals that it cost $20 to acquire a name that is not yet a buyer.

Once the catalogs are mailed to the inquirers, it is possible to multiply the response rate by the number of catalogs mailed to determine that eight catalog orders with an average order value of $75 were received, generating gross sales of $600. Gross sales multiplied by margin before advertising, less the cost of mailing the catalog, indicates a loss of $40 and a loss per name of $5. Together, the company invested $25 in each new buyer generated by the two-step promotion.

Again the three observations produce dramatically different results, all of which may be acceptable, depending on a company's criteria.

Measuring the cost of acquiring a customer is the first step in determining what you can afford to spend. Some companies are willing to spend $20 to acquire a customer who will earn (in profits) $20 in the next year. Other catalogs are willing to spend 150 percent of a customer's first-year earnings because they are relatively certain it will pay off over a three-year purchase cycle. Determining what you can afford is a matter of balancing the cost of acquiring a customer against what a customer is likely to spend over three years—called *customer lifetime value.*

Lifetime Value (LTV)

By tracking customers based on original source, and following the sales results of promotions sent to each customer source grouping, it is easy to determine the value of a customer after one, two, and three years. Three years will give you a reasonable number for comparison with other new customer media. Exhibit 8.12 shows the lifetime value calculation, the value today of future profits from a group of customers.

Our hypothetical catalog has 1,000 customers from a specific source code that it wishes to track. Year one starts with 1,000 buyers who spend $500 each, or $500,000 in total sales. When cost of goods (50 percent, or $250,000), fulfillment (12 percent, or $60,000), and advertising (25 percent, or $125,000) are subtracted from total sales, $65,000 is the remaining profit contribution. This represents a first-year LTV of $65 per customer.

In year two, 50 percent of the customers make purchases of $500 to generate sales of $250,000. From those total sales, cost of goods, fulfillment, and advertising are again subtracted, leaving $32,500. There is a 20 percent cost of money or time value of money, as though a catalog needed to borrow extra dollars to finance its selling effort. The true net present value profit is $27,083, or $27.08 for each of the original 1,000 customers. When this year's profit is added to profits from year one, there is a cumulative LTV of $92.08.

Lifetime Value of a Customer

	Year 1	Year 2	Year 3
Sales			
Customers	1,000	500	300
% Customers Who Buy Again	50%	60%	70%
Sales per Customer	$500	$500	$500
Total Sales	$500,000	$250,000	$150,000
Costs			
Cost of Goods Sold–%	50%	50%	50%
Actual Cost of Goods–$	$250,000	$125,000	$75,000
Fulfillment Cost–%	12%	12%	12%
Actual Fulfillment Cost–$	$60,000	$30,000	$18,000
Advertising Cost–%	25%	25%	25%
Actual Advertising Cost–$	$125,000	$62,5000	$37,500
Profits			
Profit Contribution (before overhead)	$65,000	$32,500	$19,500
Time Value of Money Discount Factor	100%	120%	144%
Net Present Value Profit	$65,000	$27,083	$13,542
Annual Lifetime Value (LTV) per Customer	$65.00	$27.08	$13.54
LTV (Cumulative)	$65.00	$92.08	$105.63

EXHIBIT 8.12

In year three, 60 percent, or 300 customers, spend $500 each. When cost of goods, fulfillment, and advertising are again subtracted, $19,500 remains, which is further reduced for the time value of money. The net present value profit for year three is $13,542, or $13.54 for each original customer, resulting in a cumulative LTV of $105.63.

Lifetime value helps determine what the catalog can spend to get a new customer. Most catalogers like to be able to recoup any investment for new customers in the first year. In the example here, the cataloger could pay up to $65 for a new customer and still break even in the first year.

Lifetime value can also be used to compare customers by original source code. For example, a catalog can compare the LTV of customers who first bought from a space ad in a newspaper supplement against customers who first heard about the catalog on the Internet or responded to a list rental. If new Internet buyers bought more over time than new list rental buyers, the catalog knows that it is worth spending more (per customer) to gather new buyers via the Internet.

Often the best place to gain new customers is from the sources that have the highest initial average purchase. For example, if space ad buyers have an average first purchase of $50, they are likely to make small purchases in the future as well. Likewise, if list rental buyers spend an average of $500 on their first purchase, they are likely to make large purchases in the future. Calculating lifetime value by source can uncover a potentially huge difference in future profits. It's possible to acquire plenty of names at breakeven that have no back-end value at all. You may discover that spending more for a better-qualified customer will yield many more profits over time. Use this formula to fine-tune your prospecting efforts and build a house list of names with real value.

The New Customer Acquisition Circulation Plan

It's a good idea to build a circulation plan for every catalog mailing. The prospect circulation plan in Exhibit 8.13 details a prospecting mailing in women's apparel. The catalog asked two list brokers for recommendations in order to get a complete perspective on available lists and mailing approaches. A number of list categories were identified for testing, including high- and mid-ticket apparel, apparel plus sizes, domestics (towels, sheets, linens, etc.) and children's apparel, business lists, clubs and continuities, low- and mid-range gifts, and mid- and high-priced gifts. At least one list from each category will be tested, with more tested from categories in which higher response is anticipated. The work sheet identifies the lists selected, their description, quantities available, and the final lists tested to mail.

A unique source code is identified for each list. For example, in the source code MS00A, The "MS" stands for *Maryland Square*, "00" is the *year 2000*, and "A" is the **first mail drop**. When first-time customers respond to that mailing, this "original source code" will be assigned to and maintained in the database record of all customers on the Maryland Square list whose first purchase came in drop A of the 2000 mailing.

Once lists are selected, use this form to forecast percentage response, average order value (AOV), and sales per catalog anticipated from each list. The first forecast for a catalog will be a "best guess," but the forecast will improve with each catalog edition. This forecast helps plan the merchandise buys, call center and warehouse staffing, and financial needs for the promotion. Later, you can add columns to indicate actual percentage response, AOV, and sales per catalog, or append the source frequency report discussed next.

Using the Source Frequency Report to Compare List Performance

The source frequency report in Exhibit 8.14 on page 135 analyzes results of both prospect and customer list mailings. Use it at the end of a campaign to discover how each list pulled.

This spreadsheet report ranks lists by sales per piece mailed. Data fields show the list's name, source code (the unique code applied to every list), description, quantity mailed, orders received, and sales, average order value, and percentage response of each list. It can also be sorted by subgroups to show results from buyers, inquiries, gift recipients, catalog requesters, rental lists, and so forth, or ranked by average order value, percentage response, or sales per catalog.

Prospect Circulation Plan

Mail date: 12/18 In-home date: 12/29–1/2

List	Source Code	Selection	Broker	Quantity Available	Quantity Input M/P	Final Quantity	Forecast % Response	Forecast Orders	Forecast AOV	Forecast Sales	Forecast $/Catalog
High Ticket Apparel											
AB Lambden		Last 3-mo. M/O buyers		27,000							
Appleseed's	AP00A	Last 3-mo. M/O buyers	B	85,000	7,500						
Bila of California		Last 6-mo. M/O buyers		45,000							
Brooks Brothers Women's		Last 6-mo. M/O buyers		16,000							
Clifford & Willis		Last 6-mo. M/O buyers		421,000	7,500						
Eddie Bauer—All Week Long		Last 3-mo. M/O buyers		128,000							
J. Crew		Last 3-mo. M/O buyers		655,000	denied						
Maryland Square	M500A	Last 6-mo. M/O buyers		123,000							
Nordstrom Catalog		Last 3-mo. M/O buyers	B	60,000	7,500						
Orvis		Last 3-mo. M/O buyers, female		109,000							
Simply Tops		Last 3-mo. M/O buyers		32,000							
Spiegel Masterfile	SP00A	Last 3-mo. female apparel & access	A	1,749,000	7,500						
Studio Collection		Last 3-mo. M/O buyers		43,000							
Tweeds	TW00A	Last 3-mo. M/O buyers	B		7,500						
Victoria's Secret	V500A	Last 3-mo. M/O buyers	A	600,000	7,500						
Mid-Ticket Apparel											
Bedford Fair		Last 3-mo. M/O buyers		150,000							
Chadwicks of Boston	CB00A	Last 3-mo. M/O buyers	A	1,430,000	7,500						
Damark		Last 3-mo. M/O buyers, female		40,000							
Frederick's of Hollywood	FH00A	Last 3-mo. M/O buyers, female	B	180,000	7,500						
Haband	HA00A	Last 3-mo. M/O buyers, female	B	84,000	7,500						
James River Traders	JT00A	March, April, May M/O buyers	B	101,000	7,500						
Newport News	NN00A	Monthly, $50+ M/O buyers	A	260,000	7,500						
Old Pueblo Traders	OP00A	Last 3-mo. M/O buyers	B	305,000	7,500						
RBM Apparel	R800A	Last 12-mo. M/O buyers	B	1,380,000	7,500						
Willow Ridge		Last 1-mo. M/O buyers		38,000							
Wintersilks	W500A	Last 3-mo. M/O buyers	B	65,000	7,500						
Apparel Plus Sizes											
Just Right		Last 12-mo. M/O buyers		50,000	denied						
Lane Bryant	LL00A	0-60-day hot line	B	to follow	7,500						
Lola Landers Fashion Place		Quarterly hot line	B	80,000	denied						
Roamans Catalog		0-90-day hot line		to follow	denied						
Silhouettes	SH00A	Last 6-mo. M/O buyers	B	142,000	7,500						
Domestics											
Children's Wear Digest		Last 3-mo. M/O buyers		23,000							
Company Store	CS00A	Last 3-mo. M/O buyers, female	A	85,000	7,500						

EXHIBIT 8.13
The New Customer Acquisition Circulation Plan

Mail date: 12/18 In-home date: 12/29–1/2

List	Source Code	Selection	Broker	Quantity Available	Quantity Input M/P	Final Quantity	Forecast % Response	Forecast Orders	Forecast AOV	Forecast Sales	Forecast $/Catalog
Domestics (continued)											
Domestications	DO00A	Last 3-mo. M/O buyers, female	A	1,245,000	7,500						
Hanna Anderson	HA00A	Last 3-mo. M/O buyers	A	68,000	7,500						
Playclothes	PC00A	Last 3-mo. M/O buyers, female	A	111,000	7,500						
Talbots Kids		Last 3-mo. M/O buyers	A	63,000	7,500						
Business-to-Business											
Burdines Credit Card		Last 3-mo. M/O buyers		421,000							
Careertrack Seminars	CT00A	Last 3-mo. women at business addr	A	to follow	7,500						
Daytimers		Quarterly, female, M/O buyers		63,000							
CMG Professional	CM00A	Last 3-mo. women at business addr	A	675,000	7,500						
Women's Direct Response	WD00A	Quarterly, female MOB at business addr	A	63,000	7,500						
Club/Continuities											
BMG CD Club	BM00A	Active female, omit heavy metal & r	A	to follow	7,500						
Columbia House		Young Sounds, female MOB		to follow							
Cosmetique	CQ00A	Last 3-month, 2× + M/O buyers	A	200,000	7,500						
Doubleday Literary		Monthly payers, female, $50+		75,000							
Harlequin Books	HQ00A	Active paid members	A	500,000	7,500						
Quality Paperback		Active, female paid members		300,000							
Low/Mid Gift											
Abbey Press	AP00A	Last 6-mo. M/O buyers	B	86,000	7,500						
Armchair Shopper	AS00A	Last 3-mo. M/O buyers, $25+	B	48,000	7,500						
Colorful Images		Last 6-mo. M/Or buyers, $50+		90,000							
Current Stationery	CU00A	Last 3-mo. M/O buyers, $50+	A	92,000	7,500						
Fingerhut		Monthly, female, apparel, cash, MOB		105,000							
Fingerhut		Monthly, female, apparel, cash, MOB		420,000							
Oriental Trading	OT00A	Last 3-mo. M/O buyers, $50+	B	120,000	7,500						
Personalized Products	PP00A	Last 3-mo. M/O buyers	B	120,000	7,500						
Mid/High Gift											
Casual Living	CK00A	Last 3-mo. M/O buyers, $50+	B	70,000	7,500						
Charles Keath		Last 3-mo. M/O buyers		100,000							
Horchow		Last 3-mo. M/O buyers		75,000							
Lillian Vernon	LV00A	Last 3-mo. M/O buyers, $50+	A	450,000	7,500						
Paragon		Last 3-mo. M/O buyers, $40+		66,000							
Potpourri	PO00A	Last 3-mo. M/O buyers	A	123,000	7,500						
Total				**14,253,000**	**255,000**						

EXHIBIT 8.13 (continued)
The New Customer Acquisition Circulation Plan

Source Frequency Report

		Code	List	Quantity Mailed	Orders Received	Sales	Average Order	Percent Response	$ Per Catalog
1	House	SU001A	2000 Subscribers 7/00	13	6	$ 176	$29	46.2%	$13.54
2	Multis	MB005B	3+-Time multibuyers	1,280	166	$ 8,456	$51	13.0%	$ 6.61
3	House	IN003C	2000 Inquiries	1,353	173	$ 7,704	$45	12.8%	$ 5.69
4	House	BU00A	2000 Buyers	2,783	334	$ 15,022	$45	12.0%	$ 5.40
5	House	BU003C	1999 Buyers	13,440	1,327	$ 66,678	$50	9.9%	$ 4.96
6	Multis	MB005A	2-Time multibuyers	11,508	890	$ 43,254	$49	7.7%	$ 3.76
7	House	BU003B	1998 Buyers	33,824	2,274	$ 111,681	$49	6.7%	$ 3.30
8	Contin.	CM006	Rental List O	9,167	536	$ 24,298	$45	5.8%	$ 2.65
9	House	SU003E	Subscribers GBP	2,000	79	$ 4,962	$63	4.0%	$ 2.48
10	New Test	OC004	Rental List N	3,217	172	$ 7,900	$46	5.3%	$ 2.46
11	Contin.	AC006A	Rental List M	37,155	1,475	$ 78,633	$53	4.0%	$ 2.12
12	Contin.	CL006	Rental List L	58,828	2,585	$ 116,919	$45	4.4%	$ 1.99
13	House	IN003A	1999 Inquiries	5,860	306	$ 11,299	$37	5.2%	$ 1.93
14	New Test	HC004	Rental List K	4,404	192	$ 8,120	$42	4.4%	$ 1.84
15	House	SU003B	1998 Subscribers	9,045	372	$ 15,932	$43	4.1%	$ 1.76
16	Contin.	CS008	Rental List J	5,000	194	$ 8,511	$44	3.9%	$ 1.70
17	House	BU003D	Buyers preceding 1997	7,228	246	$ 11,824	$48	3.4%	$ 1.64
18	Contin.	FD006	Rental List I	11,834	497	$ 18,931	$38	4.2%	$ 1.60
19	New Test	HS004	Rental List H	3,949	146	$ 5,689	$39	3.7%	$ 1.44
20	New Test	LA004	Rental List G	4,718	151	$ 6,664	$44	3.2%	$ 1.41
21	House	IN003E	1998 Inquiries	16,091	488	$ 22,099	$45	3.0%	$ 1.37
22	Contin.	SW006	Rental List F	14,680	461	$ 19,461	$42	3.1%	$ 1.33
23	Contin.	NF006	Rental List E	20,401	645	$ 26,438	$41	3.2%	$ 1.30
24	New Test	LB004	Rental List D	4,803	153	$ 5,764	$38	3.2%	$ 1.20
25	New Test	TH002	Rental List C	5,000	155	$ 5,736	$37	3.1%	$ 1.15
26	Contin.	JH006	Rental List B	19,358	467	$ 21,431	$46	2.4%	$ 1.11
27	House	IN003B	1997 Inquiries	2,588	84	$ 2,851	$34	3.2%	$ 1.10
28	House	SU003C	1997 Subscribers	11,752	247	$ 9,570	$39	2.1%	$ 0.81
29	New Test	PP007	Rental List A	5,000	99	$ 3,946	$40	2.0%	$ 0.79
30	House	SU003D	Subscribers before 1996	11,463	183	$ 6,989	$38	1.6%	$ 0.61
			Grand Total	337,742	15,103	$696,938	$46	4.5%	$ 2.06

EXHIBIT 8.14

The report can be used with the breakeven analysis discussed in Chapter 13 to identify lists that are meeting the preestablished goals. Together, they help you compare and improve list results from campaign to campaign.

Understanding the Seasonality of Prospect Mailings

Every catalog has good and bad seasons. Successful catalogs concentrate their prospecting in their best months and minimize new customer acquisition efforts in the "off season." The seasonality chart in Exhibit 8.15, compiled by the Kleid list brokerage and management organization, represents a composite of all mail-order efforts in all industries by month.

Business catalogs and consumer catalogs will have very different response curves. Every industry also will be different, and the only way to assemble this information is to do test mailings throughout the year. As tests reveal which months are best and which are not as good, you can build your own seasonality chart. One suggestion is to calculate, through testing, a monthly ranking of response to both customer and prospect mailings. Give the top month, say October, a rank of 100 percent, and derive a percentage ranking for every other month. If the figures in the exhibit were accurate for your catalog, your ranking would look like this:

October	100%
November	97%

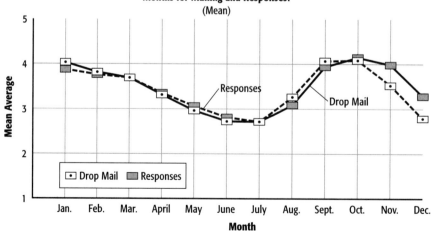

Seasonality Chart

On a Scale of 1–5 (1 = Worst; 5 = Best), What Are Your Best and Worst Months for Mailing and Responses?
(Mean)

EXHIBIT 8.15

September	96%
January	94%
February	92%
March	90%
April	85%
December	85%
May	80%
August	80%
June	75%
July	70%

Use your seasonality curve to determine when to mail and improve forecasting and overall results.

KEY STRATEGIES FOR SUCCESSFUL PROSPECTING

The following strategies will improve a catalog's chances of building the customer list faster and smarter:

- Put aside some budget dollars for testing alternative media.
- Don't ignore the creative design and copy of new media. It is as critical as the design of your catalog.
- Be tenacious in tracking source codes. With sophisticated ink-jet technology used for labels and internal order forms, there is no reason not to capture 90 to 95 percent of source codes. Don't spend a nickel on new prospecting media if you aren't doing a good job in tracking.
- Measure costs and results by source, and calculate long-term customer value now. It might just change how you look at prospecting.
- Build purchase-history information by source so you can get smarter in future new customer acquisition.
- Fill all catalog requests within twenty-four hours. The faster you can reply to a new catalog request, the greater the response rate.
- Be careful to age nonbuying catalog requests and inquiries so that you are not mailing them forever. Most catalog requests are quite "cold" by the end of eighteen months.
- Don't be discouraged if your first or second venture isn't a smash hit. As you test products, offers, lists, and the creative presentation, you will be able to increase results and fine-tune your prospecting efforts.

CHAPTER 9

Building, Managing, and Mailing Your Customer Database

Building the buyer file is a core competency and a major factor in ensuring catalog profitability. Unless you are a retailer with a large charge-card buyer list, a university with detailed lists of alumni names, or a cataloger with an existing catalog and thousands of potentially complementary names, you will probably start with only a few names or no names at all.

It takes three to five years to build a buyer list that can sustain the company. In the beginning, you must rely on renting outside names or generating new buyers from alternative media. As orders come in and the buyer list grows, fewer outside names will be needed. The mix of prospect to house names in a catalog's first five years might look like this:

	Year 1	Year 2	Year 3	Year 4	Year 5
% of New, Outside Names	100%	80%	60%	40%	30%
% of Buyers & Other House Names	0%	20%	40%	60%	70%
Total	100%	100%	100%	100%	100%

The ratio between outside, nonbuyer names and catalog buyers says a lot about the health of a new catalog. Prospecting costs money, but the buyer list generates the profitability to pay the shareholders, finance the growth of the business, and pay overhead, salaries, and general and administrative costs. The faster you convert prospects to repeat customers, the more quickly you can replace above-the-line expenditures on list rentals with bottom-line profits. Catalog sales will also benefit, because the buyer list will perform two to ten times better than nonbuyer and rental names.

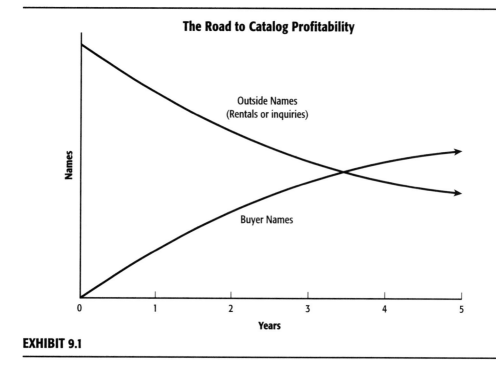

EXHIBIT 9.1

Of course, you will always need to invest some money in outside lists. New names are always needed to replace customers who have become inactive, died, moved, or changed lifestyle. They are also a source of growth for the catalog and the house file. But in general, the road to catalog profitability is paved with buyer names, as Exhibit 9.1 illustrates.

Too many catalogs underutilize or undermail their customer names. Too often, they treat every customer alike and fail to differentiate the type and volume of mailings to their best customer segments. Reaching customers and giving them an opportunity to purchase more often is not something nice to do—it is a must-do! This chapter explains how the house list can be mailed more profitably and reach customers more effectively.

The Customer List: A Cataloger's Most Valuable Asset

Most established catalogers consider their customer list to be their most important and valuable asset. Some even carry the value of buyers on the balance sheet, although most elect not to because of state laws on taxation of assets. Inventory, a building, equipment, a gifted staff—all of these are important, but they don't represent equity. To the investment world and potential investors, your company's equity is its house list. Estimating the value of that list will help estimate the value of your company.

There are three ways to value the customer list. In the *cost replacement method*, you simply multiply the number of buyers on your list by how much it cost to acquire those names. If your catalog has 100,000 buyers and it cost you $10 on average to get a customer, your customer list is worth a million dollars.

A more accurate valuation using this method results when you discount buyers that are more than a year old. Here's an example:

50,000	last-12-month buyers × $10 = $500,000
30,000	13- to 24-month buyers × $7.50 = $225,000
20,000	25-month buyers and older × $4.50 = $90,000
	Total Buyer List Value = $815,000

The ***future buying potential method*** looks at lifetime value (LTV) of customers or future propensity to buy products. This calculation assumes that you are tracking customers by original source code and maintaining buyer purchase history over time. To estimate list value using this method, multiply the number of buyers by the average purchase potential over the next three years. Thus, 100,000 buyers × $70 three-year average LTV = $7 million customer list value.

Again, this method can be fine-tuned by discounting older buyers as shown:

50,000	last-12-month buyers × $70 = $3,500,000
30,000	13- to 24-month buyers × $50 = $1,500,000
20,000	25-month buyers and older × $25 = $500,000
	Total Buyer List Value = $5,500,000

A third method of valuing the customer list is to look at the ***list rental potential*** over a two- or three-year period. Usually only buyers in the most recent twelve months have much list rental potential, but if half of the list is last-twelve-month buyers, the rental value is considerable, because it shows that the catalog continues to reactivate customers and bring in new buyers. The calculation is quite simple. Multiply the number of last-twelve-month buyers by an average list rental fee by the number of times the list manager can rent the names (sometimes called ***list turns*** or ***turnover***). Thus, 50,000 last-12-month buyers × $100/M × 20 turns = $100,000.

Strong rental lists will turn their last-twelve-month-buyers file between twenty and thirty times per year. Twenty percent of the profits goes to the list broker, 10 percent to the list manager who promotes your list, and 10 percent covers list fulfillment, leaving 60 percent as net profit contribution to the catalog's bottom line.

Using any combination of the three valuation methods discussed here will give a cataloger a sense of what the buyer list is worth.

The Hierarchy of Customers

Not all buyers are equal, as Exhibit 9.2 shows.

A customer starts out as a ***suspect***—someone who falls within the definition of your target audience but hasn't been contacted yet. Suspects become ***prospects*** when they can be found on certain lists or when they respond to a space ad, leave behind a card at a trade

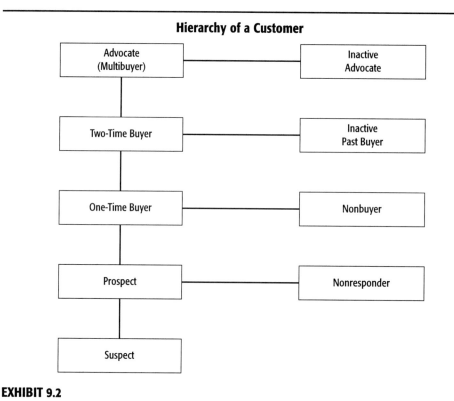

EXHIBIT 9.2

show, or contact your catalog on your website. Prospects who meet the general characteristics of your target audience can be identified and selected.

There are three hurdles in the process of nurturing suspects and prospects. Hurdle number one is getting prospects to become *one-time buyers*—people or companies that respond to a catalog mailing, make a purchase through television or a space ad, or ask for a catalog and are then converted to a buyer. Often these people are called "tryers" rather than buyers because they are trying, or testing, you out. They wish to try your products for quality. They want to try your customer service and fulfillment. They want to find out if your catalog company is worth doing business with in the long run.

The second hurdle in the customer hierarchy is getting one-time customers back for a second purchase. Many marketers consider this the most important transaction in the entire buying chain. *Two-time buyers* send you an important message—that "you're OK." They like your products and are coming back to purchase more. Your customer service and fulfillment is satisfactory. While they are not yet totally loyal customers, the second purchase is a vital step on the way to becoming one.

The third hurdle is getting two-time customers to become your ***advocates***—multibuyers who purchase regularly from your catalog. Advocates recommend their friends and colleagues to receive a catalog. They have high RFM (recency, frequency, and monetary) scores, meaning that they have purchased recently, made numerous purchases, and spent high dollar amounts. You can expect higher response rates and higher average order values from this group. You can also rely on them for research advice on new products, services, or changes to the catalog. They are a solid sounding board for advice and are the financial backbone of the catalog. When catalogers talk about the 80/20 rule—the fact that 80 percent of their business comes from 20 percent of the customers—this is the group they mean.

Building and maintaining a house list takes work, and not every new name will be successful. Only 50 percent or so of one-time buyers ever come back to the catalog for another purchase. Some two-time buyers will become inactive after their second purchase. Even the best buyers have attrition or may end up inactive. The challenge of the smart catalog marketer is to attack each of these buyer groups with specific communication initiatives to improve repurchase activity and customer loyalty.

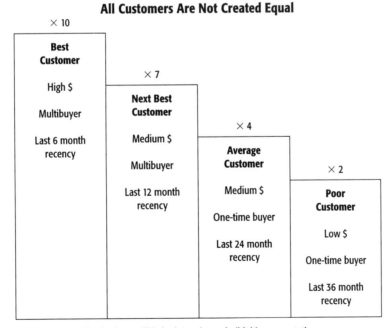

All Customers Are Not Created Equal

The database will help determine or build this segmentation

EXHIBIT 9.3

Exhibit 9.3 illustrates the RFM concept of recency of purchase, frequency of purchase, and lifetime monetary value of purchases. It likens customers to a staircase, with loyal multiple buyers who have spent more and purchased recently on the top stair. The next stair belongs to less recent customers who have spent less and have purchased in the last seven to twelve months. Another step down are one-time buyers who have spent higher dollars and have purchased in the last thirteen to twenty-four months. Lowest of all are buyers who spend little, are one-time purchasers, or haven't purchased in quite a while.

Not long ago, while developing circulation plans for a craft catalog client, my firm segmented its customer database into four groups similar to the ones shown here and used them for test mailings. The top customer segment pulled 32 percent with a $69 AOV, or $22.08 in sales per catalog mailed. The second-best customer segment pulled 17 percent with a $63 AOV, or $10.71 in sales per catalog mailed. The third customer segment pulled 7 percent with a $57 AOV, or $3.99 in sales per catalog mailed. The lowest customer segment pulled just slightly better than outside rental names, with a 2.5 percent response and a $53 AOV, or $1.33 in sales per catalog mailed. The best outside rental lists, the names that have proven to be good responders (called continuations), pulled just over 2 percent with a $52 AOV, while new test rental lists were below these numbers.

This "stair-step phenomenon" occurs with customer mailings over and over. Understanding this principle enables you to work the buyer list harder—a must for successful catalogers.

The Buyer List Inventory

It is nearly impossible to plan circulation or mailings, as discussed in later chapters, without an accurate summary or accounting of how names on the buyer file fall in the various RFM segments. Exhibit 9.4, the house list summary, exemplifies how the buyer list is segmented. Most fulfillment systems, even simple PC-based varieties, are capable of generating such a chart. As the new catalog tracks orders, it can build a customer purchase history file that includes how much customers spend, how often they purchase, and when they last bought—RFM or recency, frequency, and monetary.

The buyer list inventory should be updated before every mailing. In successful mature catalogs, typically a person on the marketing or database staff produces a report like this monthly or, in the case of a company like Fingerhut with 10 million twelve-month buyers, weekly.

The chart shows a breakout of all buyers by:

- Recency of purchase—in this example, new to file (in the last month), three-month segments up to six months, six-month segments in the first year, and twelve-month segments beyond that time

House List Summary
Month Ending 01/31/00

Total Buyer Segments:

Buyers Recency	Frequency				Monetary								Recency Total
	1 Time	%	2+ Times	%	<$50	%	$50–100	%	>$100	%			
New This Month	8.5	68	4.0	32	3.0	24	6.5	52	3.0	24			12.5
2–3 Months	15.0	63	9.0	38	6.0	25	12.0	50	6.0	25			24.0
4–6 Months	48.0	71	20.0	29	19.0	28	35.5	52	13.5	20			68.0
7–12 Months	50.0	69	22.0	31	20.0	28	35.0	49	17.0	24			72.0
13–24 Months	90.0	69	40.0	31	35.0	27	75.0	58	20.0	15			130.0
25–36 Months	85.0	74	30.0	26	30.0	26	65.0	57	20.0	17			115.0
36 Months +	60.0	71	25.0	29	25.0	29	40.0	47	20.0	24			85.0
Subtotals	**356.5**	**70**	**150.0**	**30**	**138.0**	**27**	**269.0**	**53**	**99.5**	**20**			
											Total Buyers		**506.5**

Change in Buyer Segments:

Recency	1/31/00	12/31/99	% 1-Month Change	1/31/99	% 12-Month Change
New This Month	**12.5**	**11.5**	9%	**10**	25%
2–3 Months	**24.0**	**23**	4%	**20**	20%
4–6 Months	**68.0**	**65**	5%	**35**	94%
7–12 Months	**72.0**	**70**	3%	**65**	11%
13–24 Months	**130.0**	**128**	2%	**115**	13%
25–36 Months	**115.0**	**112**	3%	**55**	109%
36 Months+	**85.0**	**81**	5%	**30**	183%

Monetary	1/31/00	12/31/99	% 1-Month Change	1/31/99	% 12-Month Change
<50	**138**	**135**	2%	**90**	53%
$50–100	**269**	**262**	3%	**180**	49%
>$100	**99.5**	**97.5**	2%	**60**	66%

EXHIBIT 9.4

- Frequency of purchase by one or two-plus times
- Monetary amount (lifetime sales) sorted by level

The report compares the count at the end of the current month with the previous month and with the same month a year previous.

Tailor the chart to your catalog's needs and make it a basic tool for planning upcoming mailings, judging the number of new buyer names being added to the file, and determining whether the customer list is being properly maintained and updated.

Using Visual RFM Segmentation to Strengthen the House List

An even more revealing tool than the house list summary is an RFM (recency, frequency, monetary) chart for house buyers. It gives you an in-depth look at your list so you can begin to differentiate among poor, average, good, and great customers. The RFM chart will be different for every mailer because each catalog has different price points and purchase frequencies. An office or computer supply catalog might get six or more purchases a year from good customers, while a gift catalog is likely to get only one or two orders per year.

Exhibit 9.5 shows a visual RFM segmentation for a hypothetical catalog. Each customer cell contains the number of names or pieces mailed, percentage response, and sales per catalog ($/Book). The best cells are in the upper right-hand corner, where customers

Visual RFM Segmentation

Recency		Frequency = 1 Monetary Range			Frequency = 2 Monetary Range			Frequency = 3 Monetary Range		
		0–$49	$50–$99	$100+	0–$49	$50–$99	$100+	0–$49	$50–$99	$100+
0–30 Days	Number Mailed	1,350	450	360	675	338	321	293	899	1,347
	$/Book	$5.45	$6.10	$7.45	$8.18	$9.16	$11.18	$13.63	$15.27	$18.62
	% Response	10.90%	12.21%	14.89%	16.35%	18.31%	22.34%	27.25%	30.52%	37.23%
31–90 Days	Number Mailed	2,612	871	697	1,306	653	620	568	1,179	1,724
	$/Book	$4.10	$4.59	$5.60	$6.15	$6.89	$8.40	$10.25	$11.48	$14.01
	% Response	8.20%	9.18%	11.20%	12.30%	13.78%	16.81%	20.50%	22.96%	28.01%
4–6 Months	Number Mailed	3,811	1,270	1,016	1,906	953	905	828	845	1,057
	$/Book	$3.60	$4.03	$4.92	$5.40	$6.05	$7.38	$9.00	$10.08	$12.30
	% Response	6.80%	7.62%	9.29%	10.20%	11.42%	13.94%	17.00%	19.04%	23.23%
7–9 Months	Number Mailed	3,916	1,305	1,044	1,958	979	930	851	869	1,086
	$/Book	$2.95	$3.30	$4.03	$4.43	$4.96	$6.05	$7.38	$8.27	$10.08
	% Response	5.90%	6.61%	8.06%	8.85%	9.91%	12.09%	14.75%	16.52%	20.15%
10–12 Months	Number Mailed	4,002	1,334	1,067	2,001	1,001	950	870	888	1,110
	$/Book	$2.55	$2.86	$3.48	$3.83	$4.29	$5.23	$6.38	$7.15	$8.72
	% Response	5.10%	5.71%	6.97%	7.65%	8.57%	10.45%	12.75%	14.28%	17.42%
13–18 Months	Number Mailed	7,950	2,650	2,120	3,975	1,988	1,888	1,728	1,764	2,204
	$/Book	$2.05	$2.30	$2.80	$3.08	$3.45	$4.21	$5.13	$5.75	$7.01
	% Response	4.10%	4.59%	5.60%	6.15%	6.89%	8.40%	10.25%	11.48%	14.01%
19–24 Months	Number Mailed	8,120	2,707	2,165	4,060	2,030	1,929	1,765	1,801	2,252
	$/Book	$1.70	$1.90	$2.32	$2.55	$2.86	$3.48	$4.25	$4.76	$5.81
	% Response	3.40%	3.81%	4.65%	5.10%	5.71%	6.97%	8.50%	9.52%	11.61%
25–36 Months	Number Mailed	7,653	2,551	2,041	3,827	1,913	1,818	1,664	2,198	1,622
	$/Book	$1.45	$1.62	$1.98	$2.18	$2.44	$2.98	$3.63	$4.07	$4.96
	% Response	2.90%	3.25%	3.96%	4.35%	4.87%	5.94%	7.25%	8.12%	9.91%
36–48 Months	Number Mailed	15,347	5,116	4,093	7,674	3,837	3,645	3,336	2,404	2,255
	$/Book	$1.25	$1.40	$1.71	$1.88	$2.11	$2.57	$3.13	$3.51	$4.28
	% Response	2.50%	2.80%	3.42%	3.75%	4.20%	5.12%	6.25%	7.00%	8.54%
48–60 Months	Number Mailed	14,391	4,797	3,838	7,196	3,598	3,418	3,128	2,192	1,990
	$/Book	$0.70	$0.78	$0.96	$1.05	$1.18	$1.43	$1.75	$1.96	$2.39
	% Response	1.40%	1.57%	1.91%	2.10%	2.35%	2.87%	3.50%	3.92%	4.78%
60 Months+	Number Mailed	16,302	5,434	4,347	8,151	4,076	3,872	3,544	2,616	2,520
	$/Book	$0.55	$0.62	$0.75	$0.83	$0.93	$1.13	$1.38	$1.55	$1.89
	% Response	1.10%	1.23%	1.50%	1.65%	1.85%	2.25%	2.75%	3.08%	3.76%

EXHIBIT 9.5

have purchased in the last thirty days, made the most lifetime purchases, and spent the most lifetime dollars. The worst cells are in the lower left-hand corner, where customers are less frequent, have made fewer purchases, and have spent less than $50 lifetime.

By ranking a catalog's customers, this chart can be used as a data mining tool to help improve campaign results and develop a relationship marketing program. Use it to:

- **Determine how deep you can mail in the next program.** By knowing the breakeven that will produce an 18 percent contribution to overhead and profit, you can mail the cells that meet the criteria and not mail those that don't. If $3.00 sales per catalog is the breakeven goal that produces a 10 percent pretax profit, for example, you can draw a line in the chart like the one in Exhibit 9.6 and mail only those cells that earned $3.00 in sales per catalog.

Visual RFM Segmentation Showing $3.00 Breakeven

Recency		Frequency = 1 Monetary Range			Frequency = 2 Monetary Range			Frequency = 3+ Monetary Range		
		0–$49	$50–$99	$100+	0–$49	$50–$99	$100+	0–$49	$50–$99	$100+
0–30 Days	Number Mailed	1,350	450	360	675	338	321	293	899	1,347
	$/Book	$5.45	$6.10	$7.45	$8.18	$9.16	$11.18	$13.63	$15.27	$18.62
	% Response	10.90%	12.21%	14.89%	16.35%	18.31%	22.34%	27.25%	30.52%	37.23%
31–90 Days	Number Mailed	2,612	871	697	1,306	653	620	568	1,179	1,724
	$/Book	$4.10	$4.59	$5.60	$6.15	$6.89	$8.40	$10.25	$11.48	$14.01
	% Response	8.20%	9.18%	11.20%	12.30%	13.78%	16.81%	20.50%	22.96%	28.01%
4–6 Months	Number Mailed	3,811	1,270	1,016	1,906	953	905	828	845	1,057
	$/Book	$3.60	$4.03	$4.92	$5.40	$6.05	$7.38	$9.00	$10.08	$12.30
	% Response	6.80%	7.62%	9.29%	10.20%	11.42%	13.94%	17.00%	19.04%	23.23%
7–9 Months	Number Mailed	3,916	1,305	1,044	1,958	979	930	851	869	1,086
	$/Book	$2.95	$3.30	$4.03	$4.43	$4.96	$6.05	$7.38	$8.27	$10.08
	% Response	5.90%	6.61%	8.06%	8.85%	9.91%	12.09%	14.75%	16.52%	20.15%
10–12 Months	Number Mailed	4,002	1,334	1,067	2,001	1,001	950	870	888	1,110
	$/Book	$2.55	$2.86	$3.48	$3.83	$4.29	$5.23	$6.38	$7.15	$8.72
	% Response	5.10%	5.71%	6.97%	7.65%	8.57%	10.45%	12.75%	14.28%	17.42%
13–18 Months	Number Mailed	7,950	2,650	2,120	3,975	1,988	1,888	1,728	1,764	2,204
	$/Book	$2.05	$2.30	$2.80	$3.08	$3.45	$4.21	$5.13	$5.75	$7.01
	% Response	4.10%	4.59%	5.60%	6.15%	6.89%	8.40%	10.25%	11.48%	14.01%
19–24 Months	Number Mailed	8,120	2,707	2,165	4,060	2,030	1,929	1,765	1,801	2,252
	$/Book	$1.70	$1.90	$2.32	$2.55	$2.86	$3.48	$4.25	$4.76	$5.81
	% Response	3.40%	3.81%	4.65%	5.10%	5.71%	6.97%	8.50%	9.52%	11.61%
25–36 Months	Number Mailed	7,653	2,551	2,041	3,827	1,913	1,818	1,664	2,198	1,622
	$/Book	$1.45	$1.62	$1.98	$2.18	$2.44	$2.98	$3.63	$4.07	$4.96
	% Response	2.90%	3.25%	3.96%	4.35%	4.87%	5.94%	7.25%	8.12%	9.91%
36–48 Months	Number Mailed	15,347	5,116	4,093	7,674	3,837	3,645	3,336	2,404	2,255
	$/Book	$1.25	$1.40	$1.71	$1.88	$2.11	$2.57	$3.13	$3.51	$4.28
	% Response	2.50%	2.80%	3.42%	3.75%	4.20%	5.12%	6.25%	7.00%	8.54%
48–60 Months	Number Mailed	14,391	4,797	3,838	7,196	3,598	3,418	3,128	2,192	1,990
	$/Book	$0.70	$0.78	$0.96	$1.05	$1.18	$1.43	$1.75	$1.96	$2.39
	% Response	1.40%	1.57%	1.91%	2.10%	2.35%	2.87%	3.50%	3.92%	4.78%
60 Months+	Number Mailed	16,302	5,434	4,347	8,151	4,076	3,872	3,544	2,616	2,520
	$/Book	$0.55	$0.62	$0.75	$0.83	$0.93	$1.13	$1.38	$1.55	$1.89
	% Response	1.10%	1.23%	1.50%	1.65%	1.85%	2.25%	2.75%	3.08%	3.76%

EXHIBIT 9.6

- **Identify problem cells that need specialized or personalized communication.** Using this chart, you could send a special reactivation message to inactive buyers who have not made a purchase for twelve to eighteen months, and a customized message designed to spur a larger purchase to one-time buyers whose only purchase was below $50.
- **Identify cells that should receive additional mailings.** It makes a great deal of sense to remail the cells with the highest RFM values. A good industry rule of thumb is that remailings of the same catalog or one with minor cover changes will pull 50 percent to 60 percent of the original mailing. If your breakeven is $3.00 in revenue per catalog, it is possible to find a great number of cells that can be expected to generate more than $6.00 in sales per book and warrant a second (or even third) mailing.
- **Thank your good customers.** When did you last send your best customers a note thanking them for their business and loyalty? This RFM segmentation can identify them immediately.

Circulation Planning for the House List

Circulation or *circulation planning* is the process of building the mailing schedule for the year (a macroplan) and the details of a specific catalog promotional campaign (a microplan). Magazines and newspapers use the term to describe building a subscriber base for a publication. In cataloging, the term refers to the process of building the customer list and contacting names during the year.

Circulation planning covers:

- What you are mailing (what format, offer, proposition, etc.)
- To whom you are mailing (prospects, catalog inquiries, buyers)
- When you are mailing (what season, what month)

Exhibit 9.7 shows a circulation or mailing plan for a consumer or business catalog. The plan starts by identifying the particular season (in this case, fall/holiday) and the mail dates and in-home dates. For years, catalogs considered the mail date important and hoped the catalog would get decent delivery by the United States Postal Service. Today, the *in-home* date is more significant, because by presorting, bagging, and tagging catalogs using carrier-route coding, printers can plan for and control the in-home date within a two- or three-day window.

The rest of the columns are also of importance. "List" indicates the particular segment of the customer list to be mailed. "Source Code" is the mailing or sales code assigned to each particular segment of the file, normally ink-jetted on the back cover and order form of consumer catalogs. "Selection" indicates the particular list selection or segment being mailed; "Qty. Avail." is the quantity of names available in this segment for this mailing; "Final Qty." is the number of names available after the merge-purge.

Fall/Holiday Customer Circulation Plan

Mail date: 9/1 In-home date: 9/11–15

List	Source Code	Selection	Final Quantity	Forecast % Response	Forecast Orders	Forecast AOV	Forecast Sales	Forecast $/Catalog
2000 4th Qtr Buyers–Bus.	BB10D	10+ Gift–Business	2,717	12.00%	326	$500	$ 163,020	$60.00
2000 4th Qtr Buyers–Bus.	BB20D	5–9 Gift–Business	1,466	8.00%	117	$250	$ 29,320	$88.00
2000 4th Qtr Buyers–Bus.	BB30D	2–4 Gift–Business	2,096	5.00%	105	$ 98	$ 10,270	$ 4.90
1999 4th Qtr Buyers–Bus.	BB40D	10+ Gift–Business	554	4.50%	25	$450	$ 11,219	$20.25
1999 4th Qtr Buyers–Bus.	BB50D	5–9 Gift–Business	514	3.50%	18	$200	$ 3,598	$ 7.00
1999 4th Qtr Buyers–Bus.	BB60D	2–4 Gift–Business	1,262	2.75%	35	$175	$ 6,073	$ 4.81
1998 4th Qtr Buyers–Bus.	BB70D	10+ Gift–Business	417	2.50%	10	$200	$ 2,085	$ 5.00
1998 4th Qtr Buyers–Bus.	BB80D	5–9 Gift–Business	384	1.50%	6	$150	$ 864	$ 2.25
1998 4th Qtr Buyers–Bus.	BB90D	2–4 Gift–Business	1,033	0.75%	8	$120	$ 930	$ 0.90
Subtotal–Business			**10,443**		**650**		**227,379**	**$21.77**
2000 4th Qtr Buyers–Cons.	CB10D	10+ Gift–Consumer	861	10.00%	86	$300	$ 25,830	$30.00
2000 4th Qtr Buyers–Cons.	CB20D	5–9 Gift–Consumer	3,036	8.00%	243	$175	$ 45,504	$14.00
2000 4th Qtr Buyers–Cons.	CB30D	2–4 Gift–Consumer	16,997	5.00%	850	$125	$ 106,231	$ 6.25
1999 4th Qtr Buyers–Cons.	CB40D	10+ Gift–Consumer	198	4.25%	8	$250	$ 2,104	$10.63
1999 4th Qtr Buyers–Cons.	CB50D	5–9 Gift–Consumer	980	3.75%	37	$180	$ 6,615	$ 6.75
1999 4th Qtr Buyers–Cons.	CB60D	2–4 Gift–Consumer	8,823	3.50%	309	$120	$ 37,057	$ 4.20
1998 4th Qtr Buyers–Cons.	CB70D	10+ Gift–Consumer	152	2.50%	4	$250	$ 950	$ 6.25
1998 4th Qtr Buyers–Cons.	CB80D	5–9 Gift–Consumer	735	1.25%	9	$125	$ 1,148	$ 1.56
1998 4th Qtr Buyers–Cons.	CB90D	2–4 Gift–Consumer	7,567	1.25%	95	$ 85	$ 8,040	$ 1.06
Subtotal–Consumer			**39,349**		**1,640**		**230,479**	**$ 5.86**
Other Buyers								
Spring 2001 Buyers	CB100D	2×+ buyers–Consumer	4,386	4.50%	197	$ 60	$ 11,842	$ 2.70
Spring 2001 Buyers	CB110D	1× buyers–Consumer	4,471	1.75%	78	$ 60	$ 4,695	$ 1.05
Fall '00 Buyers	CB120D	2×+ buyers–Consumer	13,100	6.00%	786	$ 85	$ 66,810	$ 5.10
Fall '00 Buyers	CB130D	1× buyers–Consumer	18,644	3.50%	653	$ 85	$ 55,466	$ 2.98
Spring '00 Buyers	CB140D	2×+ buyers–Consumer	2,820	3.25%	92	$100	$ 9,165	$ 3.25
Spring '00 Buyers	CB150D	1× buyers–Consumer	4,850	1.25%	60	$ 80	$ 4,830	$ 1.00
Fall '99 Buyers	CB160D	2×+ buyers–Consumer	5,366	2.50%	134	$ 90	$ 12,074	$ 2.25
Fall '99 Buyers	CB170D	1× buyers–Consumer	7,837	2.00%	157	$ 85	$ 13,323	$ 1.70
Spring '99 Buyers	CB180D	2×+ buyers–Consumer	1,684	1.00%	17	$ 85	$ 1,431	$ 0.85
Spring '99 Buyers	CB190D	1× buyers–Consumer	4,137	0.75%	31	$ 70	$ 2,172	$ 0.53
Subtotal–Other Consumer Buyers			**67,275**		**2,205**		**181,807**	**$ 2.70**
Total Mailing			**117,067**	**3.84%**	**4,495**	**$142**	**$ 142**	**$ 5.46**

EXHIBIT 9.7

"Forecast % Resp." is the predicted percent response for each list; "Forecast Orders" shows total orders forecast for each list segment, or the final quantity multiplied by the forecast percentage response. "Forecast AOV" forecasts the average order value for the list segment; "Forecast Sales" shows how much each list segment is expected to purchase (derived by multiplying forecast orders by forecast AOV); and "Forecast $/Catalog" forecasts revenue per catalog mailed, derived by dividing forecast sales by final quantity, or multiplying forecast percentage response by forecast AOV.

Mailing Your Customer List More Often

Most catalogers undermail their customer list. Catalog mailers who do head-to-head tests typically find that more mailings actually improve the response of customer names. Catalog buyers like to receive mail and like to respond to it. Obviously, this is where the customer hierarchy comes in. If a cataloger is contemplating one or two additional catalog mailings for the year, it is more logical to mail to the people or companies at the top of the buyer hierarchy.

Fingerhut again is a case in point. During the 1970s, a group of statistical analysts suggested increasing the number of mailings to the customer file from twenty to thirty times per year. I thought they were crazy until I looked at their numbers and logic. By segmenting the customer list based on past purchase activity, especially product category, recency, frequency, and dollars spent with Fingerhut, we set up a yearlong test using last-twelve-month buyers with at least two purchases. The control group got the standard twenty promotions for the year. The test group received thirty promotions. We knew that additional mailings would increase sales, but we didn't want to dilute the bottom-line results with marginal promotions.

Everyone pitched in. Merchandising supported the test with quality products, and the creative team added ten mailings to their already hectic creative schedule. The results? Sales increased as expected, and the contribution to overhead and profit (the profit left after subtracting cost of goods, fulfillment, and advertising from net sales) met the corporate goal. The test was an overwhelming success and helped Fingerhut leapfrog to a new sales plateau. By the time I left the catalog company, Fingerhut was mailing its list more than fifty times a year and looking for ways to double that number of promotions.

Remember the old expression "If you don't use it, you'll lose it"? Mailing a list more often helps keep customers active and recent. Names more than twelve months old cause a list to deteriorate dramatically in value. Mailing as often as possible gives your customers plenty of opportunity to stay in the most recent segment of your list.

Database Management

As Exhibit 9.8 illustrates, the database lies at the heart of the cataloging process. A cataloger starts by capturing information from customers or prospective customers and build-

Catalog Marketing = Database Marketing

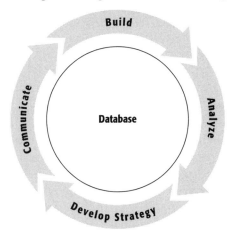

EXHIBIT 9.8

ing the information base—the essence of what growing a catalog is all about. Customer information is then analyzed, categorized, and organized for the next catalog mailing. The third step, also driven by database information, is developing the mailing strategy, offers, and timing of mailings on a macro basis for the year, and a micro basis by campaign. In the final step, you are communicating with your prospects and customers via the catalog. Some respond with orders; others do not. This closes the loop of the database process by generating information from the mailing to add to the database. The database and catalog cycle have come full circle. It is an ongoing, continuous process.

The database is generated by the catalog management system—also called a ***fulfillment system***—which facilitates every aspect of a catalog's day-to-day business, including order entry, inventory management, and shipping and receiving. It also provides reports related to promotion campaign analysis, media or list analysis, RFM, and square-inch analysis.

Every start-up cataloger needs a professional fulfillment or catalog management system. Choose software that will best fit your needs for at least five years, and then consider what hardware is needed to support it. You don't want to have to switch systems (or, if fulfillment is outsourced, suppliers), since moving transaction data between systems is difficult. Most catalog management software can be purchased in a sample version inexpensively. Before making any decisions, try out at least two different companies' software so you'll be sure to get something with which you will be comfortable.

Too many start-up catalogers neglect to purchase a catalog management or operating system. They tell themselves that their business is unique and that no off-the-shelf system will work, or are told by advisers and general marketing consultants that existing software doesn't tie into their accounting system the way they want, isn't specifically designed for their industry, or doesn't run on the platform that the information systems department likes best. But in 999 out of 1,000 cases, start-up catalogers will be better served with an existing fulfillment system software package than they will by attempting to design their own. A full-scale catalog management package can exceed $100,000, but some of the less expensive, PC-based programs have enough horsepower to run a $10 million catalog business.

Another mistake common to catalogers who farm out their fulfillment is using an operating system that is not designed for catalogs. Many noncatalog companies use direct marketing promotions to sell a single item, offer prizes, or support sales contests. These "single-promotion" operating systems do not assign unique customer numbers and require the rekeying of each customer's data for every subsequent order. For a one-shot promotion, this is not a problem, but for follow-up sales, it is severely limiting.

The best catalog management systems work on-line, or in "real time." They update all information as transactions take place, so that customer service people can confirm that items are in inventory or access customer purchase history to solve problems. The systems can also generate reports on demand, facilitating decisions about everything from purchasing to mailing strategy.

How to Organize Information

To be useable, data must be stored in an organized fashion. Normally, this means inputting information in database files in rows and columns that can easily be stored and retrieved. The rows, called records, store information about one item in the customer file, be it products in the product file, or customers in the customer file. The columns, called fields, store specific information about each item. All the names in the customer file will be stored in one field (column) in the file, all the zip codes will be in one column, and so on.

Don't attempt to store data in anything but database software. Storing customer names in a label format in word processing software causes problems later, when data must be rekeyed to be used elsewhere, and updates become difficult or impossible.

Besides names and addresses of buyers and prospects, the house list or database contains purchase information, product information, sales information, including vendor identification and when and where the product was sold, as well as offer (stimulus) information. The house list comprises six major tables that hold information, each with a distinct function. Exhibit 9.9 outlines the major tables and their fields. Most catalog fulfillment software includes these fields and tables and many others, so you don't have to reinvent the wheel.

The *customer table* is where all the data necessary to contact the customer are stored. If a cataloger is said to have 50,000 records in its customer file, what this means is that there are 50,000 people in the database. Normally, both prospects and customers are stored in the customer table. The difference is that customers have a purchase history, and prospects do not.

Database Layout

Customer

Customer ID	←→ **Key Field**
Prefix	
First Name	
Middle Name	
Last Name	
Title	
Company	
Address One	
Address Two	
City	
State or Province	
Zip or Postal Code	
Day Phone #	
Evening Phone #	
Fax #	
E-mail Address	
Original Source Code	
Date Entered in the System	
Do Not Rent	
Do Not Promote	
Change of Address	
First Purchase Date	
Last Purchase Date	R
Total # of Purchases	F
Total $$ of Purchases	M
Gift Giver (Shipper vs. Ship-to)	

Invoice Detail

Customer ID	←→ **Key Field**
Invoice Number	←→ **Key Field**
Salesperson ID	←→ **Key Field**
Source Code	←→ **Key Field**
Order Date	
Method of Payment	
Gross sales	
Discounts	
Other Charges	
Net Sale Amount	

Invoice Detail

Invoice Number	←→ **Key Field**
SKU (Item Number)	←→ **Key Field**
Invoice Line Number	
Ship Date	
Quantity	
Total Price	

Product

SKU (Item Number)	←→ **Key Field**
Product Classification (Category)	
Cost per Unit	
Shipping Weight	
Description	

Salesperson

Salesperson ID	←→ **Key Field**
Salesperson Name	
Department of Division	

Offer

Source Code	←→ **Key Field**
Description	
Media	
Number of Offers Made (Reach)	
Cost per Reach	

EXHIBIT 9.9

In addition to name, address, phone, fax, and E-mail contact information, the customer table has summary data about the customer. The table also contains the original source code, which indicates the first offer or stimulus that brought the customer into the database. While a sales or marketing source code will go with each transaction, the original source code stays with the customer record forever.

Recency, frequency, and monetary history (RFM) is also stored in the customer record, along with the date the name entered the customer table. This allows for easy classification of customers by purchase history. Be aware that first purchase date and date entered are not necessarily the same.

The customer table is also where "do not rent" and "do not promote" are tracked. This process is getting to be more and more important as consumer privacy becomes a larger issue.

Being able to track gift givers (shipper versus ship-to) can be important for certain types of catalogs, such as gift and food mailers.

This file also tracks address changes and updates. Changes are made when customers notify the catalog of a change of address or when the house list is run through the U.S. Postal Service NCOA program (National Change of Address). When customers are mailed, their names and addresses must be put through CASS (Coding Accuracy Support System) address standardization to qualify for postal discounts. A "clean" database is one that should accurately code at the 95 percent level or better. Additionally, most fulfillment software permits customers to be sorted by name, address, and often phone number to avoid duplicate entry. As a result, there should be no more than 5 percent duplication in the customer table.

The ***invoice header*** describes the total transaction—who made the purchase, which salesperson made the sale, when the sale was made, what offer or stimulus was associated with the sale, and how much was spent. Note especially the Gross Sales, Discounts, Other Charges, and Net Sales Amount fields. It is important to know which is which when counting sales dollars!

The ***invoice detail*** comprises what was purchased, how many units were purchased, when the order was shipped, and the total price by item before discounts. Often, catalogers try to have only one transaction file and omit detailed product information. This is a big mistake, as this level of data will be sorely needed in future marketing efforts.

The ***product table*** includes what was sold, what category the product is in, what the cost of the product is, and often the shipping weight of the product. This can be important when you're reviewing shipping and handling charges.

The ***salesperson table*** designates the person or group making the sale. It may have a salesperson's ID, or it may be categorized by store, or by state.

The ***offer table*** indicates the stimulus used to motivate customers or prospects to action. Where the offer was made (mail, newspaper, radio, Internet), cost of placing the offer, and a description of the offer can be found here.

Many problems with data that are blamed on the database are really human error problems. Computers don't forget source codes, misspell customer names, and duplicate customer entries—people do. Accuracy is important to database marketing and management. Before you set out to fix a database problem, make sure that you actually have a database problem!

Mining the Data

The database is a priceless source of primary data—purchase history and RFMP information—that can be used to contact customers more effectively. Secondary data—demographic information such as marital status or household size and income—can be gathered through customer surveys but more frequently come from other sources. To reduce expenses and improve targeting, maximize the use of data already collected by "mining the data," and purchase additional primary or secondary data only when it is necessary.

During the first months a cataloger is in business, mining the database is simply a matter of pulling lists and reviewing sales and response by source code. Once a catalog has been operating for a year or so, not all customers and prospects should receive the same communications with the same frequency. This is the time to take advantage of the information stored in the database.

The first place to look to develop appropriate segments is the buying habits of one-time, two-time, and three-time-plus buyers. Buyers who have made multiple past purchases are far more likely to buy again, can be communicated with more often (at a profit), and tend to spend more per order. (Be sure to track and follow up with buyers who have made multiple purchases.)

The next place to develop appropriate customer segments is low-dollar versus higher-dollar customers. Typically, customers who start out with small orders tend to continue making small orders. Be sure you are making the right offers to each group, as you don't want a database full of low-dollar buyers!

Sometimes divergent product lines such as men's and women's clothes may attract very different buyers. Look at the types of products associated with different buyers. Buyers may ultimately require very different communications to be targeted effectively.

A database may contain distinctly different buyer types, such as businesses and consumers. While business customers are generally more difficult to acquire (have a higher acquisition cost), they are more loyal over time (have a higher lifetime value). Look for clear, obvious distinctions related to buying behavior when analyzing your buyers.

To find out more about your customers, you can overlay or add secondary data such as demographic and lifestyle information to customer data for a few cents per name in the United States. The same information can be added to prospect lists in order to pinpoint the best potential customers.

Keep in mind that the purpose of the database is to support communication, and if the database is mined effectively, different customer segments will be communicated with differently. Use the knowledge contained in the database to find ways to communicate with good customers more often and not-so-good customers less often (or not at all).

The Data Warehouse

A data warehouse is an off-line system designed to store and easily manipulate large data sets. Data warehousing is important for new catalogs that begin with names of buyers from other channels. Disney, Paws (Garfield catalog), and Jeep are good examples of companies that developed catalogs to reach names they already had from another selling channel. Catalogers with these "affinity" names need a data warehouse to receive, manage, store, and output all the data from all the sources they already control. It would be too cumbersome to have tens of thousands (or even millions) of names in a fulfillment system when most will never become catalog buyers. The data warehouse can provide the best names for catalog prospects by quickly identifying names that are on more than one list, have bought a similar product in the past, or meet other criteria that the cataloger sets.

Data warehousing is not list management. List managers house data for the purpose of renting names, and some prepare files for merge-purge. The data warehouse's focus is managing data. While some catalogers manage data warehouses themselves, most prefer to outsource this function to a specialist. It is a different skill set from running a fulfillment system, a letter shop, or an MIS function.

❖ KEY POINTS

- The buyer file is your most valuable asset. Select a method of appraising your list's value, and use it regularly to benchmark your company's performance.
- Remember the customer hierarchy when you plan mailings, and build your communications and contact strategy to convert prospects to regular customers.
- Use RFM and RFMP to segment your customer list as it grows. By carefully capturing and maintaining customer purchase history, you will be able to differentiate among—and mail appropriately to—good, average, and poor buyers.
- Let your computer create a house list summary or inventory before every mailing. As your list grows, run a summary monthly.
- Invest in the best catalog management system you can in order to "slice and dice" customers during your mail or circulation planning.

CHAPTER 10

Using the Database to Maximize Sales and Profits from the Customer List

The database stores knowledge gained by listening to the customer.

Catalogers have to listen well. In order to make a sale and ship an order correctly, they have to capture the customer's name, address, and other relevant data. Like the old saying "Actions speak louder than words," catalogers can listen to what people say *and* what they do. That's why a database-driven company is like a good listener. The database is like a pair of ears that helps the company listen carefully. Good listeners may not be the flashiest or the most polished speakers, but they will eventually find the "right" things to say, by knowing the interests of their audience.

A database of purchase history information can be used to support and improve customer communications. If the information is "mined" effectively, it can help companies design custom strategies for communicating with different customer segments, so that you communicate with good customers more often and not-so-good customers less often. However, if buyer data are not used effectively (if catalogers only hear but do not listen), this advantage turns into nothing more than an expense.

This chapter shows you how to use what you've heard to create targeted, personalized, successful customer communications that get first-time buyers to make a second purchase, reactivate inactive customers, and develop loyalty. You'll also discover how to integrate every aspect of the catalog business into planning a successful campaign.

How to Get First-Time Buyers to Make a Second Purchase

Industry statistics indicate that only 50 percent of first-time buyers ever make a second purchase. Here are seven practical ideas to improve the conversion of new catalog buyers.

1. **Reach new customers with a special communication quickly.** Start by making the customers' first order special. Include a special note acknowledging customers' first

order and thanking them for placing it, or a short (no more than one page), postage-paid survey inquiring about their ordering process and demographics. This is a perfect time for an incentive on the next purchase—perhaps a $5-off coupon, a 15–20 percent discount, free shipping, or a proven premium with the next order. The offer should stand out physically in the package and be attractive enough to motivate a new customer to keep it and use it. An expiration date within sixty to ninety days of receipt is ideal. Don't forget to include a new catalog (or at least a new order form) in the box shipment.

2. **Consider a special phone call to new customers.** Try calling a new customer the week after he or she places a first order. Don't try to sell anything, but thank the person for ordering. This is also an opportunity to find out how the customer viewed the ordering process. Questions might include:

   - How helpful and courteous was the phone operator?
   - Did the order arrive in a timely manner?
   - Was the physical shipment satisfactory?
   - Was the product everything you expected?
   - What is the likelihood that you will buy again from a future edition of the company's catalog?
   - What other products would you like to see in the catalog?

   If problems are detected, this is the time to correct them. Managers must be empowered to remedy any problem to a customer's satisfaction.

   Several years ago, a fashion and general products catalog studied the lifetime value of 10,000 people who had returned their first product purchased compared with 10,000 who kept their first product. After three years, the lifetime value of people who retained their first purchase versus those who returned the product was 400 percent higher. Something had gone wrong with those who returned their initial products: they were unhappy with product quality, product value, or customer service practices. Unless you can fix a problem immediately, you might as well strike those buyers from your active mailing file.

3. **Mail a special catalog to new customers right away.** Sounds like overkill, especially if you included a new catalog in the box shipment—but try it! Surprisingly, new buyers will outperform most buyer segments if they receive a new catalog immediately. Gear the catalog to new customers with appropriate call-to-action offers and messages.

4. **Isolate first-time buyers and build a separate mailing strategy.** Fingerhut found out in the 1980s that building separate mail plans for new, one-time buyers dramatically increased the rate of conversion to two-time buyers. Here's how the process worked: New customers didn't go onto the buyer list until they had made two purchases. First-time buyers (Fingerhut called this group "the Middle End") were isolated and sent a series of mailings, almost every other month, for a period of eighteen months. It worked like crazy! Fingerhut built a new profit center and was successful in converting a much greater proportion of first-time buyers to second-time buyers than

ever before. At the end of eighteen months and eight or nine special promotion efforts, customers who still hadn't purchased were removed from the regular customer mailing list.

5. **Tailor a special edition of the customer list catalog for new buyers.** New customers are half buyer and half prospect. They have made a purchase, but they are still trying you out and subsequently have a much lower response rate and AOV than buyers. Consider using a special wraparound, and test different messages and offers to convert new buyers. Testing here is important to find out what motivates these new buyers to make that second purchase.

6. **Consider testing a noncatalog or a series of noncatalog mailings to convert these customers.** Who says that a format other than a catalog can't work as a conversion vehicle? Try testing solo mailings (a single product or narrow range of similar products) or a "multimailer" (an unbound collection of products similar to those mailed by American Express). Don't limit yourself to a second catalog mailing when another format might work even better.

7. **Give someone in your company the responsibility to ramrod the conversion process.** In order to test, standardize, and continue a conversion process or system throughout the year, someone has to be assigned responsibility for the task. Because this is a marketing function that requires cooperation from creative, merchandising, fulfillment, and operations, responsibility might be assigned to a task force of people from these disciplines.

How to Reactivate Inactive Customers

An inactive buyer is a customer who has not made a purchase in a certain period of time. Depending on the nature of the company and its products, a buyer may be termed inactive after twelve, twenty-four, or thirty-six months. Some mailers refer to inactivity as *attrition*—these are lost souls, never to return. But that's a pretty severe judgment! If treated right, many past buyers can be salvaged.

To reactivate or not . . . that is the question. Some catalogers think that older, inactive buyers are a gold mine, an asset to their company. After all, once you have a relationship with a customer, why give up on it! Others contend that reactivating customers isn't worth the effort, because their value is marginal, and the company should spend its promotional dollars getting new buyers.

Those in favor of reactivation believe that the reactivation process goes on with every mailing of the catalog. After all, don't most catalogers mail many of their inactive buyers at least once or twice a year? It is not unusual to see business and consumer catalogers making four- and five-year-old buyers produce profitable results. It's easier and less expensive to approach a past customer than it is to obtain a new buyer.

There are two secrets to successful reactivation. First, don't delay the communication process! Even though two-, three-, or even four-year-old inactive buyers produce profitable results, they will do better if mailed sooner. Second, don't treat every inactive buyer the same. Segment inactive buyers as carefully as you segment better buyers.

Those who argue against reactivation say that they are already mailing older customers once or twice a year and getting good results. Why bother with the time and expense of special communications and incentives? Won't these buyers just wait until you offer them an incentive that they can't pass up, and then sit on their hands again? Instead of designing special reactivation communications, these companies prefer to invest their money finding new buyers with whom to start fresh.

These are good emotional arguments, but the way to prove them is to *measure* the cost of obtaining a new customer versus reactivating an old one, and then tracking that customer segment over time to determine its long-term value. Just because reactivation produced gangbuster results for another catalog does not mean it necessarily will give you similar results. You need to find out for yourself.

Start by building a hierarchy of inactive buyers based on past purchase activity. Your hierarchy may look like this:

- twelve- to twenty-four-month multibuyers with high dollars spent
- twelve- to twenty-four-month multibuyers with medium dollars spent
- twelve- to twenty-four-month multibuyers with low dollars spent
- twenty-five- to thirty-six-month multibuyers with high dollars spent
- twenty-five- to thirty-six-month multibuyers with medium dollars spent
- twenty-five- to thirty-six-month multibuyers with low dollars spent
- thirty-seven- to forty-eight-month multibuyers with high dollars spent
- thirty-seven- to forty-eight-month multibuyers with medium dollars spent
- thirty-seven- to forty-eight-month multibuyers with low dollars spent
- twelve- to twenty-four-month one-time buyers with high dollars spent
- twelve- to twenty-four-month one-time buyers with medium or low dollars spent
- twenty-five- to thirty-six-month one-time buyers with high dollars spent
- twenty-five- to thirty-six-month one-time buyers with medium or low dollars spent
- thirty-seven- to forty-eight-month one-time buyers with high dollars spent
- thirty-seven- to forty-eight-month one-time buyers with medium or low dollars spent

In effect, you are using a reverse RFM (recency, frequency, monetary) segmentation to determine who your best customers are to reactivate. Some catalogers make this entire group pay out for them.

Next, design your communication test strategy. I recommend a three-way test such as:

- Control: Straight catalog mailing, no special message, no offer or incentive
- Test A: Catalog mailing with special message but no offer or incentive
- Test B: Catalog mailing with special message and an incentive to reactivate

Be sure to mail test quantities of sufficient size to read the results. If you mail 1,000 catalogs each in three test cells and get a 2.5 percent response, you're in trouble. Response from only 25 people per test cell is not sufficient to draw statistically valid conclusions about whether a special message and/or an incentive would be worth the additional costs.

The next step is to plan your promotional vehicle. You have a number of options for conveying your reactivation message. Consider putting the catalog in an envelope with a letter, or using a plastic envelope that lets the cover and your reactivation message show through. A wraparound can work well, especially if you do some selling on the inside of the wrap. A simple cover change or a "dot whack" on the cover can also convey your message. Whatever the methodology, it should not be subtle: you want the customer to see your message.

Develop your message. Since you are dealing with past buyers, starting softly with the message makes sense. Open with "We Miss You" and increase the intensity with each mailing: "We Want You Back as a Preferred Customer," "Don't Let This Be Your Last Catalog," and finally, "Last Chance!"

Verify the names being mailed. This is especially important in business catalogs, because contact people in companies move all the time. Instead of mailing catalog after catalog without knowing whether the person is still at the company or in the same job, why not initiate a call to the company to verify the contacts on your buyer database? You will also be able to add names of people who are new to the company and should receive the catalog. For consumer lists, use the USPS's National Change of Address (NCOA) file in your merge-purge and add the "Address correction requested" postal endorsement to your mailing.

Mail and track the catalog test. Make sure each list segment is carefully source-coded so you can track the results and determine any significant difference. If tracking is a problem, as it is with many business catalogs, you may need to look up each respondent in your database to verify the correct source code. Tracking customers is much easier with buyers than with prospects or names that are not on your house list.

Once the mailing is complete, summarize the results and draw your conclusions. Make certain the files of each test cell are marked to track over time and determine the longer-range impact of the reactivation activity. Finally, retest to verify results. Every catalog mailing needs to contain some reactivation testing to apply constantly what has been learned. "Test back" to the same lists that were part of the original test to verify results. Be sure to track long-term buyer activity to determine the value of each buyer segment. The long-term question is, "Do reactivated names continue to perform well, or are they motivated only by an incentive and then become dormant again?" It takes a minimum of twelve to twenty-four months to evaluate the activity of each list segment.

Reactivation is not an emotional issue; it's one that should be tested and measured. There are two key measurements of reactivated lists: what are the sales per catalog mailed (not just percent response or average order value) in the initial test, and how do these list segments perform over the next twelve, twenty-four, and thirty-six months? With special messages and incentives, dramatic response gains of 25 percent to 50 percent are not uncommon.

Remember, reactivation communication can't wait. Start as early as the thirteenth month of inactivity. Don't wait until buyers are dead and cold to let them know they are missed.

Consider a Loyalty Marketing Program

Gaining customer loyalty is a problem for catalogers. Although few catalogers make money or even avoid losing it on the first purchase, only 50 percent of first-time buyers ever come back for a second purchase. Customers are fickle. Like retailers, manufacturers, and packaged goods companies, catalogers need to build loyalty among their customers.

Building customer loyalty is the process of generating repeat purchase activity with one's buyers. It is having "top-of-mind presence"—having your catalog be the first one buyers think of when they shop for a product or service. Relationship marketing is a primary loyalty-building tool. By using your customer database information to initiate regular, consistent, and thorough communications, you can persuade prospects to become customers, stimulate one-time customers to buy a second time, and build repeat purchase activity.

Loyalty programs are not for everyone. As Exhibit 10.1 demonstrates, a loyalty program is not the answer for catalogs whose products or services are totally unique and not available anywhere else on the planet. Although this kind of catalog still needs to find target customers and build the right communication and contact strategy, every dollar it puts into a loyalty program to keep customers coming back will probably be wasted. Customers will come back anyway!

The converse also applies: the less unusual a product or service, the greater the need for a loyalty program, and the more likely that program will work. Just think of the loyalty programs designed around such commodity products as airline seats, motel rooms, long-distance telephone service, credit cards, fast-food meals, and movie theater seats.

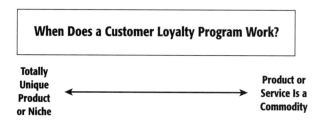

EXHIBIT 10.1
The more your product or service is a commodity, the greater the need for a loyalty program.

Catalogers are becoming innovative in developing loyalty programs that keep buyers from purchasing elsewhere. Consumer, business, and retail catalogers are using the following techniques to build and enhance customer loyalty with their buyers:

- Frequent-buyer programs
- Co-ops or rebate programs based on the year's purchase activity
- Birthday and anniversary clubs
- Preferred-customer programs
- Special pricing based on annual purchases
- In-house credit
- Gifts
- First opportunity at special sales
- Preferred shipping and customer service perks
- Newsletters
- Customer advisory boards

The more the program can be tailored and positioned specially to your company, the better. Involve your customers in building a program. After all, they are the ones who will tell you with their purchases whether it is a success or not. Another strong caveat is that you must take the time to think, plan, and research the concept before jumping into the water.

Use your database to identify the customers to whom a loyalty program should be offered, usually those with the best long-term lifetime value.

Customer loyalty programs produce many positive results. Customers react to more targeted, personalized communications and loyalty efforts with higher response rates and greater average-order values. They like the interaction and perceive it almost as "partnering." And sales and profits increase because the catalog is more selective in whom it mails. Good customers receive more communications, and prospects and poorer customers receive fewer. In sum, customers feel good about the relationship with your company, and it's a "win-win" proposition.

Loyalty programs don't always work, however. You may spend a great deal of time and capital building an elaborate, database-driven loyalty program only to find that you're getting sales that you would have gotten anyway. You may find that customers don't really want a relationship with your company. Inadequate systems and operations can result in miserable tracking and not enough customer history to segment buyer groups. You may offer the wrong perks or benefits and fail to turn on your customers. Or your program may become so complex in its benefits, offers, and methods of redemption that customers simply don't understand it.

One last word of advice: Before you initiate a loyalty program, consider its long-term implications. Think through your exit strategy, or beware. The major airlines never dreamed of what they were getting themselves into when they created frequent-flyer programs—and there's no way in sight they can ever drop them.

Traditional Versus Integrated Campaign Planning

Exhibits 10.2 and 10.3 contrast the traditional method of planning a catalog campaign with the emerging "integrated" method.

The traditional method of catalog business planning is linear. The merchandising team reviews the past catalog's results, analyzing product sales. Likewise, the creative team kicks off the campaign about ninety days or so from mail date after receiving input from the product people about new items and changes in creative approach. Together, these two groups develop the pagination and proceed with the catalog design, copy, photography, and page production.

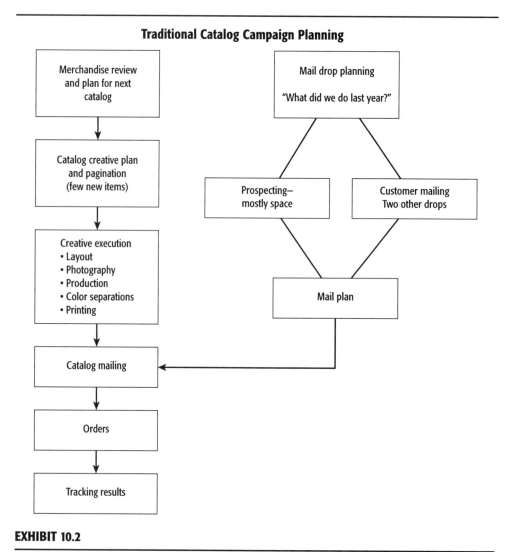

Traditional Catalog Campaign Planning

EXHIBIT 10.2

Integrated Campaign Planning Using Merchandising, Creative, Database, and Circulation

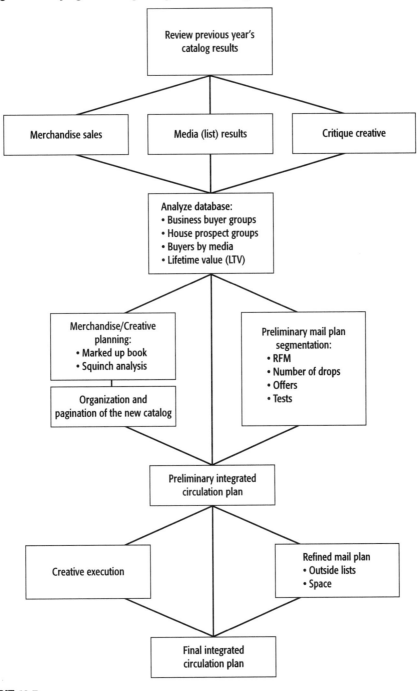

EXHIBIT 10.3

On another planet, or so it would seem, the marketing department or people responsible for circulation planning build a plan in light of last year's results. The "What Did We Do Last Year?" syndrome is unfortunately the primary method of determining how a new campaign will be planned. Especially in companies that outsource some functions, there typically is little contact between circulation and creative until the production people ask how many pieces are being mailed. That input generally takes place well along in the creative process and gives little or no thought to versioning, personalization, or special offers. Circulation determines what prospect mailings, if any, will be mailed and similarly plans how many mailings will go to customers and how deep to mail the list.

If everyone is quite good at his or her respective job, this process works just fine. Each team pays strict attention to the results from the previous season's (or year's) activity, and life is good, profits are reasonable, and the catalog continues to grow. But there is a better approach: integrating all four competencies—merchandise, creative, database, and circulation—in order to plan more effective campaigns. As Exhibit 10.3 shows, this approach is highly oriented to the customer list and specifically to improving its response. Let's review how this process differs from the traditional approach.

The first difference is that instead of every team working in its own little world, the campaign planning is done on an integrated basis. Results of all aspects of last season's or last year's mailings are analyzed by team members from all four areas. Together, they examine:

- Merchandise results (item sales, dollar sales, and square-inch analysis by item, product category, price point, etc.)
- Media results (list response, other new customer acquisition efforts via the Internet, space, TV, package inserts, card decks, customer referrals, etc.)
- Creative execution—analyzing why certain design or photo treatments sold better than others and looking at square-inch analysis to determine how to improve catalog productivity

A second difference is that the team as a whole takes a step backward and looks at the customer database for indicators of how the customer list can be better segmented to improve results. Using lifetime value and an RFMP chart as a guide, it is possible to identify problem segments that need special attention and communication (say, first-time buyers or low-AOV buyers), customer segments such as inactive buyers that require special messages, and opportunity segments such as advocates who have made five, ten, even twenty lifetime purchases, or new buyers who purchased four or five times from you in the past year.

The next step is to plan, as a team, the merchandising, creative, and marketing approach to reaching customers. Instead of having a simple five-line mail plan, you will find that you're looking at problem and opportunity segments and totally changing the manner in which you communicate with customers.

A Sample Mailing Scheme Based on the New Integrated Campaign Planning

The integrated approach to campaign planning has been used by a number of catalogers with outstanding results. Exhibit 10.4 illustrates an example of an integrated mailing scheme. This cataloger previously mailed three drops of its catalog during the holiday season. It was suggested that the top "advocate" group could profitably sustain a fourth mailing with ease. Thus, the basis of the mailing sequence to top-level customers was to reach them four times. Each cover was planned accordingly, with the last being a special "There's still time . . . to order."

One goal of the mailing sequence was to reach the top buyers—those with the highest RFM values—more often. Buyers who had made four or five purchases were given priority over two- or three-time buyers or those who had only one purchase. Multibuyers who had purchased in the last six months were given priority over those whose last purchase was seven to twelve months or thirteen to eighteen months ago. Finally, multibuyers who had spent the most (lifetime dollars spent or monetary level) were given priority over buyers with lower lifetime purchase levels. If you were developing a loyalty plan or frequent-buyer program, this lower-lifetime-purchase-level group would be the one to which it should be targeted.

This mailer tackled three problem segments with three different strategies. By studying the database, the cataloger decided to target buyers whose initial purchase was less than $25 but who made second and perhaps third purchases in that range. In order to stimulate a $50 average order value from this group, the cataloger made a special offer—50 percent off shipping and handling for any order over $50—and placed it on a cover dot whack for drop #1 and drop #3, and printed a personalized letter on the cover for drop #2.

Buyers whose initial purchase was $26 to $50 and who continued to make low second and later purchases were offered free shipping and handling on any order over $75, to increase their average order value to $75. The offer was included in a cover dot whack for drop #1 and drop #3 and in a personalized letter on the cover for drop #2.

Buyers who had not purchased in more than eighteen months were aged by six-month segment (eighteen to twenty-four months, twenty-five to thirty months, thirty-one to thirty-six months, etc.) and segmented by one-time and two-or-more-time purchasers. They were offered free shipping and handling with any order over $50, to reactivate them as active buyers with a minimum $50 AOV. Like the other two messages, this one was included on a cover dot whack for drop #1 and drop #3 and in a personalized letter on the cover for drop #2. Different wording was used each time, beginning with the low-key "We Miss You" and graduating by the third mailing to the message, "Last Chance."

This cataloger also designed a strategy to solicit first orders with an average order value of $50 or more from catalog requesters. Their copies of the catalog included a cover dot whack on all three drops that said, "Try us and we'll give you 50% off shipping and handling with your first order of $50 or more." The message was also communicated on a catalog wrap.

Integrated Mailing Scheme

Customer Segment	Drop One	Drop Two	Drop Three	Drop Four
Best Customers	**Cover One** Customer Image Renewal Letter 1	**Cover Two** Product Renewal Letter 3	**Cover Three** Christmas Scene	**Cover Four** There's Still Time Letter on Product Background
$0–25	**D-1** Dot whack on **Cover 1** with 50% Shipping–$50+	**Cover 4-a** 50% Shipping $50+ Letter on Product Background	**D-6** (same as D-1; new color) Dot whack on **Cover 3** with 50% Shipping–$50+	
$26–$50	**D-2** Dot whack on **Cover 1** with Free Shipping–$75+	**Cover 4-b** Free Shipping $75+ Letter on Product Background	**D-7** (same as D-2; new color) Dot whack on **Cover 3** with Free Shipping–$75+	
Reactivation	**D-3** "We Miss You" Dot whack on **Cover 1** with Free Shipping–$50+ ('94–'95; $50+ buyers)	**Cover 4-c** We Miss You Free Shipping $50+ Letter on Product Background ('94–'95; $0+ buyers)	**D-8** Add "Last Chance" Wrap to **Cover 3** with Free Shipping–$50+ ('94–'95; $0+ buyers)	
Prospects/ Requesters	**D-4** "Try Us" Dot whack on **Cover 1** with 50% Shipping–$50+	**D-10** (same as D-4; new color) "Try Us" Dot whack on **Cover 2** with 50% Shipping–$50+	**D-9** (same as D-4; new color) "Try Us" Dot whack on **Cover 2** with 50% Shipping–$50+	

EXHIBIT 10.4

First-time buyers should always be identified and treated like a separate group in a mail plan. Although it is not shown in the exhibit, this cataloger offered $10 off a second purchase over $50 (an offer good for thirty to sixty days) as an incentive. A $10 certificate was included in the shipment, along with a questionnaire on how the company handled the first order. Ten days later, the company followed up with a phone call to make sure everything had been received and to say thank you for the order.

This mailing scheme is applicable to every catalog, be it business, consumer, retail, or hybrid. The goal in planning circulation should be twofold: to build stronger communication with your best customers, and to identify and address problem segments in your house file. By promoting your best customers more often and more personally, you are building on the 80/20 rule, expanding revenues and profits from the most profitable 20 percent of the house list. By communicating with names in your problem segments, you are attempting to move the 80 percent into the 20 percent category and improve the future revenue and profit stream.

Catalogers should keep several caveats in mind when designing an integrated mailing plan. First, this scheme must be managed and carefully coordinated with your printer and/or mailing house. Source codes, dot whacks, cover changes, and drop timing like those shown must be precise and totally understood and monitored, or Murphy's Law (if something can go wrong, it will) can take over. Second, offers must be tested; don't automatically assume they will work for your catalog. Test every offer against no offer to prove that it is paying for the additional cost. Test dot whacks, catalog wraparounds, personalization, and cover changes to ensure that you are getting the gain you need to pay for the additional message.

Make certain that your test groups aren't so small that results are impossible to read from a statistical standpoint. If your total buyer list is 15,000 or 20,000, keep it simple; don't overcomplicate your mailing plan. A simple RFM can take you quite a way in identifying the customer segments that can be profitably promoted.

Tracking results is critical to measuring performance. If your catalog is not at the 90+ percent tracking level, fix this problem first. Get some professional help in looking at your database and starting the process of analyzing your best, average, and problem segments.

❖ KEY POINTS

- Concentrate special communications on new, first-time buyers. Reach them quickly, perhaps even by phone, and remail them as soon as possible. Create a catalog edition for new buyers. Work hard to get your new buyers to make a second purchase.
- Build a reactivation plan and strategy for buyers who have gone twelve months or more without a purchase. Special messages to coax good customers back to the fold really work. In most cases, it is far more productive and cost effective to reactivate an older buyer than to get a new customer.

- Explore ways to keep your best customers coming back. A customer loyalty program can help. Remember, customer loyalty is not bought. It is earned every time you have a transaction or communication with a customer.
- Seek to integrate your catalog campaigns rather than allowing creative, merchandising, circulation, and database functions to work independently. The integrated approach focuses intently on the customer list and improves sales and response.

CHAPTER 11

Fulfillment and Customer Service

About ten years ago, Anheuser Busch asked me to conduct a creative critique of its collectible catalog. The company wanted to know whether the catalog design and layout were maximizing revenues. As I assessed the catalog's graphics, photography, use of color, eye-flow techniques, and use of hot spots, one element jumped out at me: "Allow 4 to 6 Weeks For Delivery" was prominently printed on the back cover and order form.

In the early 1990s, the standard order turnaround in the industry was five to seven days. Telling prospective buyers on the back cover and the order form that orders would take much longer than usual to reach them was tantamount to telling them Anheuser Busch didn't care about customer service! The company had no desire to damage its considerable brand and image. It quickly upgraded its fulfillment process to meet prevailing standards.

In the 1960s and 1970s, only a handful of catalogers paid fulfillment and customer service much attention, focusing on marketing instead. The fulfillment era began in the 1980s. No longer was good fulfillment "nice to have." Suddenly, it was a significant competitive advantage that distinguished winning catalogs from the also-rans. Fulfillment could no longer be given short shrift.

Today, quality fulfillment and customer service, along with outstanding creative execution and superior merchandising, constitute the "brand tripod" on which a brand is built and strengthened. A catalog company's fulfillment is judged by standards set by catalog leaders such as Lands' End and Williams-Sonoma on the consumer side and Quill, Viking, and Dell on the business side. Same-day service is becoming a reality. Smaller catalogs and start-ups must understand that quality customer service and fulfillment is not an option if they want to stay in business. It is a core competency, a "must-have" skill. In the next decade, fulfillment will continue to differentiate the winners from those catalogs that are struggling to attain the profitability they expect.

Why Fulfillment Is Important

Fulfillment matters for five reasons:

1. **Superior fulfillment can set your catalog apart from the competition.** If you are looking for ways to differentiate your company from others, start with fulfillment.
2. **Cost-efficient fulfillment has a major impact on profitability.** While a smaller cost center than cost of goods or catalog production and printing, fulfillment is nonetheless a variable cost that must be controlled and managed. Small and medium-size catalogers are especially prone to the lack of cost control.
3. **Quality fulfillment helps prevent repeat customer inquiries, complaints, and calls from the better business bureau.** Good fulfillment does it right the first time. Eliminating mistakes in order entry; pick, pack, and ship; and back orders will prevent customer service tangles later.
4. **Fast fulfillment increases the chance of a reorder and reduces returns.** In the food-by-mail business, the faster the order can be shipped, the greater the likelihood of a second order in the all-important holiday gift-giving season. If your catalog's returns are higher than you might expect, look at fulfillment turnaround time.
5. **Outstanding fulfillment and customer service are major building blocks of a catalog's brand.** Your catalog can have terrific, well-priced products and the best creative presentation, but if your attitude toward customers is indifferent or poor, you will not be able to build strong brand identity and brand equity. Remember, quality fulfillment is one of the three elements of a strong brand, as important as good merchandising and strong creative.

Understanding the Fulfillment Process

Understanding the fulfillment process outlined in Exhibit 11.1 will equip you to judge the quality of your fulfillment and customer service operation.

Orders and Inquiries

The fulfillment process begins when an order, an inquiry about an order, or a catalog request is received by the company or its outsourced telemarketing or fulfillment service contractor. Phone orders are normally keyed directly into the catalog's order management system, while mail and fax orders are typically batched in groups of twenty-five or fifty and then keyed into the system. Internet orders are downloaded electronically into the catalog's order management system.

Phone order or inquiry information is verified for completeness and correctness. Name, mailing address, shipping address, phone number, credit card information, item

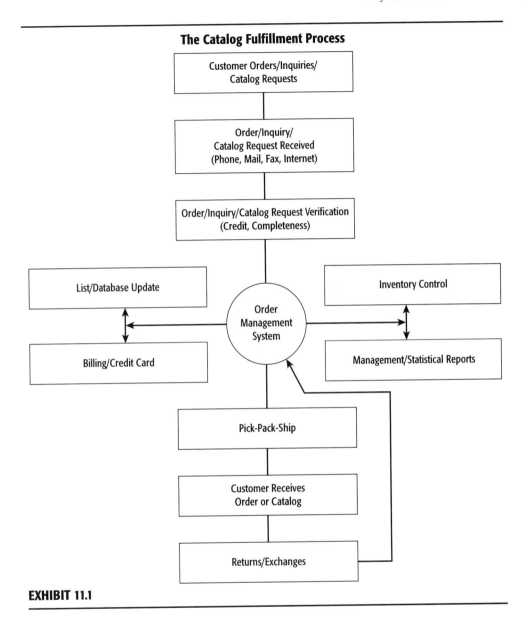

The Catalog Fulfillment Process

EXHIBIT 11.1

number, color, and size information are checked. This information must be input correctly for the order to ship properly and for the customer file to be complete.

Mail and fax orders are keyed into the operating system. This work is often done in downtime by phone operators or other clerical employees. Internet orders typically undergo an electronic pre-edit process during which specific information is automatically verified.

Taken together, this order management system is the "nerve center" of the catalog's operations, and from the system, five distinct functions evolve.

Pick, Pack, and Shipping of Orders

After an order is placed, the computer generates a pick ticket for the warehouse staff to use in preparing the order for shipment. At each stage of the pick and pack process, the order is checked for completeness. Most orders are shipped via United Parcel Service (UPS) or the United States Postal Service (USPS), with expedited shipments (overnight or second-day) using these carriers and others. When the customers receive the order, three things can occur:

- The customer keeps the product.
- The customer calls customer service with a question about the product.
- The customer returns part or all of the shipment, and the return is processed by the warehousing function and reentered into the system for credit or refund to the customer.

Credit Card, Billing, and Banking

Credit cards are processed electronically using a third-party clearinghouse or local bank. Authorizations are submitted prior to shipment, and deposits are made upon shipment confirmation. Credit card costs (discount rate) range from 1.5 percent to 3 percent, depending on the credit card and the nature of the transaction. To keep costs down, select a national third-party clearinghouse to provide this off-line function. Turn to your local bank, and you'll pay much more.

Business catalogs and some consumer catalogs will invoice customers when prior credit has been established. Orders paid by check or money order are reconciled by the order-entry function and deposited in the bank. Very large orders paid by check—$150 or more—should be held until the check clears the bank.

List/Database Update

When the order is entered, updated product purchase history is added to the customer record. Most systems will maintain RFM (recency or date of last purchase, frequency or number of lifetime purchases, and monetary or lifetime dollar purchases) as well as P (product category and item purchased) for each customer. This information is updated continuously and forms the basis of future RFMP segmentation of the customer list. For new customers, the original source code is captured at this time; for previous buyers, the code indicating which catalog they are ordering from is also captured. This information must be captured accurately for the database to be used for future customer communications.

Inventory Control

Inventory control, discussed in Chapter 3, is also a fulfillment function. After merchandise is received in the warehouse and quality and quantity are checked, receiving information is entered into the computer, which deducts orders from inventory as products are shipped. Most fulfillment operating systems have an on-line, real-time stock status report showing items on hand, on order, and ready to ship. Some catalog systems also have an inventory forecasting capability that compares orders received against an anticipated response curve and projects total demand by item for the catalog.

Statistical or Management Reports

The catalog management system produces all the reports that management needs to run the business. Besides basic inventory reports, the system should produce a square-inch or space analysis report on merchandise sold. Media or source frequency reports are used by marketing to determine which customer and prospect lists are producing what level of order response and average order values. Fulfillment numbers and ratio reports tell management how the operations people are doing in handling orders. Accounting and sales reports are available for the catalog's financial function. Every type of report needed by the catalog's staff to manage the business should be available from the operating system.

Fulfillment Options for New Catalogs

There are four ways a new or growing catalog can handle fulfillment.

1. **Contract with a full-service outside fulfillment provider or contractor.** A popular choice among new or emerging catalogs, hiring a full-service provider offers many advantages. Relying on an experienced fulfillment contractor to provide fulfillment systems, management reports, telephone operations, and equipment frees a start-up catalog to focus on merchandising and marketing, key factors in growing the company. Outsourcing fulfillment also means that capital need not be invested in a building, fulfillment racks, conveyor systems, a computer, and so forth, because the fulfillment provider pays for and amortizes the cost over a number of clients.

   Operating costs are primarily variable; the fulfillment company will charge per call, per order, or per item handled. The company will charge one fee for a catalog request and another fee for an order, with one price for the initial item and a price for all subsequent items. Paying per order is the best way to control costs.

   There are disadvantages to consider as well. For one thing, a limited number of qualified vendors are available. Many companies can fulfill literature or one-of-a-kind solo products, but few vendors have the total call center, warehouse, systems, and trained staff to be considered for a multiple-product catalog. If you are new, it may be difficult to persuade one of the qualified vendors to work with you, because many avoid new catalog start-ups like the plague. They know that new ventures typically are underfinanced, have small volumes, and may not be around in three years. They are reluctant to invest the effort in setting up the computer system and the warehouse operation for a venture that might fold. You may be forced to work with a second-tier fulfillment contractor whose practices and systems do not include the type of database, accounting, inventory, marketing, and financial reporting that a catalog needs. An alternative is to partner with an existing catalog whose fulfillment system you can tie into.

Giving operational control of fulfillment to an outsider is always risky. The company may not adequately control costs, causing the real cost of fulfillment to exceed acceptable industry standards.

2. **Build an in-house fulfillment function.** In the long run, most catalogers want to own and control their fulfillment functions. Service will probably be better when management controls this operation. Your own people will know your products and can cross-sell, up-sell, and solve problems better. Call center, warehousing, pick and pack, and computer systems can be tailored to meet the specific requirements of the catalog. Profits will increase, too. Outside fulfillment vendors are in business to make money. Owning your own facility directs the markup or profit paid to vendors to your bottom line, not theirs.

But investing in a complete fulfillment operation is expensive. There are major capital expenditures in constructing a building and purchasing telephone equipment, computers, operating systems, racking, conveyor systems, shipping systems, and so forth. Also, it may take nine to twelve months to design and build a fully-integrated fulfillment function. Then you must hire and train call center and warehouse staff, investigate and select telephone systems, think about packing materials—all issues that direct management attention away from the merchandising, marketing, and financial aspects of the business.

3. **Employ an outside call center to take and process orders, and handle the back-end portion of the business inside.** Many new business-to-business catalogers opt for this option because they already have a warehousing and shipping capability. Even if the system is set up for volume orders, it can be adapted to the "onesies and twosies" of a catalog operation.

4. **Handle the front end of fulfillment (order taking, call center, and systems), and outsource the back-end function of warehousing and shipping.** Many catalogers feel that the most sensitive aspect of customer contact comes when the buyers call on the phone. Strong telemarketing and customer service people can build confidence, support up-selling and cross-selling, answer customer queries, provide technical support, and solve problems. The more complex and technical your product, the more this option makes sense. If your company already has a strong telephone operation, this may be the course for you.

Fulfillment Operating Costs

	In-House Operation	Employ Full-Service Contractor
Sales per Order	$52.43	$52.43
Cost per Order		
Direct Labor (including benefits)		
Order Processing	$1.40	$4.50*
Distribution	$1.60	$2.50*
Total Direct Labor	$3.00	$7.00*
Shipping	($2.39)	($2.39)
Data Processing	$1.00	**
Telephone	$0.60	$0.60
Banking	$1.44	$1.44
Supplies & Other Miscellaneous Costs	$1.00	$0.75
Fixed Costs	$1.50	$0.50
Total Operating Costs	$6.15	$7.90
% of Sales	12%	15%

*Processing Fees
**Included in Processing Fees

EXHIBIT 11.2

Fulfillment Operating Costs

Exhibit 11.2 compares the costs of operating an in-house fulfillment operation and out-sourcing the total fulfillment function to a full-service provider. These estimates indicate what a medium-size or large catalog company might expect to pay; fulfillment costs for start-up and smaller catalogs will be considerably higher because they must invest in new facilities or pay setup charges to the fulfillment provider.

Fulfillment is charged as a percent of sales. This example showing 12 percent to 15 percent of net sales (after deducting shipping and handling income from the customer) is where catalogs (at maturity) typically need to be to generate a reasonable EBIT (earnings before interest and taxes), or pretax profit.

Measuring Your Performance Against Industry Fulfillment Standards

A good catalog always compares its performance with industry benchmarks in order to detect and correct fulfillment problems. According to fulfillment consultant Bill Spaide, a former partner of Stanley Fenvessy, author of the definitive book on this subject, *Fenvessy on Fulfillment*, the following are the fulfillment standards that catalogers should expect to meet today, whether they outsource fulfillment or handle it in-house.

Turnaround Time

It should take twenty-four hours or less to respond to customer service mail or E-mail, ship an order, or process a return. "In today/out tomorrow" is the standard and should be your goal.

Call Center Service

Phone orders represent the bulk of today's orders. It is essential to have well-trained, accommodating, capable people on the phone. Gruff, surly, or incompetent phone operators tell customers that your company doesn't value them.

In a world of answering machines and voice mail, people expect phones to be picked up promptly. Eighty percent of all calls should be answered within twenty seconds. Letting the phone ring ten or even fifteen times before picking up a call hardly welcomes a customer! Busy signals are even worse. No more than 2 or 3 percent of calls should be "abandoned" by customers who are put on hold during busy hours. The customer may call back—or the order may be lost forever. Staff your call center to handle high volumes of calls during peak order seasons and hours.

Accuracy is an important quality of call center service. Call center staff need to accurately enter order information such as color, size, item number, and credit card number. No worse than a 1 percent error rate is acceptable.

While 10 to 15 percent of orders will require service inquiries or adjustments, no more than 2 percent should result in serious complaints. Ninety percent of customer service calls should be handled completely while the customer is on the line. Customers shouldn't have to make a second call to resolve a problem, or expect to be called back about one.

Some orders will be canceled. Track the ratio of cancellations to orders and cancellations to sales, to detect and correct problems. Cancellation rates vary by type of catalog; apparel cancellations, for example, are higher than gift cancellations. If the benchmark in your industry product segment is 5 percent but your company is experiencing 8 percent cancellations, you may have problems with vendor delivery, inventory management, or customer credit.

Order Fill Rate

Order fill rate measures the efficiency of your inventory management. *Initial fill rate* indicates how many orders can be filled from the first inventory order before triggering a reorder or a backorder situation. Apparel catalogs should be able to fill 80 to 85 percent of initial orders; hard goods catalogs should be able to fill 95 to 98 percent. The difference between apparel and hard goods reflects the greater number of SKUs in color and size in apparel and the difficulty in managing apparel inventory.

The *final fill rate* tells how many orders were filled at the very end of a catalog cycle after all orders are in and all inventory purchases have been made. Apparel catalogs should strive for a final fill rate of 95 to 98 percent of all orders; hard goods catalogs should be able to fill 99+ percent of all orders.

Net Return Rate

While product returns are a cost of doing business, they need to be maintained at a reasonable level. Track the ratio of your returns to orders and returns to sales, to make sure you are not exceeding the following industry standards for returns:

Apparel:	15 to 30% of orders
Hard goods:	3 to 5% of orders
Gifts, general merchandise:	8 to 10% of orders
PC software and hardware:	5 to 10% of orders
Specialty products:	2% of orders
Business-to-business:	3 to 5% of orders

Returns must be processed promptly. Don't let them pile up! Customers should be able to expect the appropriate credit within a week. Accuracy is also an issue; processing a return with a wrong item number or wrong account number will lengthen the cycle and create more problems.

Operating Performance

An efficient warehouse staff will ensure that orders are picked, packed, and shipped promptly. Hire extra workers during peak seasons to ensure that orders are turned around in a day—not three or four. Industrywide, about 85 percent of full-time employees have more than six months of service; during peak seasons, more than 50 percent of the workers in any catalog company will be temporary and part-time. Backlogs in fulfillment should never exceed one day.

Whether you use full-time or part-time employees, their "pick and pack" error rate should be less than 1 or 2 percent of all orders. Ensure quality control by designating separate crews of "pickers" who fill orders and "packers" who pack orders. Packers can check items against the pick ticket to make sure an order is accurate and complete.

How frequently inventory turns over depends upon how frequently you mail. A catalog that mails monthly will turn over inventory faster than one that mails quarterly. The industry standard for inventory turns is four to six times per year.

Operating Costs—Direct Labor

Inbound telemarketing:	$.40 to $.45 per minute
Order processing:	$1.25 to $1.50 per order
Distribution:	$1.25 to $1.50 per order

Total fulfillment operating costs should fall between 15 and 18 percent of net sales. To keep your costs in line, track both call center and fulfillment center labor costs as a percentage of sales.

"Do It Right the First Time"

Keep this popular industry adage in mind as you manage the fulfillment function. Mistakes at any point in the fulfillment process will trigger problems that take time and money to resolve. Make every step of the fulfillment operation as accurate as possible, and you can keep most orders out of the time-consuming customer service cycle of responding to problems, returning or exchanging products, adding products back to inventory, and adjusting customer accounts.

❖ Key Points

- Quality fulfillment enhances the company's brand; inferior fulfillment will weaken or destroy it. Fulfillment can also differentiate your catalog from the competition, control costs and improve profitability, reduce customer service calls and inquiries, and make repeat business more likely.
- Customers measure all catalog companies—even start-ups—by the service delivered by the top-performing catalogs. Design your system to meet those standards in your very first catalog, and benchmark your service by constantly comparing your costs and performance with that of mature catalogers.
- Fulfillment may be outsourced, but keep in mind that only a handful of full-service catalog fulfillment providers have all the operating systems in place.
- Fulfillment is the Achilles' heel for many of today's Internet marketers. As Internet sales grow, product fulfillment will increase in importance. Catalogers with smooth fulfillment operations stand to benefit from this trend.

CHAPTER 12

Testing

Oh, how catalog marketers long for the solo mailing environment where testing is easy. Solo testing is really a "piece of cake" because only one element at a time is tested: product, size or format, price point, envelope, copy theme or platform, offers, brochure layout and size, or timing of mail drops. Catalog testing is much more complicated. In fact, I think that catalogs are by far the most difficult of all direct mail formats in which to test.

Three questions must be addressed when catalogers think about testing:

- What can you test, and how do you measure results?
- When is the optimum time to test?
- How do you plan and organize a test?

These topics, along with a look at common mistakes of catalog testing, are the gist of this chapter. More information about testing merchandise can be found in Chapter 2; about offer testing in Chapter 4; and about list testing in Chapter 8.

Five Stages of Catalog Testing

Five distinct stages in catalog testing are particularly applicable to new ventures: research, pretesting, in-the-mail testing, postanalysis, and retesting. Let's look at them one at a time.

Stage One: Research

Before launching a catalog, a company needs to understand everything it can about the target audience(s), the general catalog marketplace, the particular product line market, and the competition. For a new venture to succeed, management needs to know every aspect of the companies with whom the catalog will compete and every possible habit, attitude, and buying behavior of the customer. This research, which takes place more often in libraries than in the field, is often part of a feasibility study or a new business planning effort. The greater the effort at this stage, the better prepared a new catalog will be to proceed to the next two steps.

Stage Two: Pretesting

By now, the catalog concept is starting to take shape. The product line and particular items have been identified, and some initial creative concepts have been developed. The merchandise and creative concept are presented to target customer groups, often through focus groups of eight to ten people, led by an experienced moderator, that give feedback on various catalog merchandise and creative concepts. Another technique often used is mall intercepts, or one-on-one interviews with people who qualify as the target audience. Both types of research help catalogers gauge prospective customers' overall receptivity to the catalog concept, and fine-tune product categories, pricing, offers, format, size and number of pages, covers, page or spread layouts, and copy style.

Stage Three: In-the-Mail Testing

Stage two gives the cataloger sufficient information to complete the product sourcing and selection and the creative effort. The circulation plan is complete and the mailing planned. Now is the moment of truth. It is one thing for customers to react to concepts; it's another to find out whether they will buy your product. In-the-mail tests will tell you.

In most cases, in-the-mail testing means mailing a completed catalog, with results applied to subsequent editions. In-the-mail testing quantifies which lists and other media are best for the catalog, when and how often to mail, which offers are most appealing to your target audience, and which products are winners.

Stage Four: Postanalysis

The catalog has now been out ten or twelve weeks. Customers have reacted, and you can start to get a feel for how the catalog has done. This postanalysis stage asks four main questions:

- How did the catalog's lists perform?
- What merchandise sold?
- Which offers increased response and average order value?
- What months performed best?

In effect, the catalog is asking what happened and why. "Why" is the most difficult question to answer. Some catalogs will do mail or telephone surveys to get customers' reaction at this point. Others will survey nonrespondents and attempt to find out why prospects didn't buy from the catalog. Conclusions are drawn so that they can be applied to the next stage of testing.

Stage Five: Retesting

By stage five, merchandise, list, and offer results have been analyzed, and a new catalog has been created. You should start to get smarter during the second mailing by building on the winning products, price points, and creative techniques and remailing the lists that produced the best results. Retesting is reaffirming what the first in-the-mail test has shown you and improving on that information.

Every catalog mailing should test something, and after every mailing, the results should be studied closely. Merchandise catalogs with distinct seasons may have to wait a season to apply the results as they learn which products sell better in spring or fall. Even catalogs with stable product lines have something to learn. They may not change products, but they may discover how to repaginate or reallocate space for better results.

What Do Catalogers Test and How Do They Measure Results?

Catalogers need to plan and prioritize their testing to obtain the greatest return on their investment. Don't waste time on minutiae that reveal only nice-to-know answers that won't make any difference in your business. Set priorities, and test important things first.

Merchandise is the most important area to test, because it is fundamental to the long-range health of a catalog. Every catalog needs to devote catalog space to testing new merchandise. While it's nearly impossible to accomplish true A/B testing of new items as in a solo mailing format, the square-inch analysis presented in Chapter 2 will help pinpoint each product's contribution to profit. Allocation of space for new items is normally based on historical results of similar items in a category and price point. The tricky part is accurately reading the sales results of tests and determining whether to expand, contract, or just continue the item.

There are several ways to measure merchandise tests. Product performance may be measured on units sold and sales produced, units sold per thousand catalogs mailed, or financial contribution based on amount of advertising space allocated to the product (square-inch or space analysis).

Lists are the second most important variable to test. Response can differ significantly from rental list to rental list; variances of 200 percent and 300 percent are not uncommon. All house lists (buyers, inquiries, gift recipients, etc.) need to be included in list testing, covered in greater detail in Chapter 8. It is unlikely that a cataloger will mail all of its house names every season, making continual segment testing of the house list a must.

List testing is complex. With outside lists, the tighter the selection, the better. For example, don't just test mail-order buyers, but test last-three-month or last-six-month hot-line buyers, with a gender and dollar select applicable to your catalog. If the tightest select doesn't work in your prime season, then you can scratch the list with a clear conscience, knowing that you've given it the best shot.

List results may be measured by:

- Sales per catalog mailed compared with other outside lists or house lists
- Sales per catalog mailed compared with breakeven (with different goals for prospecting versus house-owned names)
- Cost to obtain a buyer
- Value of a buyer measured over twenty-four or thirty-six months

Offers, the third most important test variable, are relatively easy to test. Using covers, cover wraps, dot whacks, and the order form, it is not difficult to test one offer against another or versus no offer. In my judgment, most catalogers underutilize offers and under-test offers and therefore are missing an opportunity to improve their mailing and financial results. The most important quantitative measurement of a test offer is whether it paid for itself, and whether it beat the control (often no offer). Another criterion is to compare response and average order value against breakeven.

Timing of mailings is another component to test. Experienced, mature catalogs that mail every month know their best months and seasons. New and growing catalogs that are attempting to expand their mailings and home in on the most important months to mail need to test timing. How early in the fall can your catalog be mailed: September? How about August? July? Testing timing of both prospect and customer lists can pay enormous dividends.

The most effective way to judge timing tests is to compare actual results with prime months. For example, by testing a list such as last-twelve-month multibuyers that is common to all mailings, you can compare the response to catalogs mailing in July, August, and September with response from the best month(s).

While catalog *format* is important, it is not often tested head-to-head against the control format. For example, if your catalog's control is digest size, it may pay to test a full-size format (i.e., 8⅜″ × 10⅞″). Williams-Sonoma and Peruvian Connection both switched from digest to full-size format after testing both. Measuring results is expensive but not difficult. Just measuring sales per catalog by split-mailing the new test format against the control isn't enough, however. The ideal is to mail a test format (e.g., a digest control catalog) against a new format (e.g., a full-size catalog), using both buyer and prospect lists. It is conceivable that one format will work better for prospecting while the other is better for the customer list or house list.

Catalog *covers, wraps, and dot whacks* are becoming more important factors to test. Dot whacks that send targeted messages to customers and prospect segments are inexpensive to apply and test. Cover changes are also easy to test and have produced gains of 30 percent and 40 percent, especially among mature catalogs that mail multiple books per year. Catalog wraps used in the reactivation process with special messages such as "We Miss You" or "Last Chance" also can produce major gains in sales per book. The new cover or wrap should be tested directly against the control cover, and results should be measured in sales per catalog and the value of the name obtained or reactivated by the test cover or wrap.

Pricing is one of the most difficult variables to test in cataloging. A meaningful test requires the production of two separate catalogs—a control and a test catalog with different prices or pricing schemes in each. I know of only one instance in which the entire black plate of the catalog was changed to test a single pricing scheme versus three-part discount pricing. The test was expensive, but the results were dramatic . . . showing nearly a 30 percent difference in sales per catalog.

Tests in catalog *design and layout* can produce major response differences. It would be great to test the number of products per page, a grid layout versus an asymmetrical or free-form layout, illustrations versus photography, or different styles of copy or type, but this level of testing is far too expensive. Most catalogs use focus group or other one-on-one research instead.

Testing design techniques requires complete production of two catalogs; results are measured by comparing sales per catalog. Results need to be significantly different in order to justify switching to a new design standard. Most catalogers test design changes a second time to confirm that the gain in sales is consistent.

Catalog *personalization* is relatively easy to test and can make big differences. New techniques in laser personalization for front and back covers can give your catalog a feeling of one-to-one communication. (See Exhibit 12.1 for an example.) Smaller ink-jet messages on the back cover, in my judgment, have been overused and get less customer attention. Results can be measured by comparing sales per catalog with special message versus no message. Test this technique on all list segments—buyers, nonbuyer house names, and outside prospect lists.

Order forms can be easily and inexpensively changed or modified for testing. Use them to test offers, special price or discount concepts, sale of close-out merchandise, and the like. Measuring results is a straightforward matter of comparing sales per catalog on each test segment.

When to Test

Every edition of a catalog should include some testing. Merchandise testing should be done continuously; testing and measuring results by item, product category, and amount of space used will consistently produce a stronger product line.

Test outside lists (prospecting) in the prime season, less often in slower seasons. Unless your catalog has no seasonality, don't prospect in the less productive season. Test the house list, especially older, inactive buyers and inquiries, throughout the year.

Offers and covers, wraps, and dot whacks should be tested in the appropriate season. In other words, offers or covers for the spring season need to be tested in the spring. You won't get an accurate reading if you test them in the fall or summer. Formats, prices, and major design changes should be tested when a catalog is new or when a serious repositioning is contemplated, although simpler, less costly formats may be used in the off-season to keep in touch with customers. The thirty-six-page holiday Garfield catalog, for

EXHIBIT 12.1
Catalog Personalization

example, is reduced to a sixteen-page book and mailed only to steady customers during other seasons. Personalization or order form testing can be ongoing and done as needed throughout the year.

How to Test

Testing is a quantitative discipline. To achieve the results that keep the catalog growing in sales and profits, the test must be properly set up in order to be statistically accurate and measurable, and the proper conclusions must be drawn from the results.

Tests for most catalog variables follow several common rules:

- Have a control to test against (usually your standard catalog).
- Ensure that each test segment is being mailed to the same universe—for example, last-twelve-month buyers who have purchased two or more times.
- Test only one variable at a time. Don't attempt to test an offer, a list segment, and timing simultaneously!
- Mail sufficient quantities for the test to ensure that you have statistical accuracy to read results.
- Follow the foregoing rules on when to test.
- Give each test a unique source code for tracking purposes, and stress with your telephone staff how critical source code capture is to the business.

Exhibit 12.2 shows two test grids (simple and complex) to illustrate these points.

Common Testing Mistakes

Testing is the lifeblood of a catalog—but there are hazards that you should do everything you can to avoid.

Mistake #1: Not Testing at All

Testing catalogs is tough, and some catalogers would just as soon skip it. Each catalog mailing is like producing a new control. Every catalog contains merchandise, copy, and photographs that are new as well as some that have been picked up from previous editions; covers and page or spread layouts are almost always new.

Nevertheless, your catalog has a control format along with size, shape, number of pages, copy style, and lists that consistently work. Within that scope, every opportunity to improve your performance through testing can improve the bottom line. Success at the bank is the most important criterion for your catalog. Don't give up on testing. Think of ways to improve your catalog through testing with each issue.

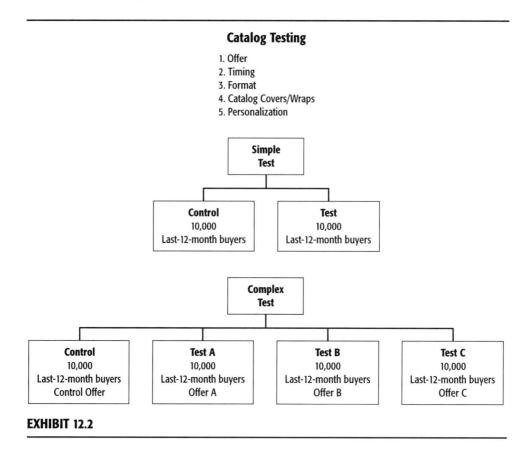

Catalog Testing

1. Offer
2. Timing
3. Format
4. Catalog Covers/Wraps
5. Personalization

EXHIBIT 12.2

Mistake #2: Not Testing Different Media to Build the Customer List

Don't confine your testing to rental lists only. As response declines, mailers need to examine and test alternative strategies to build their customer lists. Test new sources of names, especially those that share postage costs or don't require them. Chapter 8 lists a number of alternative media that can generate inquiries or orders.

Mistake #3: Testing Quantities That Are Too Small

I have a simple rule of thumb for determining test quantities called the "rule of 100." For each test cell or segment, you should have a minimum of 100 responses for any level of statistical reliability and validity. If you expect a 2 percent response, you need to test 5,000 names to get 100 responses to a cell. If you expect a 1 percent response, you need to test 10,000 names to get 100 responses. This is problematic for business mailers who traditionally get small responses like .3 percent; to end up with 100 responses, they would need to test 33,333 names per test cell! Many times, there aren't enough names available from either the house list or outside rented lists.

It makes no sense to build a circulation plan with test cells that can't be read. Watch your test cell sizes, and you will be happier with your results.

Mistake #4: Neglecting to Track Responses

If your catalog has trouble accurately tracking response, forget about testing until that problem is under control. Small and medium-size catalogs are often horrible in tracking results, even in the simplest list or offer mailings. If you are not capturing 95 percent of the responses and have a strong sense that your results are accurate, don't waste the time on establishing elaborate tests. Concentrate on getting those results right in the first place.

❖ KEY POINTS

- Testing should take place in every new edition of a catalog. Keep in mind the hierarchy of variables when you plan tests, and focus on variables that make the most difference to your bottom line.
- Consider the statistical implications of every test before conducting it. If in doubt, consult your statistics book or a consultant.
- Almost all catalogs make some mistakes in testing, but the cardinal sin is the inability to track source codes. No source codes means no reliable results!

CHAPTER 13

Financial Measurement

Cataloging is a very quantitative undertaking—a fact not widely understood by owners and managers of new catalog ventures, who often focus on merchandising without grasping the financial implications of their decisions. I believe everyone in a catalog company should have a reasonable understanding of the numbers, and at least one person should have strong financial and analytical expertise.

Some of the most successful catalog companies with which I've been associated made a concerted effort to brief nonstatistical or nonanalytical people on the fundamental tools that measure catalog success. Writers, art directors, and merchandisers don't have to prepare elaborate spreadsheets or circulation plans or develop a lifetime value chart for customers, but they do need to understand financial models, the profit and loss statement, and breakeven and how these elements guide management of a catalog's business.

The Financial Model

Every cataloger needs to create a financial model for its business. Although industry and product category models exist, no single financial model applies to all consumer or business catalogs. You will need to build your own around your catalog's unique cost of goods, returns, and cancellations.

Exhibit 13.1 presents consumer catalog financial models for three quite different industry examples: gift/hard goods, apparel, and electronics. These three models represent what a catalog would like to achieve as a minimum. They also represent mature catalog companies, not start-up or second-year operations. Let's look at the model category by category.

The most important figure in a financial model is the bottom line: pretax profit. In a mature catalog environment, the bottom-line goal of every consumer catalog should be

Consumer Financial Model

	Gift/Hard Goods	Apparel	Electronics
Gross Merchandise Sales	115%	135%	113%
Less returns	5–10%	15–25%	5–10%
Less cancellations	3–5%	5–10%	1–3%
Net Sales	100%	100%	100%
Less cost of goods	45–47%	50%	60%
Gross Margin	53–55%	50%	40%
Less fulfillment	12%	15%	10%
Less advertising	25%	17%	15%
Contribution to Overhead & Profit	16–18%	18%	15%
Less fixed costs (G&A)	8%	8%	5%
Pretax Profit	8–10%	10%	10%

EXHIBIT 13.1

10 percent pretax profit, or 10 percent EBIT (earnings before interest and taxes). New catalogs strive to meet this level or goal by the fifth year. Some take ten years, others three years; some mature catalogers never achieve it, some because their industry has lower margins and they can't achieve it, and others, especially privately held companies wishing to avoid taxes, will purposely try to minimize their profits. If a new catalog's financial projections don't come close to a 10 percent pretax profit, the cataloger needs to seriously question the venture's feasibility. Will a 5 percent pretax profit be enough to attract financial support from investors, or to justify the owner's investment?

Gross merchandise sales represents gross demand by customers for products offered in your catalog—in other words, total orders, whether they are filled or not. For gift/hard goods companies, gross demand is typically about 15 percent higher than net sales, or 115 percent. Sometimes shipping and handling income is included in gross sales; more often, as shown here, it is not included in gross sales but under gross margin as an offsetting cost against fulfillment.

Returns and cancellations are subtracted from gross sales. Returns represent product returned for credit or refund. Exchanges—customers exchanging one product for another—also cost money, but they are not considered a reduction of gross sales. Returns and exchanges occur throughout the catalog cycle. For the gift/hard goods model, returns will typically run 5 percent to 10 percent; in apparel, returns of 15 percent, 20 percent, or even 25 percent are not uncommon.

Cancellations come in two varieties: those related to payment, and those related to product availability. If customers give you bad checks or their credit cards are wrong, maxed out, or fraudulent, the sale cannot be completed. Neither can it be completed if product is not available because of a vendor delivery problem or because the order arrived at the end of the catalog cycle when forecast inventory is depleted. Orders can be canceled when items are on back order and customers elect not to wait. Cancellations vary by product category, with higher numbers in apparel than in gift/hard goods.

Net sales is what is left from gross demand after returns and cancellations are deducted. This is what you take to the bank! Final net sales cannot truly be read until all demand is complete and returns are in, usually about six months after the catalog drop. In all cases, net sales are the starting point (100 percent) from which all other costs are figured. In each of the financial models, net sales is 100 percent.

Cost of goods represents the total cost of product, freight to your warehouse (freight-in), plus any cost incurred for end-of-season product markdowns and remaindering. Cost of goods varies dramatically by type of company, ranging from 60 percent for consumer electronics to slightly under 50 percent for gift/hard goods. Because cost of goods is such a large cost factor in the entire financial model, it is a principal driver of catalog economic success.

The amount left after cost of goods is subtracted from net sales is ***gross margin***, another critical economic driver of success. Cataloging is a "margin-driven" business. Improve the margin by 1 percent, and that gain drops directly through to contribution to overhead and profit. Lose a single point in margin, and it directly affects bottom-line profitability.

Fulfillment is subtracted from gross margin. Fulfillment represents the total cost of receiving customers' orders, inquiries, and catalog requests, and shipping products to them. Order entry, the catalog operating system, warehousing, pick-pack-ship, handling returns, even credit card authorization and customer inquiries and complaints, are allocated to this cost center. Fulfillment also has an income side, because most catalogs credit shipping and handling revenue from customers to fulfillment. This allows the catalog to determine what it costs to fulfill an order, service a complaint, or ship a catalog to a requester. For mature catalogs, the net cost of fulfillment must be managed in the 10 percent to 15 percent range. Controlling this cost will always be a battle for younger catalogs, whether they outsource fulfillment or handle it in-house.

Advertising, which includes list rentals, prospecting, creative costs, even printing and binding, represents a huge percentage of catalog costs. For new ventures and catalogs in their formative years, it is even more important because so much of the advertising is being allocated to new customer acquisition and building the buyer list.

The leverage of advertising is threefold. Fixed costs of creating the catalog and developing color separations are enormous for catalogers mailing only a few hundred thousand catalogs. For example, if a catalog's fixed cost is $50,000 and only 200,000 of the test catalog are being mailed, fixed costs represent $250 per thousand, or 25¢ per catalog mailed. If the same catalog with the same $50,000 fixed cost is mailed to 1 million names, fixed costs drop to $50 per thousand, or only 5¢ per catalog.

The second element of leverage is the percent response. The higher the response, the lower advertising is as a percent of sales. Two examples illustrate this point. Imagine one cataloger, primarily in the prospecting mode, that mails 90 percent of its catalogs to rental names. Its variable printing, mailing, and postage costs are $600 per thousand, or 60¢ per piece to mail 500,000 catalogs, for a total of $300,000. It pulls 1 percent, with a $100 average order value (AOV), or 5,000 orders and $500,000 in revenues, making advertising 60 percent of sales.

Now imagine a second consumer cataloger that mails 60 percent of its catalogs to buyers. It has the same variable printing, mailing, and postage cost of $600 per thousand, which means 60¢ per piece to mail 500,000 catalogs, or $300,000. It pulls 3 percent, with a $100 average order value (AOV), or 15,000 orders and $1,500,000 in revenues. Here, advertising is 20 percent of sales.

The third way that advertising has leverage concerns printing economies. The greater the number of catalogs mailed, the lower the unit cost. Catalogs with smaller quantities mailed will always fight the higher per-piece cost in the mail. In contrast, the larger, more mature catalogs have better bargaining power and more leverage to reduce the cost in the mail because of their higher volumes.

Advertising is expensive for new or growing catalogs that mail smaller quantities. Remember, the model in Exhibit 13.1 represents a mature catalog that is mailing to a higher percentage of house and buyer names and therefore is able to drive its cost, as a percent of sales, to 25 percent or lower.

What is left from gross margin after subtracting fulfillment and advertising is called ***contribution to overhead and profit***. This is a key economic benchmark against which the catalog and its marketing managers and merchandising people are measured. After all, marketers and merchants have little influence and impact on the fixed costs or general and administrative costs of the catalog company, but they can impact all the results above this line. Since most mature catalogers like to limit their fixed costs (also called ***overhead***, or ***general*** and ***administrative costs***) to 6 percent to 8 percent, this line in the financial model is an important control point. With an overall goal of a 10 percent pretax profit, this contribution line in the model must be achieved, or the pretax goal will never be realized.

List rental income is normally reported at the bottom of the financial model after contribution to overhead and profit.

Pretax profit is the starting point (as a goal) and the ending point (after all expenses are deducted from revenue). As noted, this line is sometimes referred to as ***EBIT***, or earnings before interest and taxes. Every company's tax situation is different, so this is typically the line for which a catalog's general management is held accountable.

The business-to-business catalog financial model in Exhibit 13.2 follows the same format as the consumer financial model but reveals some significant differences. Returns and cancellations on business catalogs are lower than on consumer catalogs, and the cost of goods will have wider swings, depending on whether the business is a wholesaler, a distributor, or an end seller. Some companies will have large margins; those selling computer equipment and accessories may have 10 percent or even 5 percent margins.

How to Use the Financial Model

Financial modeling provides new and growing catalogers with economic benchmarks and goals for which to strive.

Business-to-Business Financial Model

	Business Gifts	Work Apparel	Computer/ Electronics
Gross Merchandise Sales	110%	115%	113%
Less returns	3–5%	5–10%	5–10%
Less cancellations	3–5%	3–5%	1–3%
Net Sales	100%	100%	100%
Less cost of goods	45–47%	50%	60%
Gross Margin	53–55%	50%	40%
Less fulfillment	12%	15%	10%
Less advertising	25%	17%	15%
Contribution to Overhead & Profit	16–18%	18%	15%
Less fixed costs (G&A)	8%	8%	5%
Pretax Profit	8–10%	10%	10%

EXHIBIT 13.2

To start your year-to-year financial model, pull out your five-year profit and loss projections. If you have done adequate financial planning for your catalog, you have conservative, optimistic, and midrange or most likely scenarios. Use your financial projections to define where you think your catalog will be in a mature environment and build a simple year-by-year financial model for years one, two, and three. Determine the gap between year three and maturity. If projections indicate that your catalog will fall short of its goal, you may need to make adjustments.

Financial models can also tell you something about the competition. Research and construct an estimated financial model for each public company in your product category sector. Compare it with your three-year and mature models, and identify where there are major variances. If a competitor's cost of goods or advertising is ten points lower than yours, find out why!

Update your financial model annually, and use it to assign goals to those responsible for controlling costs and meeting sales and marketing projections. If your five-year goal is to decrease the cost of goods half a percent every year, make the merchandising department responsible for the achievement. Likewise, the advertising and marketing team can be charged with annual cost-cutting goals.

The Profit and Loss Statement

The profit and loss statement (P&L), sometimes called an *income statement*, can be used to measure results of a specific catalog promotional campaign or a month, a quarter, or a year. The format is similar to the financial model, except the P&L goes into much greater depth, as you can see from Exhibit 13.3. Use it to identify where changes and improvements need to be made.

Promotion Campaign–Profit and Loss Statement

Category	Plan	% of Net Sales	vs.	Actual	% of Net Sales
Gross Sales	$2,097,472	114.0%			
Returns	$ 147,139	8.0%			
Cancellations	$ 26,856	1.5%			
Net Sales	**$1,837,191**	**100.0%**			
Cost of Merchandise	$ 734,876	40.0%			
Freight In	$ 38,393	2.1%			
Markdowns/Excess	$ 56,421	3.1%			
Shrinkage	$ 9,865	0.5%			
(Co-Op Advertising)	$ (55,938)	−3.0%			
(Cash Discounts)	$ (30,143)	−1.6%			
Cost of Goods	$ 753,474	41.0%			
Gross Margin	**$1,083,717**	**59.0%**			
Call Center Fees	$ 50,876	2.8%			
Order Receipt & Order Entry	$ 71,463	3.9%			
Systems/Computer Processing	$ 88,269	4.8%			
Warehousing	$ 55,287	3.0%			
Pick, Pack, & Ship	$ 79,157	4.3%			
Credit Card Fees	$ 32,151	1.8%			
(Shipping & Handling Income)	$(139,909)	−7.6%			
Fulfillment	$ 237,294	12.9%			
Catalog Creative (fixed)	$ 123,328	6.7%			
Color Separations (fixed)	$ 63,107	3.4%			
Printing–Catalog & Order Form	$ 188,123	10.2%			
Lists & List Processing	$ 9,812	0.5%			
Binding, Addressing, & Mailing	$ 16,894	0.9%			
Postage	$ 145,963	7.9%			
Other Fixed Costs	$ 39,845	2.2%			
Advertising	$ 587,072	32.0%			
Contribution to Overhead & Profit	**$ 259,351**	**14.1%**			
General Management	$ 35,619	1.9%			
Building, Maintenance, & Utilities	$ 67,765	3.7%			
Capital Charges	$ 5,535	0.3%			
Divisional or Company Allocation	$ 16,618	0.9%			
Outside Services (consultants)	$ 29,500	1.6%			
Overhead, or General & Administrative	$ 155,037	8.4%			
Pretax Profit (EBIT)	**$ 104,314**	**5.7%**			

EXHIBIT 13.3

The P&L is most often used to plan a particular catalog campaign. The left-hand side of the format is the plan, showing as much detail as possible. The right-hand side includes space where the actual results can be added at the end of the mailing cycle.

Like the financial model, the P&L shows gross sales (excluding shipping and handling income), returns and cancellations, net sales (excluding shipping and handling income), and gross margin. The cost of goods is shown in much greater detail including cost of merchandise, freight-in cost, markdowns taken, and shrinkage in the warehouse due to theft or damage. The cost of goods is offset by credits for co-op advertising and freight allowances from vendors and discounts for early bill payments to vendors. (Some vendors claim that they never give allowances but will negotiate a more preferred price. Two sides of the same coin.)

The P&L statement breaks out specific fulfillment costs and offsets those costs with shipping and handling income charged to and paid for by the customer. Advertising and overhead or administrative costs are also broken down in great detail. Overhead or general and administrative costs are typically not allocated to each promotional campaign, but assigned to the monthly, quarterly, or annual income statement.

As in the financial model, the contribution to overhead and profit is the benchmark against which each catalog mailing campaign is measured.

How to Use the Catalog Profit and Loss Statement

Smart catalogers build a plan for each mailing campaign that forecasts anticipated sales in units and dollars, list response, AOV and sales per catalog mailed, advertising costs (both fixed and variable), and fulfillment cost per order. All of these costs along with forecast returns and cancellations are plugged into a P&L format similar to the one shown. At the end of the catalog cycle, the actual sales and costs are entered into the P&L. Note and explain variations between the plan and actual results. The forecast of the first catalog will be little more than grasping at thin air, but by following this regimen, you will narrow the gap between plan and results with succeeding catalogs.

The Breakeven Analysis

Like a forecast, a breakeven analysis is performed *before* a promotional campaign. The breakeven really works a profit and loss statement backward by solving for two important variables: the percentage response needed for a mailing to break even, and the sales dollars per catalog mailed needed to break even. Sales per catalog mailed (sometimes expressed as sales per 1,000 catalogs mailed) is the critical measurement of a catalog's success. A breakeven can be used to measure the overall success of a campaign or to measure the performance of rental lists, Internet catalog requests, or various selections of the buyer list that may have been segmented by RFMP (recency, frequency, monetary, and product category).

Breakevens are typically performed at three different levels:

- Level one, the variable cost level, or 0 percent level, is used to judge prospects. Breakeven at this level covers all variable costs but not overhead and does not generate contribution to profit.
- Level two, the overhead or 7 percent to 10 percent level, is applicable to older-year customers and nonbuyer house names. Breakeven at this level covers all variable costs and overhead but generates no profit contribution. The numbers at this level correspond to your overhead costs; in other words, if your catalog's overhead is 8 percent of net sales, then you will calculate breakeven based on 8 percent.
- Level three, the fully loaded or 17 percent to 20 percent level (depending on overhead costs), assumes that the catalog is seeking a 10 percent pretax profit. Use this level to measure performance of the best catalog buyers—for example, last-twelve-month customers. This breakeven level covers all variable costs, overhead, and 10 percent pretax profit contribution.

The breakeven analysis chart in Exhibit 13.4 details the three different levels of breakeven and the calculation for solving for the variables of percent response and sales per catalog. Figures in all three columns are the same except for the calculation used to solve the breakeven at the three levels.

Examples A, B, and C assume an average unit price of $33.33 for products being sold in the catalog. The catalog is expecting 1.5 units per order, making the average order value $50.00 ($33.33 × 1.5 = $50.00). Cancellations are expected to be 1 percent, (1% × $50.00 = $.50), and returns are expected to be 10 percent, (10% × $50.00 = $5.00), producing net sales per order of $44.50 ($50.00 less $.50, less $5.00 = $44.50). The cost of goods is 50 percent, or $22.25 ($44.50 × 50% = $22.25); fulfillment is $12.00 per order, with fulfillment income (shipping and handling paid by the buyer) at $5.00 per order. Net fulfillment expense is $7.00 ($12.00 less $5.00), which results in a contribution (before promotion, overhead, and profit) of $15.25 at the 0 percent level ($44.50 less $22.25, less $7.00).

The in-mail cost per promotion piece is $.50, which represents the variable cost of printing, postage, binding, and mailing. Some companies will add fixed creative costs (layout, copy, photography, computer page production, and color separations) to this calculation.

The breakeven formula is cost per promotion (each piece in the mail) divided by the contribution. At 0 percent, or variable breakeven, that is $.50 divided by $15.25, which equals .0327868, or 3.3 percent, the percentage response needed to achieve variable breakeven. Sales per catalog is determined by multiplying the percent response times the net order sale (3.3% × $44.50 = $1.46 revenue or sales per catalog mailed). With these two figures, the catalog can judge the success of all mailings, especially new customer acquisition.

The other levels of breakeven are done in a similar manner. Contribution is arrived at by multiplying the net order sale by 10 percent or 20 percent and subtracting that figure from the 0 percent or Example A contribution. In Example B, the contribution is 10 percent: 10% × $44.50 = $4.45; subtracting $4.45 from the 0 percent contribution of $15.25

Breakeven Analysis by Order

	Example A 0% Breakeven	Example B 10% Breakeven	Example C 20% Breakeven
Average Unit Price	$33.33	$33.33	$33.33
Average Units per Order	1.5	1.5	1.5
Average Order Value (AOV)	$50.00	$50.00	$50.00
Cancellations = 1%	$ 0.50	$ 0.50	$ 0.50
Returns = 10%	$ 5.00	$ 5.00	$ 5.00
Net Sales per Order	$44.50	$44.50	$44.50
Cost of Goods = 50%	$22.25	$22.25	$22.25
Fulfillment Cost per Order = $12	$12.00	$12.00	$12.00
+ Fulfillment Income per Order = $5	$ 5.00	$ 5.00	$ 5.00
Net Fulfillment Cost per Order	$ 7.00	$ 7.00	$ 7.00
Contribution (before Promotion, Overhead, & Profit)			
Contribution @ 0% (variable)	$15.25	$15.25	$15.25
		$ (4.45)	
Contribution @ 10% (variable)		$10.80	
			$(8.90)
Contribution @ 20% (variable)			$ 6.35
Cost per Promotion–In Mail	**$ 0.50**	**$ 0.50**	**$ 0.50**

Conclusion:

Formula: Breakeven = $\dfrac{\text{Cost per Promotion–In Mail}}{\text{Contribution}}$

	Example A	Example B	Example C
Breakeven = 0% (Variable level) Sales per Catalog	3.3% $1.46		
Breakeven = 10% (Variable + Overhead level) Sales per Catalog		4.6% $2.06	
Breakeven = 20% (Variable + Overhead + Profit level) Sales per Catalog			7.9% $3.50

EXHIBIT 13.4

yields $10.80 to pay for advertising, overhead, and profit. In Example C, the contribution is $6.35. The percentage response needed to reach 10 percent breakeven in Example B is .0462962, or 4.6 percent ($.50 ÷ $10.80); in Example C, the percentage response needed is .0787401, or 7.9 percent ($.50 ÷ $6.35).

Sales per catalog is determined by multiplying the percent response by the net order sale; in Example B, 4.6% × $44.50 = $2.06 revenue or sales per catalog mailed; in Example C, 7.9% × $44.50 = $3.50 revenue or sales per catalog mailed.

How to Use the Breakeven Analysis

There are three ways to use the breakeven analysis. First, it serves as a reality check for your assumptions. It tells you whether the numbers make sense or are within the realm of reality. In Example A, the prospect breakeven and customer breakeven look quite high. But if the cataloger uses a bonus for orders over $75 or offers "order three items, get one free" to increase the AOV to $75, the breakeven improves dramatically. The breakeven calculation lends itself to "what-if" observations; for example, what if the AOV is $100, or what if cost of goods is 45 percent, or what if the promotion cost is $.42? All three of these items have a huge impact on the breakeven. An increase in AOV or a decrease of even a penny or a nickel in the cost of goods and promotion cost will lower the breakeven point. It is much easier to change average order value than response rate, and the payoff is high.

Second, the breakeven can be applied to the catalog's prospect and customer circulation plans. By forecasting each list segment's percent response, AOV, and sales per catalog and then comparing expectations with the breakeven, a cataloger can quickly tell which lists can be tested, mailed deeper, or not mailed at all.

Third, the breakeven can be used as a leverage with merchandisers and creative staff to reduce the cost of goods and advertising. Challenge merchandising staff to find new sources for best selling items, or review printing costs and identify areas where savings can be achieved.

❖ Key Points

- The financial model is a standard metric or benchmark for catalogers. A 10 percent pretax profit is a viable goal for catalogers in maturity.
- Every cataloger should feel comfortable using the financial model and the profit and loss statement in long-term planning as well as catalog-to-catalog campaign planning.
- Use the breakeven analysis as a reality check to determine what percent response and sales per catalog you need to break even at three different levels.

CHAPTER 14

Cataloging and the Internet

My formal introduction to the giant English retailer Marks & Spencer came in 1996 over lunch with the chairman in London. M&S was considering expanding its direct selling efforts by repositioning its traffic-building Home catalog into a direct selling catalog and by launching an apparel catalog. The chairman inquired about my company's credentials and then asked, "Why should M&S want to be in cataloging, anyway?" I responded, "If the Internet and selling on the Web is at all in the future plans of Marks & Spencer, catalogs will get you a good part of the way." The chairman agreed and direct selling catalogs became a reality for M&S.

A catalog can help a company establish and strengthen a presence on the Web. One site can be hard to find in the ever-expanding universe of the Web; a paper catalog can make it easier by telling customers how and where to find you. An important distinction between paper catalogs and the Internet is that paper catalogs are intrusive, and on-line catalogs are passive. Catalogers go out and solicit sales by mailing catalogs to prospects and customers based on targeted selections. In contrast, the on-line site must wait to be discovered. You can cut the waiting time by using your intrusive catalog to direct customers to your site. Use it to educate consumers about buying on-line, and create special incentives that drive sales to the Internet. Use it to strengthen your niche; the more distinct a catalog's niche, the greater its chances for on-line success and profit. Include your Web address on all of your promotional materials—catalogs, space ads, shipping materials, co-op inserts, and so on—to reinforce your presence.

A catalog is especially helpful to small or medium-size companies in pursuit of E-commerce. Through a catalog and a website, even a small company can act like a large one. A good-looking catalog gives any company immediate credibility and authority—and that translates to your website. On the Web and in the mail, David can take on Goliath. When David builds and maintains a website himself, he can sustain a Web presence much less expensively than Goliath, too.

The biggest and best-known companies are using websites to build their brand and the accompanying share of mind. They are investing millions of dollars in developing sites and links to get potential customers to visit—in some cases, without generating revenue at all. Amazon.com is spending millions and has yet to show a profit. Wal-Mart, in the year 2000, is about to unveil an enormous advertising budget to draw customers to its site. Hardly a television commercial, radio spot, or even billboard is without a Web address today.

Why? These companies know that the Internet is transforming the way goods are bought and sold. They want to reach the tantalizing Internet audience—estimated by database provider Axiom to be 477 million adults worldwide by 2002, 86 million in the United States alone. They want their share of Internet revenues, expected to exceed $1.2 trillion early in the twenty-first century. They know that the top 10 percent of all websites average more than $4 million in revenues annually, and the top 100 E-commerce websites gross between $1 million and $8 million per month, as reported by ActivMedia, an Internet research firm.

The Internet *must* be part of a cataloger's marketing mix. Business-to-business Internet selling is maturing quite nicely, but consumer and retail-oriented catalogs need to ensure that the Internet is not delayed or forgotten. The Web is evolving into a distinct direct marketing channel, and although paper catalogs will not disappear, they will inevitably decline. On-line revenues will outpace any traditional channel of selling by huge multiples. Internet sales growth will come at the expense of traditional (off-line) marketing. Catalogers who use the Internet as a complementary selling tool are going to steal market share from those who remain traditional printed catalog purists.

WHO MANAGES A WEBSITE?

An on-line marketing survey conducted by *Catalog Age* in 1999 asked catalogers that handle their websites internally which department holds decision-making authority over E-catalog operations. Sixty-five percent of respondents delegate decision-making power to the marketing department, 16 percent to the creative department, and 14 percent to the MIS department. The moral of the story: It doesn't necessarily matter who manages the site, as long as marketing, creative, and MIS are all included in the process.

Three Ingredients of Internet Success

A successful on-line catalog has three aspects: technical, graphic, and marketing. Each plays a role in the success or failure of an on-line venture. For instance, a site that is too graphically intense may load slowly and discourage participation. A site with too few graphics may be unappealing to visitors or fail to show products in a positive light. A beautifully crafted, highly engaging site is wasted if the ordering process is cumbersome and confusing. Just as success in paper cataloging comes from integrating database, circulation, merchandising, and creative, success in on-line cataloging comes as a result of the marriage of technical elements (programming), graphics (creative), and marketing (direct marketing principles).

Technical Skills

Consider the target market's "lowest common denominator" when you select browser version, monitor settings, plug-ins, and connection speeds. Cutting-edge technologies make exciting Web pages, but if the cutting edge is more than most people can afford, you may alienate more people than you impress. Design your site to meet the capabilities of your audience, not the technology. According to on-line statistics compilers StatMarket.com and e-Stats.com, in 1999, 68 percent of all Internet users used Microsoft Internet Explorer; 51 percent surfed the Net at home; 55 percent of users had a screen resolution of 800 × 600; and the most common connection speeds fell between 14.4 kBps and 33.3 kBps.

On the server side, you want to design a site that makes on-line ordering easy and beneficial. Eventually, software will allow customers to check inventory on-line to confirm whether the goods they want to order are in stock—without the assistance of a telephone clerk. Look for software that updates customer and product databases in real time instead of collecting and processing orders in batches, and offers customers the ability to track orders throughout the order and shipping process. Exhibit 14.1 shows how much-heralded Dell Computer Corporation (www.dell.com) lets customers track orders and follows up each shipment with a confirmation E-mail message telling them when their computer left the dock.

Graphics Skills

Graphically, E-catalogers must again consider the technical capabilities of the customer's computer. With advances in monitors and scanners, image presentation is better than ever. But presenting too many images or very large images makes downloading almost unbearably slow and reduces the likelihood that someone will stay at your site long enough to purchase. Making sure that image formats commonly used for on-line line art (.gif images) are optimized and reduced to a limited color palette makes image files smaller and vastly improves download times. Large images can be saved in segments, and no image needs to be displayed at a higher resolution than 72 pixels per inch unless you intend it to be downloaded and printed from the Internet for reuse. Jcrew.com is a good example: the site not only picks up photography from the printed catalog but also keeps images manageable from a size standpoint.

Marketing Skills

ActivMedia reports that between 30 percent and 100 percent of on-line revenues come from new customers—a boon for new and growing catalogers for whom building the customer list is a priority. But marketing the on-line catalog can be difficult. The million-dollar

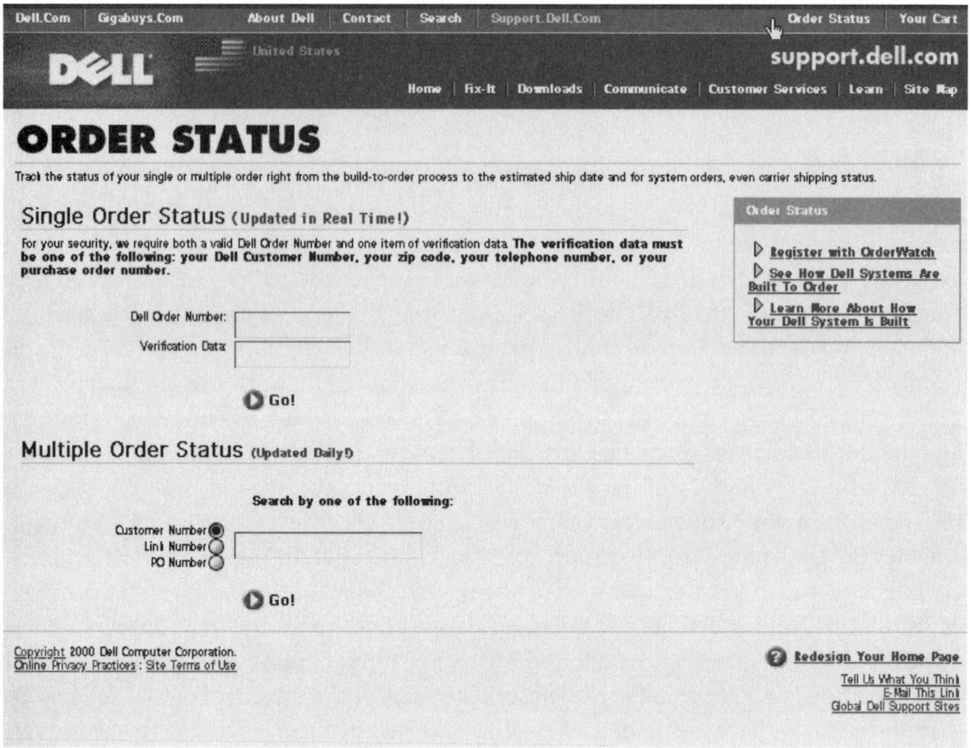

EXHIBIT 14.1
Dell Computer Corporation (dell.com)

question always seems to be "How do we get more traffic to our site?" The half-million-dollar question: "How do we keep them coming back?"

There are a number of proven techniques for generating first-time traffic to a site:

- Participate in on-line catalog portals such as CatalogCity.com (see Exhibit 14.2), CatalogSite.com, CatalogSavings.com, and CatalogLink.com that offer catalog requests and, in some cases, product sales and links to the E-catalog's site.
- Develop on-line alliances with vendors and clients in which you reciprocate placement of links on each other's sites.
- Register your site with the most applicable search engines and directories.
- Send targeted E-mail to available on-line mailing lists, making sure that the recipients on the list have opted in to the list. Opt-out E-mail is not a part of the DMA's Privacy Promise guidelines.
- Include your Web address on every piece of marketing material that goes out the door, particularly to prospects. Make your Web address as prominent as your toll-free telephone number in your catalog if you expect people to order on-line.

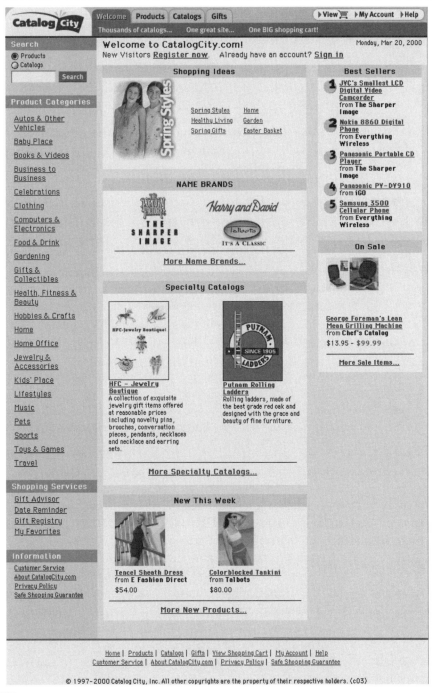

EXHIBIT 14.2
CatalogCity.com

In both the paper and the on-line catalog, profits lie in repeat business. To build repeat business in a medium that lets customers hop from your site to another one with the click of a mouse, you've got to give customers incentives to return. You need to reward customers for returning to your site.

Several of the techniques that keep on-line customers coming back are common to traditional cataloging:

- Get permission to communicate. Getting customers to opt in to an E-mail marketing program makes follow-up communication much easier. J. Crew, Victoria's Secret, and Cabella's all do an excellent job of keeping the lines of communication open with customers through all seasons. Omaha Steaks (omahasteaks.com) even sends its catalog via E-mail and provides an on-line ordering device, as Exhibit 14.3 illustrates.
- Make an offer. Drive repeat purchases with special E-mailed offers or offers made in the paper catalog to encourage on-line sales. Tweeds did this with a preprinted dot whack driving customers to www.tweeds.com/bonus for a $5-off offer for on-line purchases.
- Provide helpful customer service. Because no customer service representative will walk customers through the ordering process, your site needs to provide everything needed to order with comfort and ease. And remember the crucial element: a shopper or prospect should never be more than one click away from ordering.
- Make purchasing easy. Design an order form that captures the necessary information succinctly, including a source code.
- Keep the site fresh. Customers want to see what's new. Some E-catalogs update their sites daily with on-line specials. Use icons and special bursts to point out new items.

Refresh your content at least once a quarter and preferably much more frequently. Another technique that works remarkably well with catalog requests from the Internet is to have customers opt in and provide you their E-mail addresses. Then promptly send out the paper catalog and follow up with a special E-mail offer. In other words, reach these customers in the same manner they reached you.

The beauty of the Internet is that an organization can secure multiple addresses and operate transparently as two or more distinct organizations, not unlike catalogers that publish multiple titles. This chameleon quality means that catalogers can use the Web, among other things, as an avenue to liquidate inventory. Exhibit 14.4 is a great example of this type of operation—Andy's Garage (andysgarage.com), an independent site with an identity all its own that in reality is an on-line outlet for Fingerhut. Some marketers link sites like these; others want to keep distance between the company's upscale primary site and its over-in-the-corner liquidation center.

The most successful on-line catalogers are taking advantage of the economies that come from integrating the traditional catalog with the E-catalog. Whether sharing

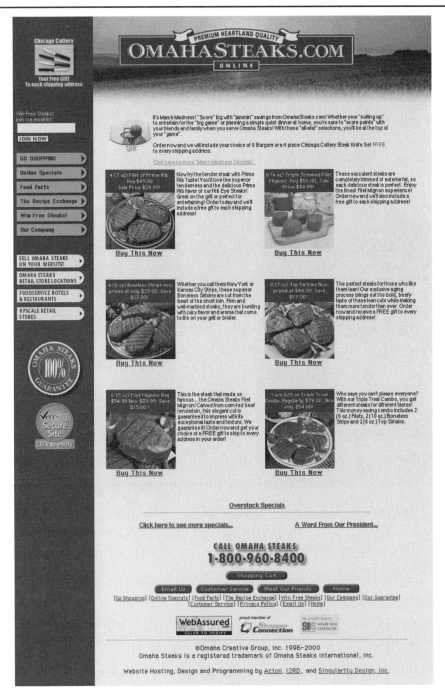

EXHIBIT 14.3
Omaha Steaks (omahasteaks.com)

EXHIBIT 14.4
Andy's Garage (andysgarage.com)

photography and copy elements or using one medium to generate sales and traffic for the other, it is undeniable that the two formats go hand in hand. A solid paper catalog goes a long way in making the Net work.

❖ KEY POINTS

- To encourage participation and sales, design a site that matches the technical capabilities of your users and makes ordering easy.
- Generate first-time traffic by participating in on-line catalog portals, registering your site with search engines and directories, and developing links to other sites.
- Include your Web address on every one of your marketing materials.
- Use special offers and E-mail messages to encourage repeat business, and update your site continually so that customers always see something new.

Appendix
Financial Model

New Catalog Start-Up Feasibility Study

The following pages present an example of a financial feasibility study for a new catalog. The model contains seven pertinent documents:

- Assumptions
- Catalog Page and Mailing Strategy
- Circulation Plan, for both prospects and customers
- Five-Year Name Flow and Revenue Plan
- Order Flow (five-year)
- Income Statement (profit and loss statement)
- Cash Flow, for years one through five

This is a hypothetical model, not based on any specific catalog. Also observe that this particular example is labeled "Most Likely Scenario." This is the financial case that represents the "middle of the road." It is recommended that three separate observations or scenarios be developed:

- Conservative Scenario—lower response percent, lower average order value, and higher costs
- Most Likely Scenario—the middle of the road
- Optimistic Scenario—higher response percent, higher average order value, and lower costs

With prudent planning, the conservative and optimistic cases should give the new cataloger the lower and upper financial limits to help judge the worth or feasibility of the venture. For each scenario, all financial assumptions need to be carefully defined before they are entered into the model.

A financial document like this can also be used by existing catalogs as part of their annual marketing planning to project costs and growth.

New Catalog Start-Up
Most Likely Scenario

Assumptions

Mailing

	Year 1	Year 2	Year 3	Year 4	Year 5
List Rentals—Test	1,000,000	100,000	100,000	100,000	100,000
List Rentals—Continuation	0	1,400,000	1,900,000	2,900,000	3,400,000
Total List Rentals	1,000,000	1,500,000	2,000,000	3,000,000	3,500,000
Net Names—List Rentals	1,000,000	1,500,000	2,000,000	3,000,000	3,500,000
List Rental Cost/1,000	$120	$120	$120	$120	$120
Internet Catalog Requests	5,000	10,000	15,000	20,000	20,000
Internet Orders (% of catalog sales)	5%	7%	8%	9%	10%

Response Rates

Response Rate—List Rentals—Test	1.0%	1.0%	1.0%	1.0%	1.0%
Response Rate—List Rentals—Continuation		1.25%	1.30%	1.35%	1.40%
Response Rate—Recent Buyers	6.0%	6.0%	6.0%	6.0%	6.0%
Response Rate—1-Year+ Buyers		5.0%	5.0%	5.0%	5.0%

Space Ads (Catalog Requests)

Annual Circulation	1,000,000	2,000,000	4,000,000	6,000,000	8,000,000
Cost of Ads/1,000	$15.00	$15.00	$15.00	$15.00	$15.00
Response Rate	0.5%	0.5%	0.5%	0.5%	0.5%
Conversion Rate (average per request)	3.0%	3.0%	3.0%	3.0%	3.0%

Creative

Creative—$/page	$1,250	$1,250	$1,250	$1,250	$1,250
Photography—$/page	$1,250	$1,250	$1,250	$1,250	$1,250
Color Separation—$/page	$650	$650	$650	$650	$650
Total Creative Cost—$/page	$3,150	$3,150	$3,150	$3,150	$3,150

Catalog Variable Costs

Catalog Printing Cost/1,000	$260	$289	$300	$340	$350
Order Form Printing Cost/1,000	$50	$50	$50	$50	$50
Mailing/Binding/DP, etc. Cost/1,000	$40	$40	$40	$40	$40
Postage Cost/1,000	$250	$250	$250	$250	$250
Total Mailing Cost/1,000	$600	$629	$640	$680	$690

Fulfillment

Fulfillment Cost per Order	$15.00	$15.00	$15.00	$15.00	$15.00
Shipping & Handling Charges Collected	$7.00	$7.00	$7.00	$7.00	$7.00
Cancellations (%)	1.0%	1.0%	1.0%	1.0%	1.0%
Returns (%)	5.0%	5.0%	5.0%	5.0%	5.0%

Average Order Value

Prospects & Internet Buyers	$100.00	$100.00	$100.00	$100.00	$100.00
Recent Buyers	$120.00	$125.00	$130.00	$140.00	$150.00
1-Year+ Buyers	$110.00	$115.00	$120.00	$130.00	$140.00

Cost of Goods Sold %	50.0%	49.0%	48.0%	47.0%	46.0%
Overhead	$200,000	$500,000	$500,000	$750,000	$1,000,000
List Rental Income/1,000	$100	$100	$100	$100	$100
Net List Rental %	60%	60%	60%	60%	60%
List Rental Turnover	0	10	15	20	20

EXHIBIT A-1

Catalog Page and Mailing Strategy

Year	Month	Catalog	Lists Mailed	No. of Pages	No. New Pages
Year 1	January				
	February				
	March				
	April				
	May				
	June				
	July				
	August	New	Prospects & Customers	36	36
	September				
	October	Remail	Prospects & Customers	36	8
	November				
	December				
		Total			44
Year 2	January	New	Prospects & Customers	44	34
	February				
	March	Remail	Prospects & Customers	44	8
	April				
	May	Remail	Prospects & Customers	44	8
	June				
	July				
	August	New	Prospects & Customers	44	22
	September				
	October	Remail	Prospects & Customers	44	8
	November	Remail	Customers Only	44	8
	December				
		Total			88
Year 3	January	New	Prospects & Customers	52	38
	February				
	March	Remail	Prospects & Customers	52	8
	April				
	May	Remail	Prospects & Customers	52	8
	June				
	July				
	August	New	Prospects & Customers	52	26
	September				
	October	Remail	Prospects & Customers	52	8
	November	Remail	Customers Only	52	8
	December				
		Total			96
Year 4	January	New	Prospects & Customers	60	42
	February				
	March	Remail	Prospects & Customers	60	8
	April				
	May	Remail	Prospects & Customers	60	8
	June				
	July				
	August	New	Prospects & Customers	60	30
	September				
	October	Remail	Prospects & Customers	60	8
	November	Remail	Customers Only	60	8
	December				
		Total			104
Year 5	January	New	Prospects & Customers	68	46
	February				
	March	Remail	Prospects & Customers	68	8
	April				
	May	Remail	Prospects & Customers	68	8
	June				
	July				
	August	New	Prospects & Customers	68	34
	September				
	October	Remail	Prospects & Customers	68	8
	November	Remail	Customers Only	68	8
	December				
		Total			112

EXHIBIT A-2

Circulation Plan

Mailing Plan–Prospects (Rented Lists)	Year 1	Year 2	Year 3	Year 4	Year 5
January		210,000	280,000	420,000	490,000
February	200,000				
March		210,000	280,000	420,000	490,000
April	200,000				
May					
June		210,000	280,000	420,000	490,000
July					
August	300,000	435,000	580,000	870,000	1,015,000
September					
October	300,000	435,000	580,000	870,000	1,015,000
November					
December					
	1,000,000	**1,500,000**	**2,000,000**	**3,000,000**	**3,500,000**

Mailing Plan–Customers					
January		11,302	33,523	66,643	120,082
February					
March				66,643	120,082
April		17,270	42,425		
May				81,009	138,187
June					
July					
August	4,537	20,875	48,078	90,309	150,158
September					
October	7,930	27,388	57,754	105,831	169,582
November			57,754	105,831	169,582
December					
Total Mailings–Buyers	**12,468**	**76,835**	**239,535**	**516,266**	**867,675**

Customer List Growth					
From Rented Lists	10,000	18,500	25,700	40,150	48,600
From Catalog Requests	728	2,519	5,046	8,104	10,984
Direct Buyers–Internet	574	1,767	3,514	6,898	10,731
Customer List–Year-End	**11,302**	**22,786**	**34,259**	**55,152**	**70,315**
Customer List–Cumulative	11,302	34,088	68,347	123,500	193,814
Attrition Rate		5%	5%	5%	5%
Net Customer List–Year-End	**11,302**	**33,523**	**66,643**	**120,082**	**187,639**

EXHIBIT A-3

Five-Year Name Flow and Revenue Plan

Prospects–Rented Lists–Test	Year 1	Year 2	Year 3	Year 4	Year 5
Quantity Mailed	1,000,000	100,000	100,000	100,000	100,000
Response Rate	1.00%	1.00%	1.00%	1.00%	1.00%
Number of Orders	10,000	1,000	1,000	1,000	1,000
Average Order $	$100	$100	$100	$100	$100
Total Segment Sales	$1,000,000	$100,000	$100,000	$100,000	$100,000
$/1,000 Catalogs Mailed	$1,000	$1,000	$1,000	$1,000	$1,000

Prospects–Rented Lists–Continuation					
Quantity Mailed		1,400,000	1,900,000	2,900,000	3,400,000
Response Rate		1.25%	1.30%	1.35%	1.40%
Number of Orders		17,500	24,700	39,150	47,600
Average Order $		$120	$120	$120	$120
Total Segment Sales		$2,100,000	$2,964,000	$4,698,000	$5,712,000
$/1,000 Catalogs Mailed		$1,500	$1,560	$1,620	$1,680

Catalog Requests					
Quantity Mailed	24,261	83,975	168,191	270,134	366,132
Response Rate	3.0%	3.0%	3.0%	3.0%	3.0%
Number of Orders	728	2,519	5,046	8,104	10,984
Average Order $	$100.00	$100.00	$100.00	$100.00	$100.00
Total Segment Sales	$72,784	$251,925	$504,574	$810,402	$1,098,395
$/1,000 Catalogs Mailed	$3,000	$3,000	$3,000	$3,000	$3,000

Recent Buyers (Last 12 Months)					
Quantity Mailed	12,468	38,418	119,767	258,133	433,837
Response Rate	6.0%	6.0%	6.0%	6.0%	6.0%
Number of Orders	748	2,305	7,186	15,488	26,030
Average Order $	$120.00	$125.00	$130.00	$140.00	$150.00
Total Segment Sales	$89,767	$288,131	$934,186	$2,168,315	$3,904,537
$/1,000 Catalogs Mailed	$7,200	$7,500	$7,800	$8,400	$9,000

Buyers (13+ Months)					
Quantity Mailed		38,418	119,767	258,133	433,837
Response Rate		5.0%	5.0%	5.0%	5.0%
Number of Orders		1,921	5,988	12,907	21,692
Average Order $		$115.00	$120.00	$130.00	$140.00
Total Segment Sales		$220,901	$718,605	$1,677,863	$3,036,862
$/1,000 Catalogs Mailed		$5,750	$6,000	$6,500	$7,000

Direct Buyers–Internet					
Number of Orders	574	1,767	3,514	6,898	10,731
Average Order $	$120.00	$120.00	$120.00	$120.00	$120.00
Total Segment Sales	$68,855	$212,060	$421,634	$827,805	$1,287,673
% of Total Orders	4.8%	6.5%	7.4%	8.3%	9.1%

Total–Catalog & Direct					
Total Order $	12,050	27,012	47,434	83,547	118,037
Average Order $	$102.19	$117.47	$118.97	$123.07	$128.26
Total Sales	$1,231,406	$3,173,017	$5,642,998	$10,282,385	$15,139,466

EXHIBIT A-4

Order Flow

	Year 1	Year 2	Year 3	Year 4	Year 5
% Orders by Mail	19%	19%	19%	18%	18%
% Orders by Phone	76%	75%	74%	74%	73%
% Orders by Internet	5%	6%	6%	8%	9%
Orders Received by Phone	2,295	5,049	8,784	15,330	21,461
Orders Received by Mail	9,181	20,196	35,136	61,319	85,845
Orders Received by Internet	574	1,767	3,514	6,898	10,731
Total Orders Received	12,050	27,012	47,434	83,547	118,037
Cancellations–%	1%	1%	1%	1%	1%
Net Orders Shipped	11,929	26,742	46,959	82,712	116,856
Sales Before Returns	$1,219,092	$3,141,287	$5,586,568	$10,179,561	$14,988,071
Returns–%	5%	5%	5%	5%	5%
Net Sales	$1,157,522	$2,982,636	$5,304,418	$9,665,442	$14,231,098
Average Order $	$102.19	$117.47	$118.97	$123.07	$128.26

EXHIBIT A-5

Income Statement

	Year 1	% of Sales	Year 2	% of Sales	Year 3	% of Sales	Year 4	% of Sales	Year 5	% of Sales
Sales										
Gross Merchandise Sales	$1,231,406		$3,173,017		$5,642,998		$10,282,385		$15,139,466	
Cancellations	$12,314	1.0%	$31,730	1.0%	$56,430	1.0%	$102,824	1.0%	$151,395	1.0%
Returns	$61,570	5.0%	$158,651	5.0%	$282,150	5.0%	$514,119	5.0%	$756,973	5.0%
Net Sales	**$1,157,522**		**$2,982,636**		**$5,304,418**		**$9,665,442**		**$14,231,098**	
Cost of Goods Sold	$578,761	50.0%	$1,461,492	49.0%	$2,546,121	48.0%	$4,542,758	47.0%	$6,546,305	46.0%
Gross Margin	**$578,761**		**$1,521,144**		**$2,758,297**		**$5,122,684**		**$7,684,793**	
Fulfillment Expense										
Fulfillment Cost	$178,938	15.5%	$401,133	13.4%	$704,391	13.3%	$1,240,673	12.8%	$1,752,845	12.3%
Shipping & Handling Income	$83,504	7.2%	$187,196	6.3%	$328,716	6.2%	$578,981	6.0%	$817,994	5.7%
Net Fulfillment Expense	**$95,434**	8.2%	**$213,938**	7.2%	**$375,675**	7.1%	**$661,692**	6.8%	**$934,850**	6.6%
Operating Income	**$483,327**	41.8%	**$1,307,207**	43.8%	**$2,382,622**	44.9%	**$4,460,992**	46.2%	**$6,749,942**	47.4%
Catalog Production (Fixed)										
Photography	$55,000	4.8%	$110,000	3.7%	$120,000	2.3%	$130,000	1.3%	$140,000	1.0%
Creative Execution	$55,000	4.8%	$110,000	3.7%	$120,000	2.3%	$130,000	1.3%	$140,000	1.0%
Color Separations	$28,600	2.5%	$57,200	1.9%	$62,400	1.2%	$67,600	0.7%	$72,800	0.5%
Catalog Expense	**$138,600**	12.0%	**$227,200**	9.3%	**$302,400**	5.7%	**$327,600**	3.4%	**$352,800**	2.5%
Mailing Expense (Variable)										
List Rental	$120,000	10.4%	$180,000	6.0%	$240,000	4.5%	$360,000	3.7%	$420,000	3.0%
Printing Cost	$269,550	23.3%	$479,974	16.1%	$722,318	13.6%	$1,287,376	13.3%	$1,656,832	11.6%
Order Form	$51,836	4.5%	$83,041	2.8%	$120,386	2.3%	$189,320	2.0%	$236,690	1.7%
Mailing/Binding/DP, etc.	$41,469	3.6%	$66,432	2.2%	$96,309	1.8%	$151,456	1.6%	$189,352	1.3%
Postage	$259,182	22.4%	$415,203	13.9%	$601,932	11.3%	$946,600	9.8%	$1,183,452	8.3%
Mailing Expense	**$742,037**	64.1%	**$1,224,650**	41.1%	**$1,780,945**	33.6%	**$2,934,752**	30.4%	**$3,686,326**	25.9%
Total Catalog Expense	**$880,637**	76.1%	**$1,501,850**	50.4%	**$2,083,345**	39.3%	**$3,262,352**	33.8%	**$4,039,126**	28.4%
Expense per Catalog	$0.85		$0.90		$0.87		$0.86		$0.85	
Space Ads	$60,000	5.2%	$120,000	4.0%	$240,000	4.5%	$360,000	3.7%	$480,000	3.4%
Internet	$100,000	8.6%	$100,000	3.4%	$100,000	1.9%	$100,000	1.0%	$100,000	0.7%
Total Promotion Expense	**$1,040,637**	89.9%	**$1,721,850**	57.7%	**$2,423,345**	45.7%	**$3,722,352**	38.5%	**$4,619,126**	32.5%
Contribution to G&A & Profit	**−$557,310**	−48.1%	**−$414,643**	−13.9%	**−$40,723**	−0.8%	**$738,640**	7.6%	**$2,130,816**	15.0%
General & Administrative Expense	$200,000	17.3%	$500,000	16.8%	$500,000	9.4%	$750,000	7.8%	$1,000,000	7.0%
Net List Rental Income	$0		$10,057		$29,989		$72,049		$112,584	
Profit/Loss from Catalog Operations	**−$757,310**	−65.4%	**−$904,586**	−30.3%	**−$510,733**	−9.6%	**$60,690**	0.6%	**$1,245,400**	8.7%

EXHIBIT A-6

Cash Flow—Year 1

	Jan.	Feb.	March	April	May	June	July	Aug.	Sept.	Oct.	Nov.	Dec.	Total
Revenue													
Net Sales	$6,395	$55,506	$83,244	$104,924	$106,333	$56,173	$30,468	$91,567	$135,572	$175,636	$180,605	$94,954	$1,121,377
Shipping & Handling Income	$461	$4,004	$6,005	$7,569	$7,671	$4,052	$2,198	$6,606	$9,780	$12,671	$13,029	$6,850	$80,897
List Rental Income	$0	$0	$0	$0	$0	$0	$0	$0	$0	$0	$0	$0	$0
Total Revenue	**$6,856**	**$59,511**	**$89,250**	**$112,494**	**$114,004**	**$60,225**	**$32,666**	**$98,173**	**$145,352**	**$188,307**	**$193,633**	**$101,804**	**$1,202,274**
Expenses													
Operations													
Inventory Purchases	$200,000	$0	$0	$29,959	$54,575	$0	$0	$74,338	$111,791	$127,882	$95,271	$0	$693,816
Fulfillment	$989	$8,581	$12,869	$16,220	$16,438	$8,684	$4,710	$14,155	$20,958	$27,151	$27,919	$14,679	$173,350
Total Operations	**$200,989**	**$8,581**	**$12,869**	**$46,179**	**$71,013**	**$8,684**	**$4,710**	**$88,493**	**$132,749**	**$155,033**	**$123,190**	**$14,679**	**$867,167**
Creative & Advertising													
Creative	$0	$0	$0	$0	$0	$0	$0	$0	$113,400	$0	$25,200	$0	$138,600
Printing/Mailing	$0	$0	$0	$0	$0	$0	$0	$0	$254,470	$0	$56,549	$0	$311,019
Order Form	$0	$0	$51,836	$0	$0	$0	$0	$0	$0	$0	$0	$0	$51,836
Postage	$0	$50,000	$625	$50,000	$0	$1,231	$0	$76,134	$1,819	$76,983	$0	$2,390	$259,182
List Rental Expense	$0	$24,000	$0	$24,000	$0	$0	$0	$36,000	$0	$36,000	$0	$0	$120,000
Other Media	$13,333	$13,333	$13,333	$13,333	$13,333	$13,333	$13,333	$13,333	$13,333	$13,333	$13,333	$13,333	$160,000
Total Promotion	**$13,333**	**$87,333**	**$65,795**	**$84,346**	**$13,333**	**$14,565**	**$13,333**	**$125,468**	**$383,022**	**$126,316**	**$95,082**	**$15,723**	**$1,040,637**
Direct Expenses	$214,322	$95,914	$78,663	$133,513	$84,346	$23,248	$18,043	$213,961	$515,771	$281,349	$218,272	$30,402	$1,907,804
Contribution to Overhead	–$207,466	–$36,403	$10,586	–$21,019	$29,658	$36,977	$14,623	–$115,788	–$370,419	–$93,043	–$24,639	$71,402	–$705,550
Overhead	$16,667	$16,667	$16,667	$16,667	$16,667	$16,667	$16,667	$16,667	$16,667	$16,667	$16,667	$16,667	$200,000
Cash Flow	–$224,133	–$53,070	–$6,080	–$37,686	$12,991	$20,310	–$2,044	–$132,455	–$387,086	–$109,709	–$41,305	$54,736	–$905,530
Cash Flow—YTD	–$224,133	–$227,203	–$283,283	–$320,968	–$307,977	–$287,667	–$289,711	–$422,165	–$809,251	–$918,960	–$960,265	–$905,530	

EXHIBIT A-7

Cash Flow—Year 2

Revenue	Jan.	Feb.	March	April	May	June	July	Aug.	Sept.	Oct.	Nov.	Dec.	Total
Net Sales	$116,734	$177,018	$188,229	$212,667	$154,676	$158,179	$166,661	$298,391	$351,802	$416,282	$428,209	$228,780	$2,897,628
Shipping & Handling Income	$7,326	$11,110	$11,814	$13,347	$9,708	$9,928	$10,460	$18,728	$22,080	$26,127	$26,875	$14,359	$181,860
List Rental Income	$838	$838	$838	$838	$838	$838	$838	$838	$838	$838	$838	$838	$10,057
Total Revenue	**$124,898**	**$188,966**	**$200,881**	**$226,853**	**$165,222**	**$168,945**	**$177,959**	**$317,957**	**$374,720**	**$443,247**	**$455,922**	**$243,977**	**$3,089,545**
Expenses													
Operations													
Inventory Purchases	$38,471	$145,817	$103,219	$128,157	$18,960	$80,941	$89,976	$275,308	$224,725	$267,169	$221,510	$0	$1,594,252
Fulfillment	$15,699	$23,807	$25,315	$28,602	$20,802	$21,273	$22,414	$40,130	$47,314	$55,986	$57,590	$30,769	$389,701
Total Operations	**$54,170**	**$169,624**	**$128,534**	**$156,758**	**$39,762**	**$102,214**	**$112,390**	**$315,438**	**$272,039**	**$323,155**	**$279,100**	**$30,769**	**$1,983,953**
Creative & Advertising													
Creative	$0	$107,100	$0	$25,200	$0	$25,200	$0	$0	$69,300	$0	$25,200	$25,200	$227,200
Printing/Mailing	$0	$211,112	$0	$49,673	$0	$49,673	$0	$0	$136,602	$0	$49,673	$49,673	$546,407
Order Form	$0	$83,041	$0	$0	$0	$0	$0	$0	$0	$0	$0	$0	$83,041
Postage	$55,325	$0	$56,068	$4,317	$0	$57,211	$0	$113,969	$5,820	$115,597	$0	$6,895	$415,203
List Rental Expense	$25,200	$0	$25,200	$0	$0	$25,200	$0	$52,200	$0	$52,200	$0	$0	$180,000
Other Media	$18,333	$18,333	$18,333	$18,333	$18,333	$18,333	$18,333	$18,333	$18,333	$18,333	$18,333	$18,333	$220,000
Total Promotion	**$98,859**	**$419,585**	**$99,601**	**$97,524**	**$18,333**	**$175,618**	**$18,333**	**$184,502**	**$230,055**	**$186,130**	**$93,207**	**$100,102**	**$1,721,850**
Direct Expenses	**$153,029**	**$589,209**	**$228,136**	**$254,282**	**$58,095**	**$227,832**	**$130,724**	**$499,940**	**$502,094**	**$509,285**	**$372,306**	**$130,870**	**$3,705,803**
Contribution to Overhead	−$28,131	−$400,244	−$27,255	−$27,429	$107,127	−$108,887	$47,235	−$181,983	−$127,374	−$66,038	$83,616	$113,107	−$616,257
Overhead	$41,667	$41,667	$41,667	$41,667	$41,667	$41,667	$41,667	$41,667	$41,667	$41,667	$41,667	$41,667	$500,000
Cash Flow	−$69,798	−$441,910	−$68,922	−$69,096	$65,460	−$150,554	$5,569	−$223,650	−$169,041	−$107,705	$41,949	$71,440	−$1,116,257
Cash Flow—YTD	−$69,798	−$511,708	−$580,630	−$649,726	−$584,266	−$734,820	−$729,251	−$952,901	−$1,121,942	−$1,229,647	−$1,187,698	−$1,116,257	

EXHIBIT A-8

Cash Flow—Year 3

Revenue	Jan.	Feb.	March	April	May	June	July	Aug.	Sept.	Oct.	Nov.	Dec.	Total
Net Sales	$213,012	$321,173	$313,601	$364,013	$290,483	$271,787	$270,664	$475,927	$562,333	$669,533	$777,542	$514,255	$5,044,322
Shipping & Handling Income	$13,200	$19,903	$19,434	$22,558	$18,001	$16,843	$16,773	$29,493	$34,848	$41,491	$48,184	$31,868	$312,598
List Rental Income	$2,499	$2,499	$2,499	$2,499	$2,499	$2,499	$2,499	$2,499	$2,499	$2,499	$2,499	$2,499	$29,989
Total Revenue	**$228,711**	**$343,575**	**$335,534**	**$389,070**	**$310,984**	**$291,129**	**$289,936**	**$507,920**	**$599,680**	**$713,523**	**$828,225**	**$548,622**	**$5,386,909**
Expenses													
Operations													
Inventory Purchases	$0	$257,193	$143,259	$223,121	$68,844	$112,509	$128,841	$425,497	$352,870	$424,287	$476,908	$0	$2,613,330
Fulfillment	$28,287	$42,650	$41,644	$48,338	$38,574	$36,092	$35,942	$63,200	$76,674	$88,909	$103,252	$68,290	$669,852
Total Operations	**$28,287**	**$299,842**	**$184,904**	**$271,460**	**$107,418**	**$148,601**	**$164,783**	**$488,697**	**$427,544**	**$513,197**	**$580,161**	**$68,290**	**$3,283,183**
Creative & Advertising													
Creative	$0	$119,700	$0	$25,200	$0	$25,200	$0	$0	$81,900	$0	$25,200	$25,200	$302,400
Printing/Mailing	$0	$324,040	$0	$68,219	$0	$68,219	$0	$0	$221,711	$0	$68,219	$68,219	$818,627
Order Form	$0	$120,386	$0	$0	$0	$0	$0	$0	$0	$0	$0	$0	$120,386
Postage	$78,381	$0	$78,386	$10,606	$0	$79,832	$0	$157,020	$11,235	$159,439	$14,439	$12,595	$601,932
List Rental Expense	$33,600	$0	$33,600	$0	$0	$33,600	$0	$69,600	$0	$69,600	$0	$0	$240,000
Other Media	$28,333	$28,333	$28,333	$28,333	$28,333	$28,333	$28,333	$28,333	$28,333	$28,333	$28,333	$28,333	$340,000
Total Promotion	**$140,314**	**$592,459**	**$140,319**	**$132,359**	**$28,333**	**$235,184**	**$28,333**	**$254,953**	**$343,179**	**$257,372**	**$136,191**	**$134,348**	**$2,423,345**
Direct Expenses	**$168,601**	**$892,302**	**$325,223**	**$403,818**	**$135,751**	**$383,786**	**$193,116**	**$743,650**	**$770,723**	**$770,569**	**$716,352**	**$202,637**	**$5,706,527**
Contribution to Overhead	**$60,111**	**−$548,726**	**$10,311**	**−$14,749**	**$175,232**	**−$92,657**	**$96,820**	**−$235,731**	**−$171,043**	**−$57,046**	**$111,874**	**$345,985**	**−$319,618**
Overhead	$41,667	$41,667	$41,667	$41,667	$41,667	$41,667	$41,667	$41,667	$41,667	$41,667	$41,667	$41,667	$500,000
Cash Flow	**$18,444**	**−$590,393**	**−$31,355**	**−$56,415**	**$133,566**	**−$134,323**	**$55,153**	**−$277,397**	**−$212,710**	**−$98,712**	**$70,207**	**$304,318**	**−$819,618**
Cash Flow—YTD	**$18,444**	**−$571,949**	**−$603,304**	**−$659,720**	**−$526,154**	**−$660,477**	**−$605,324**	**−$882,721**	**−$1,095,431**	**−$1,194,143**	**−$1,123,936**	**−$819,618**	

EXHIBIT A-9

Cash Flow—Year 4

Revenue	Jan.	Feb.	March	April	May	June	July	Aug.	Sept.	Oct.	Nov.	Dec.	Total
Net Sales	$384,935	$575,993	$653,517	$679,407	$553,227	$598,487	$539,371	$859,545	$961,762	$1,143,816	$1,342,652	$908,133	$9,200,846
Shipping & Handling Income	$23,058	$34,503	$39,147	$40,698	$33,139	$35,851	$32,309	$51,489	$57,612	$68,517	$80,428	$54,399	$551,150
List Rental Income	$6,004	$6,004	$6,004	$6,004	$6,004	$6,004	$6,004	$6,004	$6,004	$6,004	$6,004	$6,004	$72,049
Total Revenue	**$413,998**	**$616,501**	**$698,668**	**$726,109**	**$592,370**	**$640,342**	**$577,685**	**$917,038**	**$1,025,378**	**$1,218,337**	**$1,429,084**	**$968,536**	**$9,824,046**
Expenses													
Operations													
Inventory Purchases	$43,161	$450,311	$380,025	$343,657	$141,407	$323,834	$197,936	$704,950	$548,112	$708,725	$817,952	$18,375	$4,678,445
Fulfillment	$49,411	$73,936	$83,887	$87,210	$71,013	$76,823	$69,235	$110,333	$123,453	$146,822	$172,345	$116,570	$1,181,037
Total Operations	**$92,572**	**$524,247**	**$463,912**	**$430,867**	**$212,420**	**$400,657**	**$267,170**	**$815,282**	**$671,566**	**$855,547**	**$990,297**	**$134,944**	**$5,859,482**
Creative & Advertising													
Creative	$0	$132,300	$0	$25,200	$0	$25,200	$0	$0	$94,500	$0	$25,200	$25,200	$327,600
Printing/Mailing	$0	$581,067	$0	$110,679	$0	$110,679	$0	$0	$415,048	$0	$110,679	$110,679	$1,438,832
Order Form	$0	$189,320	$0	$0	$0	$0	$0	$0	$0	$0	$0	$0	$189,320
Postage	$121,661		$136,024	$0	$20,252	$121,077	$0	$240,077	$17,740	$243,958	$26,458	$19,353	$946,600
List Rental Expense	$50,400	$0	$50,400	$0	$0	$50,400	$0	$104,400	$0	$104,400	$0	$0	$360,000
Other Media	$38,333	$38,333	$38,333	$38,333	$38,333	$38,333	$38,333	$38,333	$38,333	$38,333	$38,333	$38,333	$460,000
Total Promotion	**$210,394**	**$941,020**	**$224,757**	**$174,213**	**$58,585**	**$345,690**	**$38,333**	**$382,811**	**$565,621**	**$386,691**	**$200,670**	**$193,566**	**$3,722,352**
Direct Expenses	**$302,966**	**$1,465,267**	**$688,669**	**$605,080**	**$271,006**	**$746,346**	**$305,504**	**$1,198,093**	**$1,237,187**	**$1,242,238**	**$1,190,968**	**$328,510**	**$9,581,834**
Contribution to Overhead	**$111,032**	**−$848,766**	**$10,000**	**$121,029**	**$321,364**	**−$106,005**	**$272,181**	**−$281,055**	**−$211,809**	**−$23,900**	**$238,116**	**$640,026**	**$242,213**
Overhead	**$62,500**	**$62,500**	**$62,500**	**$62,500**	**$62,500**	**$62,500**	**$62,500**	**$62,500**	**$62,500**	**$62,500**	**$62,500**	**$62,500**	**$750,000**
Cash Flow	**$48,532**	**−$911,266**	**−$52,500**	**$58,529**	**$258,864**	**−$168,505**	**$209,681**	**−$343,555**	**−$274,309**	**−$86,400**	**$175,616**	**$577,526**	**−$507,787**
Cash Flow—YTD	**$48,532**	**−$862,734**	**−$915,235**	**−$856,706**	**−$597,842**	**−$766,346**	**−$556,665**	**−$900,220**	**−$1,174,529**	**−$1,260,929**	**−$1,085,313**	**−$507,787**	

EXHIBIT A-10

Cash Flow—Year 5

	Jan.	Feb.	March	April	May	June	July	Aug.	Sept.	Oct.	Nov.	Dec.	Total
Revenue													
Net Sales	$580,050	$863,394	$977,027	$1,012,237	$862,458	$911,409	$771,012	$1,192,740	$1,326,498	$1,582,019	$1,902,414	$1,338,819	$13,320,77
Shipping & Handling Income	$33,341	$49,627	$56,159	$58,183	$49,574	$52,387	$44,317	$68,558	$76,246	$90,933	$109,349	$76,954	$765,629
List Rental Income	$9,382	$9,382	$9,382	$9,382	$9,382	$9,382	$9,382	$9,382	$9,382	$9,382	$9,382	$9,382	$112,584
Total Revenue	$622,773	$922,403	$1,042,568	$1,079,801	$921,414	$973,178	$824,711	$1,270,680	$1,412,127	$1,682,334	$2,021,145	$1,425,155	$14,198,290
Expenses													
Operations													
Inventory Purchases	$0	$604,662	$553,975	$498,022	$258,935	$464,283	$225,500	$936,651	$733,247	$962,807	$1,169,874	$97,349	$6,505,303
Fulfillment	$71,445	$106,344	$120,340	$124,677	$106,229	$112,258	$94,966	$146,910	$163,385	$194,857	$234,320	$164,902	$1,640,634
Total Operations	$71,445	$711,006	$674,315	$622,699	$365,164	$576,542	$320,465	$1,083,560	$896,632	$1,157,665	$1,404,194	$262,251	$8,145,937
Creative & Advertising													
Creative	$0	$144,900	$0	$25,200	$0	$25,200	$0	$0	$107,100	$0	$25,200	$25,200	$352,800
Printing/Mailing	$0	$758,254	$0	$131,870	$0	$131,870	$0	$0	$560,449	$0	$131,870	$131,870	$1,846,184
Order Form	$0	$236,690	$0										$236,690
Postage	$152,521	$0	$173,329	$0	$34,547	$144,720	$0	$291,289	$23,589	$296,146	$42,396	$24,916	$1,183,452
List Rental Expense	$58,800	$0	$58,800	$0	$0	$58,800	$0	$121,800	$0	$121,800	$0	$0	$420,000
Other Media	$48,333	$48,333	$48,333	$48,333	$48,333	$48,333	$48,333	$48,333	$48,333	$48,333	$48,333	$48,333	$580,000
Total Promotion	$259,654	$1,188,178	$280,462	$205,404	$82,880	$408,932	$48,333	$461,423	$739,471	$466,279	$247,799	$230,320	$4,619,126
Direct Expenses	$331,099	$1,899,184	$954,777	$828,103	$448,044	$985,465	$368,799	$1,544,983	$1,636,102	$1,623,943	$1,651,993	$492,571	$12,765,064
Contribution to Overhead	$291,675	−$976,781	$87,790	$251,699	$473,370	−$12,286	$455,912	−$274,303	−$223,976	$58,391	$369,152	$932,583	$1,433,226
Overhead	$83,333	$83,333	$83,333	$83,333	$83,333	$83,333	$83,333	$83,333	$83,333	$83,333	$83,333	$83,333	$1,000,000
Cash Flow	$208,341	−$1,060,114	$4,457	$168,365	$390,037	−$95,620	$372,579	−$357,636	−$307,309	−$24,943	$285,819	$849,250	$433,226
Cash Flow—YTD	$208,341	−$851,773	−$847,316	−$678,950	−$288,914	−$384,534	−$11,954	−$369,591	−$676,900	−$701,843	−$416,024	$433,226	

EXHIBIT A-11

Glossary

Active buyer A person or company who has responded to a promotion in a recent period of time—for example, the last twelve months.

Address correction requested (ACR) An instruction to the post office to provide the mailer with an updated postal address. It is printed on the upper left-hand corner of the mailing section under the return address of a catalog. There is a fee for this service. Also called "Address Service Requested."

Alteration A late change in copy or layout made by the cataloger and chargeable to the cataloger.

Alternative media All new customer-acquisition efforts that do not involve list rental, including space advertising, card decks, package inserts, the Internet, and so forth.

AOV Average order value.

APR Automatic picture replacement. The technique used in catalog page production in which the color separator provides the computer page production person a low-resolution scan of a photo so that it can be placed in the layout for size and position.

Back-end fulfillment The warehousing, pick-pack-ship, and return-handling aspects of the fulfillment process.

Back-end marketing Marketing to the customer list—that is, previous buyers—as opposed to front-end marketing to prospects.

Bar code A row of vertical parallel bars defining zip + 4 and destination that is printed on a catalog to facilitate the automatic processing of mail by the USPS.

Batch Accumulation of incoming orders (usually by mail or fax) for entry into the computer. Orders are normally "batched" in groups of twenty-five to fifty for control purposes.

Bindery A part of the printing facility or process that trims, gathers, folds, collates, and binds catalogs.

Binding Assembling and attaching together catalog pages. The most common types of catalog bindings are perfect-bound (glued spine) and saddle-stitched (stapled).

Black-and-white One-color printing using black ink on white paper.

Bleed Printing that goes to the edge or past the trim of the catalog.

Bleed designation Printing area outside the trim marks. This is determined by the printer and must be shown on the artwork.

Blue line A proof provided by the printer for checking type and photo positioning prior to printing. The proof is blue due to the process of burning the film image to a treated paper.

Body copy Text used to describe a catalog product, including the price and item number. Does not include headlines.

Boldface type Heavy-faced type often used for headlines or paragraph lead-ins.

Book Slang for *catalog*.

Bounce-back An offer to customers that rides in the box shipment of the order.

BRC Business reply card.

BRM Business reply mail.

Brochure A circular, pamphlet, or flyer. A general term for a promotion of less than eight to twelve pages.

Bulk mail center (BMC) A highly mechanized USPS mail facility for processing and distributing standard mail, which includes catalogs.

Bundling Putting together a number of complementary products at one price to form a special offer.

Buyer (customer) A person or company who has ordered product from a catalog.

Buyer (merchandiser) A person responsible for sourcing products for a catalog.

Card deck See **deck mailing**.

Carrier route A geographical area of approximately 350 households used by the USPS to sort and deliver mail. Mail that is presorted by carrier route receives a substantial discount.

Cash with order/cash buyer A person who responds by mail to a catalog solicitation with a money order or check enclosed with the order.

Catalog A promotion consisting of a minimum of twelve to sixteen pages and offering multiple products. Anything smaller is a *brochure* or *booklet*.

Catalog buyer A person or company who purchases merchandise or services from a catalog.

Catalog requester A person or company who requests a copy of a catalog. The catalog may be free, or there may be a charge for it.

Center spread, or center fold The middle of a saddle-stitched catalog in which an order form is often bound. A "hot spot" in the catalog.

CHAID (chi-square automatic interaction detector) An analysis based on the chi-squared test for statistical independence. CHAID looks at a variety of independent variables to determine which ones best predict the dependent variable.

Charge-back A disputed credit card transaction, usually by the credit card holder.

Charge card buyer A person or company who charges a catalog order to a credit card.

Cheshire label A mailing label prepared on plain paper, usually printed four across and eleven down, and mechanically affixed to a catalog or to an envelope or order form with applied glue.

Chromalin A type of high-resolution color separation proof in which the four primary colors (CMYK) are overlaid to produce a color reproduction.

Chrome See **transparency** and **color transparency**.

Circulation The process of planning all details of a mailing program. Describes to whom the mailing is going, when, and the quantity.

Cleaning a list Updating a mailing list with current information and removing names that are no longer mailable.

CMYK The four basic printing colors: cyan (blue), magenta, yellow, and black.

COA Change of address.

Code Also known as *source code* or *key code.* An alphanumeric series used to identify each segment of a prospect or customer mailing to track results. Source codes are attached to each address record for easy identification.

Cold list A rented list of names that a cataloger uses for prospecting.

Collation Assembly of catalog signatures as part of the binding process.

Color key A color representation provided by the color separator or printer to show the expected results of PMS printing. Each PMS color to be printed is shown separately. See **PMS colors** and **PMS printing**.

Color proof A color representation provided by the color separator or printer to show the expected results of four-color process printing. This proof can be produced for PMS proofing as well but is more expensive than a color key. See **process printing**.

Color separation A process by which a photograph or artwork is divided into the four basic colors (CMYK) for printing.

Color transparency Also called a *chrome.* A positive, full-color photographic image that can be viewed on a light table.

Co-mailing Also called commingling. A service provided by the printer in which two different catalogs similar in size and weight are mailed together to achieve postal savings.

Compiled list A type of rental list of residential or business addresses that have been gathered together from public information such as directories, registrations, and census information.

Comprehensive Also called a *comp.* A type of layout that shows a detailed representation of how a printed catalog page or spread will look. The comp can be done in four-color or black-and-white and may be produced with colored markers or with a computer.

Computer service bureau A firm that offers various services including list maintenance, merge-purge, computer letters, and personalization.

Continuity program A type of promotion in which a product is sold in multiple shipments—for example, monthly or semimonthly. Continuity programs are most commonly used by book and record clubs, collectibles, and food mailers.

Controlled circulation A class of publication that is distributed free of charge to people or firms that fit a certain profile (in an industry). Examples include *DM News, Target Marketing,* and *Catalog Age.*

Conversion Changing a prospect person or company into a buyer.

Co-op catalog A catalog that offers multiple products or pages from a variety of companies. Examples are Skymall and The Good Catalog Company.

Co-op mailing A shared mailing in which two or more offers are combined for prospecting. Postage costs are shared among participants. An example is Carol Wright.

Cost per inquiry (CPI) The total cost of a promotion or advertisement divided by the number of inquiries received.

Cost per order (CPO) The total cost of a promotion or advertisement divided by the number of orders received.

Cost per thousand (CPM) The total cost of a promotion or advertisement divided by the number of thousands reached. (*M* is the roman numeral for 1,000.)

Crop Trimming off of extraneous parts of a photo for catalog reproduction.

Cross section The selection of a group of names representative of the whole.

Data appending The addition of demographic or other relevant information to a prospect or buyer database for the purpose of segmenting and selecting names for promotion.

Data entry The process of capturing key customer or prospect information to start the fulfillment process. This is the first step in entering a catalog order or catalog request into the computer.

Database Information in a computer file on customers or prospects. It should include name; address; company name (if a business); phone, fax and E-mail numbers; complete purchase history; and sometimes demographic characteristics about households, individuals, or companies.

Database marketing The process of extracting all relevant information from customers' purchases for use in future marketing programs and customer contacts.

Deck mailing A group of postcards that contain promotional information and business-reply characteristics. Usually published by magazines, card decks are an effective alternative medium for generating catalog requests from a group of people with common demographics—for example, sales and marketing executives or food-by-mail buyers.

Decoy Also called *seed name*. A name that is intentionally added to a rental mailing list with the sole intent of tracking the use (or misuse) of the list. This procedure is known as "seeding" or "salting."

De-duping See **dupe elimination**.

Demographics Economic, social, or business characteristic information about people, households, or companies that can be used to select and segment candidates for promotion.

Direct mail The use of the USPS to send promotions to individuals or companies, with the specific intent of gaining a measurable response.

Direct marketing Also called *direct response marketing*. A method of promotion using the mail, telephone, broadcast, print, fax, or Internet to sell products or generate inquiries that is measurable and accountable.

DMA Acronym for the Direct Marketing Association, the leading trade association for companies selling via direct marketing.

Dot whack A small, stamp-like *sticker* that is affixed to catalog covers, usually to present a special message or offer. Dot whacks are normally glued to covers in the binding process.

Downscale The opposite of **upscale**. A market segment that is lower in income and discretionary buying power and that typically will not respond to luxury offers.

DPI Dots per inch. The number of dots in artwork, indicative of the resolution quality for printing or reproduction. The greater the number of dots, the tighter the printing.

Drop date Same as **mail date**, the date on which a promotional campaign is mailed.

Drop-ship The direct shipment of a product to the customer from the manufacturer, bypassing the cataloger's warehouse and inventory system.

Dummy A mock-up of a printed promotion with photography and copy in position to show the relative feel and look of a piece before mailing.

Duotone The use of only two colors in the printing process to create a piece of art that achieves greater depth with the use of lighter and darker shades of ink.

Dupe elimination The process of detecting and removing duplicate names from a single mailing list or multiple mailing lists before promotion. Also called *de-duping*.

Duplicate Also known as *dupe*. Two or more names and addresses on a mailing list that match or appear to be the same. Usually detected in the merge-purge process before mailing.

Enamel A type of coated paper with a glossy finish typically used in catalog printing.

Expire A name on a subscription list that has not renewed or is no longer an active subscriber. Subscriber mailing lists often offer separate rentals of such names.

Field A specific set of data.

File See **list**.

First-time buyer A person or company that purchases a product or service for the first time. This sale can come via response to a catalog, a space ad, an Internet offer, a solo mailing, or any other type of direct promotion.

First-class mail A designation by the USPS referring to mail that pays the highest postage and is given priority treatment.

FOB Freight on board. The cost of shipment from the originating warehouse location, e.g., the manufacturer's warehouse to the catalog distribution center.

Folio A page number placed on a catalog or brochure.

Former buyer A person or company that has previously made a purchase from your company but has failed to respond or purchase recently.

Four-color process Also called *full color*. The use of the four colors (cyan [blue], magenta, yellow, and black) in the reproduction and printing process. Also called CMYK.

FPO For position only. Low-resolution artwork in a computer layout to be used only for approvals, not for reproduction.

Free lance An independent artist, writer, or other service provider who is employed job-by-job and works for a number of different companies or agencies.

Free sheet Printing paper that contains no wood pulp.

Freestanding insert (FSI) A promotional piece that usually rides along with a newspaper. The insert can be a single promotion or coupled with other promotions and coupon offers.

Frequency See **recency/frequency/monetary**.

Friend-get-a-friend Also called *member-get-a-member*. A referral process asking existing customers to recommend friends who might like to receive the catalog.

Front-end fulfillment All the activity of receiving an order, getting it into the computer, and generating the picking documentation.

Front-end marketing Commonly refers to prospecting or new name acquisition.

Fulfillment The process of receiving orders, entering purchase or inquiry information into the computer, warehousing, pick-pack-ship, and developing all the accompanying credit, accounting, database, inventory, and management reports to run the business. Closing the loop with a customer.

Gang run Printing related or similar jobs together to save time and money.

Gathering Assembling printed and folded signatures together in the proper sequence for binding.

.gif image pronounced "giff" or "jiff", a common image format developed by CompuServe used to produce line art for the Web. Also gif 89 or gif 89a.

Gift giver A person or company who purchases product for others.

Gravure See **rotogravure**.

Groundwood A type of printing paper that contains wood pulp.

Guarantee A promise made to customers that the catalog stands behind its products and ensures the satisfaction of the buyer. The terms of the promise can vary from replacement of product to a money-back guarantee.

Halftone A plate or printed piece that involves shooting artwork through a lined screen that breaks up the art into a dot pattern.

Hickey A mark on printed material caused by foreign matter or dirt during the printing process.

High resolution See **resolution**.

Hot-line list Names on a list that are very recent—for example, the last three months, or the last thirty days. This list demands a higher or premium price because of its recency.

Hot spot One of the places in the catalog that are most likely to be seen first and by the most people. Hot spots include the front and back covers, inside front and back covers, and centerfold—especially if there is a bound-in order form.

House list The names owned by a company that can be used for a promotion. These names might include buyers, inquiries, catalog requesters, or gift recipients.

Imposition The manner in which pages are positioned in printing so that they can be correctly printed and folded.

Inactive buyer A person or company who once purchased from your company but has not been an active buyer for twelve to twenty-four months or more.

Indicia An imprinted designation issued by the USPS and used on a mailing piece or catalog. The indicia goes in the upper right corner of the addressing portion of a catalog or mailing piece and indicates that the postage has been paid into an account opened by the permit holder.

Infomercial A long television commercial in the form of an interview or discussion. May be fifteen, thirty, or more minutes.

Ink-jetting The process of applying mailing list names, addresses, and source codes to the back of a catalog or to an order form or elsewhere on a mailing piece. It is usually done in the binding process and completely computer controlled.

Inquiry A person or company who has not yet purchased from your catalog but who has requested information or a catalog. There may or may not be a charge for such a request.

Interfile duplicate A name that appears on two or more outside mailing lists.

Intrafile duplicate A name that appears more than once on the same mailing list (outside or house list).

Kerning Reducing or modifying spacing between type characters.

Key code See **code**.

Keyline Also called *mechanical, pasteup,* or *finished art.* The final assembly of artwork and copy used for making plates and/or film for printing. With increasing computer design, the terms *keyline* and *mechanical* are becoming obsolete.

Keystone margin The gross margin in which the cost is 50 percent of the selling price. Retailers typically work on a keystone margin. Example: A catalog buys a product for $5.00 and sells it for $10.00.

Kromekote A highly glossy, coated paper stock.

Label A piece of paper (plain or pressure sensitive) upon which the name, address, and source code are printed and that is affixed to the catalog, order form, or outer envelope for mailing purposes.

Layout A graphic rendering of a proposed promotion piece or catalog pages that indicates position for headlines, copy, and photography.

Leading The space between lines of copy. (Pronounced like the metal.)

Letter shop Also called a *mail house*. A service company that oversees the collation, addressing, inserting, and mailing of catalogs and other printed promotion pieces.

Lifetime value (LTV) The value of customers over time, usually two or three years, expressed in total dollars spent less the cost of goods, the cost of communicating with customers, and the cost of fulfilling customers' orders.

Line drawing A piece of artwork or sketch, usually done in pencil, that uses solid black line artwork and does not require halftone reproduction.

List Also known as *file*. Names and addresses of prospects or customers who have common purchase or demographic characteristics.

List broker A person who recommends and coordinates the rental of mailing lists from list owners or list managers.

List cleaning The process of updating and removing undesirable names and addresses from a mailing list.

List compiler A company that collects or brings together, often from public sources, various demographic, professional, or occupational information for use in mailing.

List exchange An agreement between companies to trade names, with no monetary or rental fee associated with the transaction.

List maintenance The regular updating of a list (usually the house list) to ensure that the addresses are current and deliverable. See **update**.

List manager The person or firm responsible for promoting and maintaining a list for a list owner. Requests for list rentals come to the list manager and are cleared for usage. The list manager has total responsibility for all paperwork and collection of funds in the list transaction.

List owner The company or individual who has developed a list of names of prospective buyers and who desires to rent the names to generate income.

List rental The one-time usage of a mailing list by a mailer. The list owner is paid on a dollars-per-thousand basis. The entire transaction is usually arranged by a list broker.

List sample A segment of a list that is used for testing, usually by random or "nth-name" selection.

List selection Specific segments of a mailing list used for mailing purposes that demand a higher rental fee.

Logotype Also called *logo*. The trademark or symbol of a company shown with typography or artwork.

Low res See **resolution**.

LTV See **lifetime value**.

Magnetic tape An electronic storage system for recording and maintaining bits of data through a computer. Typically used for storage of mailing lists.

Mail date The day agreed upon between a list renter and list owner for the dropping of a mailing. This date, also known as **drop date**, is defined in a list rental agreement and must be strictly adhered to.

Mail house See **letter shop**.

Mail order The transaction of business via the USPS.

Mail-order buyer A person or company who purchases products or services by mail.

Mail preference service (MPS) A service offered by the DMA that allows consumers to delete their names from mailing lists.

Mailer A firm that promotes its products or services via the mail. Also the term for a direct mail piece and for the carton in which a product is shipped to customers.

Makeready The preparation and setup of printing presses for printing, including the adjustment of inks and registration of images.

Margin The difference between the cost of goods and the selling price.

Markup The percent an item is increased from its cost to its selling price.

Marriage mail A type of co-op mailing that includes multiple promotional offers.

Match code The shortened form of data from a name-and-address record used to identify duplicate records within or between lists.

Matte finish A coated paper with a dull finish.

Mechanical See **keyline**.

Merge-purge A computer process in which a number of mailing lists are formatted and placed in zip-code sequence and then compared with each other for identifying duplicate names.

Metropolitan statistical area (MSA) A Census Bureau designation for a standard metropolitan statistical area (SMSA) that includes the group of counties that define the geography of a major metropolitan area.

Monetary See **recency/frequency/monetary**.

Moonlighter A freelance worker who is also employed full-time elsewhere.

Multibuyer A person or company who has purchased two or more times from the same catalog or company. Also called *repeat buyer*.

Multiple regression analysis A statistical technique in which various characteristics of prospects or buyers are quantified to determine their propensity to purchase or the relative profitability of ordering.

Negative The photographic image on film showing the reverse of what is viewed by the naked eye. Light colors show as dark; dark colors show as light.

Negative option An offer used by book and record clubs in which customers send back a response when they do not wish to purchase a monthly selection.

Nesting A process of placing one promotional piece inside another before insertion into an envelope, thus reducing the number of positions on an inserting machine.

Net name arrangement An agreement between the list user (the mailer) and the list owner in which the owner agrees to accept a reduced fee for the mailing list based on quantity of names taken, duplication of names between lists, and/or similar factors.

Net-net name An agreement between the list user (the mailer) and the list owner in which the mailer pays only for names mailed after the merge-purge process.

Nixie Industry jargon for *undeliverable*. A piece of mail that does not reach its intended destination due to a faulty name or address and is returned by the USPS.

Nth-name selection A list selection process in which the mailer opts to take only a fraction of the names on the list. Usually, the selection process is by random, every tenth name, or every twentieth name.

OCR Optical character reader. An electronic machine, also called an *optical scanner*, that optically reads a line of printed characters and converts each character into an electronic symbol for processing.

OF Order form.

Offer Also called the *proposition*. The terms and conditions presented to prospective buyers to motivate them to action. Offers may include special pricing, a premium, sweepstakes, reduction of shipping and handling, a discount, and the like.

Offset A method of printing that transfers ink from a metal plate to a rubber surface and then to paper.

One-time buyer A company or person who has made only one purchase from a mailer.

One-time use The usual arrangement for a list rental, stipulating that the mailer (the list renter) will not tamper with, copy, or otherwise adapt the mailing list without the permission of and further payment to the list owner.

Optical scanner See **OCR**.

"Or current resident" A line of copy used in the addressing area of catalogs to advise the postal carrier to deliver the promotion to the current household, even if the addressee has moved.

Order form Abbreviated OF, the ordering device in catalogs that is customarily inserted into the center fold of the catalog. Other options of placement are the back inside cover page and between catalog signatures.

Out of register The condition of colors used in printing being in imperfect alignment, resulting in one color with a "hanging" dot pattern and giving the image an "out of focus" appearance.

Overlay A transparent sheet that covers artwork to show distinctive artistic markings such as color usage or accessorization for photography. Also refers to the appending of outside data such as demographic information to a mailing list to enhance its value.

Overwrap Also called *wrap, outer wrap*, or *cover wrap*. A four-page cover, usually of a different paper from the catalog cover, used to present special messages or offers.

P&L A profit and loss statement.

Package An entire direct mail solicitation, which usually includes the outer envelope, letter, brochure, ordering device, business reply envelope, and sometimes a lift or special promotional letter.

Package insert A promotion that is included in the box shipment of a product. It may be from the company shipping the product or from an outside company that has purchased the use of the space.

Packer A person in a fulfillment operation who physically inserts merchandise into a carton for shipment.

Pagination The process of determining what products (or product categories) go where in a catalog and how much space each item will be given on a spread.

Pander names The names of persons who have indicated that they do not wish to receive direct mail solicitation; people who have signed up with the DMA's Mail Preference Service.

Pass-along The additional readers of a catalog that has been routed or passed from one person to another. Pass-along volume is especially important in business-to-business cataloging because of multiple people in a department of a big company or in a small company.

Peel-off label See **pressure-sensitive label**.

Pencil sketch Also called *rough*. A drawing of a planned layout for a catalog done in pencil. Initial sketches may be *thumbnails* (greatly reduced) or full-size and generally are done for two-page spreads.

Penetration The number or percentage of names on a list in relation to the total number of names available. The universe may be a state, city, SIC code, or similar set.

Perfect bound A binding method for larger catalogs in which the spine is glued, not stapled.

Personalization The use of a person's or company's name or other purchase history information on catalog covers, order forms, or opening pages.

Photostat Also called *stat*. A high-quality reproduction of camera-ready art used for offset printing.

Picker A person who selects merchandise from warehouse shelves and delivers it to a packing station for packing.

Piggyback An offer that rides along free with another offer.

Plus cover An extra four-page outer wrap or cover that is added to the inside thirty-two-, forty-eight-, or sixty-four-page catalog signatures. Usually a somewhat heavier stock is used. The opposite of **self-cover**.

PMS colors Stands for Pantone Matching System. Standard, numbered shades and colors available to printers everywhere.

PMS printing Printing that uses PMS colors only. There are no color separations, although there will be separate pieces of film for each PMS color. The printed color is solid; there are no dots as in 4-color process printing.

Poly bag A clear, plastic bag used for mailing a catalog or other promotion instead of a paper envelope.

Pop-up A three-dimensional paper promotion in which a portion of the paper "pops up" when the mailing is opened.

Positive A photographic image on film that looks exactly like the original image. The opposite of **negative**.

Positive option A type of club promotion in which customers must respond if they desire to purchase a product.

Postcard mailer Also known as a *card deck mailer*. A collection of promotional cards sent to a specific audience to generate a response. Commonly used for catalog requests.

Premium A type of offer in which the buyer receives a gift when purchasing an item or responding to a promotion. Premiums can be used to promote early ordering (a "hurry-up premium"), to increase the average order value, or just to encourage response to the promotion.

Press proof A printed piece from the press produced during the makeready after color separations, to check color and registration before the full print run is made.

Pressure-sensitive label An address label that can be peeled off the customer's address portion of a catalog or envelope and affixed to an order form. Usually these labels contain all source code information, as well as name and address. Also called *peel-off label*.

Process printing, or four-color process printing Printing using four process colors (CMYK) to create full-color images and photos.

Progressive proofs Also called "progs." A method of printing proofs that are separated by each color and then assembled to show how all four printing colors are combined.

Propping The accessories used with a product during photography to show size relationship, function, or utility of the product.

Prospect A person or company who is viewed as a potential buyer from a catalog or other promotion but has not yet purchased.

Psychographics Lifestyle or attitude characteristics of prospects or customers.

Pull See **response rate**.

Purge See **merge-purge**.

Rate card A publisher's listing of advertising rates for a publication, including discounts, cut-off dates, and the like.

Recency/frequency/monetary (RFM) A method used by catalogers and direct marketers to segment a list based on customer purchase history. *Recency* refers to the date of last purchase. *Frequency* refers to the number of lifetime purchases. *Monetary* refers to the total lifetime dollar purchases made from the catalog or company. A scoring system is built based on these three variables.

Reformatting Also called *list conversion*. Altering magnetic tapes to a common format for further manipulation. Commonly used in the merge-purge process.

Registration Alignment of color plates in printing so that all colors are sequenced and lying on top of each dot correctly. If one color plate is out of registration, the image is blurred and has bad color.

Regression See **multiple regression analysis**.

Resolution The amount of computer memory used to produce an image. "Screen" resolution (as in your computer screen) is 72 pixels/inch; low resolution is up to 150 pixels/inch; high resolution is 300+ pixels/inch. This term is often used interchangeably— and incorrectly—with *dots per inch* which is a printing term.

Response rate Also called *pull*. The percentage of orders received from a catalog or other promotional mailing.

Retouching An artistic process for improving or enhancing artwork or photographs.

Return postage guaranteed A USPS endorsement used with third-class or standard class promotions such as catalogs that tells the postal service to return the mail to the sender if it is undeliverable. There is a charge for this service.

RFM See **recency/frequency/monetary**.

RFMP *P* stands for "product category" and is added to recency, frequency, and monetary when further segmenting buyers by which type of product they have purchased. Often, product category purchase activity is highly predictive of what customers will purchase in the future.

RIP Raster imaging processing. Computer processing that produces a format for reproduction—either a proof or film. "Ripping a file" means taking a proof or printer film from a computer.

Rollout Also called *continuation*. The larger mailing of a promotion or offer following a successful test of a smaller quantity.

ROP See **run of press**.

Rotogravure Also called *gravure*. A printing method that uses etched copper cylinders. Applicable to larger catalog print runs in excess of 1 million copies.

Rough See **pencil sketch**.

Run of press (ROP) A newspaper or magazine space allocation that is within the regular pages of the publication and goes to all segments, regions, or issues.

Running charges A fee set by a list owner to cover the administrative cost of producing lists that are not ultimately used by the mailer.

S&H Shipping and handling. The charge to the customer for delivery of a package.

Saddle stitching A common type of catalog binding that uses staples to bind signatures and an order form together. Generally used with catalogs that are less than ninety-six pages.

Salting See **decoy**.

Scanning A computerized method of turning artwork or photographic images into digital data.

SCF (sectional center facility). A mechanized USPS mail-handling facility in which mail is sorted to several smaller post offices within the SCF area. The first three digits of a zip code represent the SCF.

Scitex The registered brand mark of Scitex Corporation Ltd., for a type of commonly used color separations.

Seeding, or seed name See **decoy**.

Segmentation The division of a customer or prospect list into unique parts based on common criteria such as recency, frequency, monetary, geography, business or consumer, and demographics.

Select A specific segment of a mailing list in which all names have a common denominator—for example, all have Alabama addresses, or have incomes in excess of $100,000, or have children at home.

Self-cover A catalog cover printed on the same paper as the interior signatures or pages. Part of the sixteen, thirty-two, or forty-eight pages of a catalog. The opposite of **plus cover**.

Self-mailer A direct mail promotion that is totally contained in one piece and not inserted in an envelope. It is usually a multifold piece that is not stapled.

Separation See **color separation**.

Serif and sans serif Two classifications of print fonts. A *serif* (T) is the short line crossing or stemming from the main stroke of a letter. Type without ascending or descending short lines is called *sans serif* (T).

Setup fee A one-time charge by a service bureau, fulfillment facility, or printer for establishing all the parameters for a catalog job or project.

Sheetfed A type of press that prints on sheets of paper that are fed one at a time. Usually used for smaller-quantity or higher-quality runs. Compare with **web press**.

Signature A section of a catalog, usually eight or sixteen pages, that is printed, gathered, cut, and folded as it comes off the press.

SKU (stock keeping unit) The number assigned to a product or line item and used for inventory control, data entry, order fulfillment, and catalog postanalysis. May be as specific as including color and size. For example: a style of shoes in six colors, eight sizes, and four widths has 192 SKUs ($6 \times 8 \times 4$); a black, one-size-fits-all poncho has 1 SKU.

Slim jim A catalog format that measures approximately $6'' \times 10\frac{7}{8}''$. This size was once in vogue because of special postal discounts by the USPS.

Solo mailing A direct mail promotion for a single product or product line. Usually refers to a mailing in an envelope that contains a letter, a brochure, an order form, and a reply envelope.

Source code See **code**.

Sourcing The process of searching for new catalog products from manufacturers or distributors at trade shows, by direct contact, or from an importer.

Space Advertising that uses publications (magazines, newspapers, or newsletters) to solicit an order or catalog request.

Split run Two versions of an ad offered in a publication that allows every other copy to carry a different ad. Allows for statistically accurate testing.

Split test Two segments of a mailing list, each representative of the entire list, used to test different promotions, such as varying offers or prices.

Spread Two facing pages in a catalog.

Standard industrial classification (SIC) A coding system established by the United States Department of Commerce to designate different business types.

State count The number of names and addresses from a given state in a mailing list.

Statement stuffer A type of promotion piece that rides along with another customer communication (an invoice or customer account statement), usually for the purpose of selling a product.

Stripping The positioning of negative or positive film in platemaking for printing.

Style manual A document containing detailed guidelines for presenting a catalog's layout, copy, use of color, typography, photography, and corporate logo and brand.

Suppression "Tagging" particular names on a mailing list so they will not be mailed. For example, a cataloger may wish to suppress the names of all customers who have not bought since 1997 for a particular mailing.

Suspect The lowest level in the hierarchy of a customer. Defines a household or company that matches your target audience.

Swatching The insertion of fabric samples in a mailing piece or catalog to help the customer "touch, feel, and see" the product. Also refers to the use of photographic fabric reproductions.

Syndicated catalog A type of catalog in which a company sponsors the promotion and allows other companies to include products or mail the entire catalog under their own names. Examples include Skymall, The Good Catalog Company, and Electric Odyssey (Minnesota Power).

Syndicator A firm that prepares promotions for a list owner to mail to the owner's list. Usually includes selecting and procuring the products and sometimes includes fulfillment.

Syquest The registered mark of SYQT, a brand of portable electronic storage cartridge that holds many megabytes of data. Often used for catalog pages.

Teaser The copy on the outside of an envelope, a catalog, or other direct mail promotions to get the recipient to open and read the piece.

Telephone preference service (TPS) A service of the Direct Marketing Association that permits consumers to have their names removed from phone lists.

Test quantity The number of names from a specific mailing list used for testing. Every mailer strives to select a quantity of names that will be statistically reliable and valid.

Test side, or test panel Each of the offers or segments of a split mailing. Also refers to a preset segment of a mailing list used for testing.

Three-digit zip The first three digits of a five-digit zip code which designate the sectional center facility. See **SCF**.

Thumbnail, or thumbnail sketch A miniature layout sketch of a catalog cover or spread used to give a general idea of what larger layouts will look like.

Trade publication A magazine aimed at people who are involved in a specific trade or profession.

Traffic builder A promotional piece used by retailers to encourage customers to visit their stores.

Transparency Also called a *chrome*. A transparent photograph, such as a 35 mm slide, or $4'' \times 5''$ negative that will be color separated and used for printing.

Turnover, list rental The number of times a cataloger rents its buyer file per year. Also called "list turns."

Twofer A special offer in which two of the same or similar items are sold for a price that is less than that charged for two single items. The same approach may be used with three items.

Undeliverable See **nixie**.

Universe The total number of people or companies on a specific mailing list.

Up front Getting payment for a product or service before it is shipped.

UPC Universal product code. A standard bar code that can be read by a computer.

Update The addition of recently acquired names or buyers to a mailing list to assure its accuracy.

UPS United Parcel Service.

Upscale A market with higher levels of income, lifestyle, and interests, appropriate for offers related to luxury or discretionary income.

USPS United States Postal Service.

Validation A mailing that follows an initial test mailing to verify test results before a rollout mailing.

WATS Wide Area Telephone Service. A service that provides reduced rates for volume callers and allows direct-dial calls within a certain zone of the country for a flat monthly fee.

Web press A printing press that uses rotary action and large continuous rolls of paper. Used for larger-quantity printing—usually 50,000 or 100,000 pieces and up. Compare with **sheetfed**.

White mail Mail that is not trackable by source code. This mail may contain orders or catalog requests but cannot be allocated to a specific source.

Widow In typesetting, a word or short part of a sentence on a line by itself, at the end of a paragraph.

Window envelope An envelope with a die-cut see-through area that allows for a name-and-address label or labeled device to show. May have a cellophane covering.

Zip code A five-digit set of numbers used by the USPS to designate specific post offices, stations, or branch offices. If an additional four digits are added, called zip + 4.

Zip code sequence The arranging of names and addresses in numeric sequence of zip codes (from 00000 through 99999) for mailing purposes. Third-class or standard mailing requires that mail be sorted in this manner. Further sortation to nine digits (zip + 4) is often used to sort mail to the carrier-route level.

Index